Macro Systems in the Social Environment

MACRO SYSTEMS IN THE SOCIAL ENVIRONMENT

SECOND EDITION

Dennis D. Long
Xavier University
Marla C. Holle, MSW

BROOKS/COLE
CENGAGE Learning™

Australia • Brazil • Japan • Korea • Mexico • Singapore • Spain • United Kingdom • United States

BROOKS/COLE
CENGAGE Learning™

Macro Systems in the Social Environment, Second Edition
Dennis D. Long and Marla C. Holle

Editor in Chief: Marcus Boggs

Acquisitions Editor: Marquita Flemming

Assistant Editor: Alma Dea Michelena

Editorial Assistant: Sheila Walsh

Technology Project Manager: Inna Fedoseyeva

Marketing Manager: Caroline Concilla

Senior Marketing Communications Manager: Tami Strang

Project Manager, Editorial Production: Christy Krueger

Creative Director: Rob Hugel

Art Director: Vernon Boes

Print Buyer: Barbara Britton

Permissions Editor: Roberta Broyer

Production Service: Matrix Productions Inc.

Production Editor: Aaron Downey

Copy Editor: Ann Whetstone

Cover Designer: Ross Carron

Cover Image: Forest Floor/ Getty Images

Compositor: Interactive Composition Corporation

For product information and technology assistance, contact us at **Cengage Learning Customer & Sales Support, 1-800-354-9706**

For permission to use material from this text or product, submit all requests online at **www.cengage.com/permissions** Further permissions questions can be e-mailed to **permissionrequest@cengage.com**

Library of Congress Control Number: 2006923683

ISBN-13: 978-0-495-00772-2

ISBN-10: 0-495-00772-2

Brooks/Cole Cengage Learning
20 Davis Drive
Belmont, CA 94002-3098
USA

Cengage Learning is a leading provider of customized learning solutions with office locations around the globe, including Singapore, the United Kingdom, Australia, Mexico, Brazil, and Japan. Locate your local office at **www.cengage.com/global**

Cengage Learning products are represented in Canada by Nelson Education, Ltd.

To learn more about Brooks/Cole, visit **www.cengage.com/brookscole**

Purchase any of our products at your local college store or at our preferred online store **www.cengagebrain.com**

Printed in the United States of America
2 3 4 5 6   22 21 20 19 18

CONTENTS

PREFACE

It is a privilege to share a second edition of *Macro Systems in the Social Environment* for your reading and use in higher education. Many programs and professors adopted the first version of this book to supplement traditional readings in human behavior and the social environment or to enrich macro-oriented coursework. Feedback through the years from colleagues has been consistent. As anticipated, social work educators and their students were drawn to a more comprehensive understanding of the complexities of human development. The use of social-psychological literature and sociological theory to examine infancy through later adulthood has been found to be a useful approach in altering the long-standing tradition of viewing human behavior and maturation in individualistic, psychological terms.

In a very practical sense, social work educators have also indicated the original edition of this book was helpful in addressing educational standards of the Council on Social Work Education (CSWE). From the beginning, the primary purpose of this work was to identify and highlight the relevance of larger social systems, particularly as suggested for coursework in the foundation area of Human Behavior in the Social Environment (HBSE).

The goal in writing the second edition of this book was to preserve the focus, integrity, and creativity of our original text. Inspired by Jane Jacob's *Dark Age Ahead* (2004, Random House), chapters have been updated by exploring contemporary themes: home ownership, public transportation, day care, and education. Additionally, increased import has been given to information and materials examining pressing macro social and professional issues of our time: immigration, refugee status, social security reform, language issues, the No Child Left Behind Act, family preservation services, multiracial identification, Medicare prescription drug coverage, multicultural organizational development, and cultural competence.

As in the first edition, this book has been organized in a distinctive fashion. The rationale for its format involves four elements.

First, chapters begin with a well-known media figure or fictional character to introduce various life-cycle topics, capture the attention of the reader, and encourage critical analysis of real-life people, events, and occurrences. Social significance can be found in newspaper and magazine articles, movies, television, athletic events, and nearly every aspect of life that affects students today. Professionals gain insight by critically examining and analyzing popular people, characters, and events in their everyday surroundings or popular culture.

Second, chapters are theory driven and encourage deductive reasoning. Readers examine theoretical perspectives and concepts and draw on these constructs to appraise the social environment—social situations, conditions, policies, and settings. The use of theoretical frameworks supported with selected readings is intended to direct attention away from individual pathology and family disequilibrium toward probing the larger social context.

Third, a case example is presented for consideration. Case studies allow students to ground their thoughts in practical application. Practice-based examples tend to personalize materials in a way that allows one to imagine a person, group of people, or situation. Professors, especially colleagues teaching in seminarlike settings, might consider requiring students to present chapter materials and supplement content in case examples with personal experiences. For aspiring social workers, connecting theory and research to life events is helpful for developing analytical skills for utilization in practice.

Finally, sections devoted to "Time to Think!," "Reflection on Diversity," "Applying a Social Work Framework," and "Suggested Activities" encourage analytical and critical thinking skills. "Time to Think!" sections challenge readers to think about the relevance of organizations, communities, society, and global influences in case examples. "Reflection on Diversity" sections provide various forms of human diversity. Chapters conclude with "Suggested Activities," designed to facilitate experiential learning about social systems.

New to this second edition of *Macro Systems in the Social Environment* are the "Reflection on Diversity" sections. While human diversity is an integral concept throughout the text, intentional and purposeful consideration of diversity in each chapter reinforces an appreciation of human differences in the social environment. Stimulating, thought-provoking content and paradigms for examining diversity are provided in relationship to specific developmental time periods.

As in the previous edition, noteworthy concepts and phrases are in bold type and defined. While the authors hope to appeal to the imagination of readers, recognition of key concepts and terms is also seen as an important element in social work education.

When considering the use of various social perspectives, readers need to be cognizant of two points. First, many of the theories described in this book were not developed for social work practice; they are by definition more pure than applied. Theories are, therefore, offered to yield insight to social processes. Second, although only one theory was selected to undergird each chapter, other theories could have been employed. Professors and students are encouraged to debate the merits of using alternative macro theories in each chapter. Our design is not meant to imply that a single theory should be used or imposed in social work assessment. Instead, the goal is to illustrate how a variety of theories can be useful in assessing the social environment.

Finally, the names and locales of case examples provided throughout the book have been altered to provide anonymity. Each case example was developed with two objectives: consistency with chapter themes and portrayal of realistic situations. Cases reflect a blend of years of social work practice and selective creativity by the authors. Thus, any resemblance to real people, places, or events is coincidental.

ACKNOWLEDGMENTS

The authors are grateful to many individuals who helped bring this book to fruition. Thomson Publishing provided direction, impetus, and kindly advice from the outset in the persons of Lisa Gebo and Sheila Walsh. Their steady guidance and suggestions were invaluable, and we wish to express our thanks for their many contributions.

Our appreciation goes also to Richard Welna, Ted Peacock, Thomas M. Meenaghan, Carolyn J. Tice, Neil Heighberger, P. Neal Richey, Jon Hoelter, Richard Sexton, Donald Brieland, Carolyn S. Jenkins, Margo J. Heydt, Shelagh Larkin, Ann Dinan, and Michael Meier. We are indebted to these colleagues, mentors, and friends for their contributions to our intellectual and creative spirits.

Peg Hubbard has dedicated many hours of diligent work to the preparation and technical aspects of this book. We thank Peg for her expert assistance and support.

No book should reach reader's hands without the sensitive critiques of others in the field and, though unnamed, we thank them for steering us through the shoals of omissions, exclusions, and missed opportunities. A special thanks is given to our copy editor, Ann Whetstone, and Aaron Downey at Matrix Productions.

Our parents and children have displayed extravagant pride in our efforts, and we thank them for their cheerfulness in relinquishing family time to allow us the privilege of working as son-in-law and mother-in-law on this project. Our appreciation to children/grandchildren who shared generational insights as the writing progressed.

Special thanks to spouses Joan Holle Long and Reg Holle for encouraging us to take on the challenge of authoring a second edition of this book. Their support kept us intact in every way.

MACRO SYSTEMS: THEIR IMPORTANCE AND USEFULNESS TO THE SOCIAL WORKER

Reruns of the popular television show *M*A*S*H* are familiar to many people and have become a part of American popular culture. This highly successful series depicts the life of doctors and nurses in a mobile hospital unit during the Korean conflict. Surgeon Hawkeye Pierce's recurring complaint addressed the practice of patching up young, wounded soldiers in order to send them back into the war zone. "End the war, now!" was Hawkeye's frequent shout of frustration. The sound of approaching helicopters and the cry of "Wounded!" by the unit commander's aide, Radar O'Reilly, was a reminder that although health care professionals saved lives and mended bodies, the war and casualties continued.

Enabling soldiers to recover physically and mentally at a hospital, only to return them to the battlefront, was but a microcosm of a much larger problem. If the war continued, then the wounded would also continue to arrive. Tending to the sick and injured was not sufficient; addressing the larger (macro-level) issue of the war was necessary to bring an end to the human suffering.

Social workers may feel like Hawkeye. They are educated and trained to conceptualize human behavior in a holistic and systems-oriented manner. The relationship between person and environment is a dynamic process in everyday life. People are affected by their environment, and they have an impact on their environment as well (Miley, O'Melia, & DuBois, 2001, pp. 32–33). In social work practice, environment is an encompassing term that has traditionally included social, cultural, economic, and political aspects, as well as a focus on the family with its religious and physical facets.

Although people served by social workers may not occupy military battle-fields as do the soldiers in $M*A*S*H$, they often live in social battle zones of poverty and oppression. Consumers of our services frequently experience both social and economic catastrophe. Indeed, social workers often choose the profession in order to help eliminate specific social conditions that are the source of problems for clients. To be an effective practitioner and to avoid the feeling of helplessness in dealing with large scale issues, social workers need to commit themselves to assessment and intervention with organizations, communities, societies, and global entities. Social workers must shape their practice activities to goals aimed at eliminating or reducing poverty, discrimination, and social-economic injustice.

However, confronting social problems is a complex task. Large-scale battles facing clients can take many forms. Racial, age, and gender discrimination, lack of health care and quality day care, inadequate housing and public transportation, domestic violence, poor quality education for many, and the travesty of mental health care are but a few of the failures of systems that need to be seen as more than skirmishes. These types of issues require instead strategic assaults on political and economic fronts.

To complicate matters, social problems typically compete with other causes, domestic and international, for public attention and critical resources. Public support for large-scale change can vary in relationship to social-historical periods, current events, political power, type of problem, and people affected.

As contemporary examples, recall how Americans rallied to provide much needed support and aid to the victims of September 11, 2001, the tsunami of December 2004, and the hurricanes in Florida and the Gulf Coast region in 2005. From these events, an increased awareness emerged for new and improved security and warning systems, as well as structural change involving intelligence sources and interdepartmental communication. In response to the tsunami of 2004, physical help and supplies were forthcoming from nations around the globe. In the case of the September 11 attacks, Americans were called upon to mobilize assets and energies in order to fight a newfound "War on Terrorism." As a result of hurricane Katrina and the loss of life and severe damage experienced in New Orleans and the Gulf Coast, the need for coordinated responses from federal, state, and local relief agencies became clear to U.S. citizens and government officials.

Yet, many Americans continue to suffer and perish in the United States as a result of an inferior and segregated system of physical and mental health care. Social workers employed in medical and mental health settings can empathize with Hawkeye Pierce's frustrations. A comprehensive, more universal system of health care in the United States would certainly lessen human suffering and provide healthy starts for babies and children. Social workers practicing in health-oriented agencies feel like shouting, "Create and implement an effective system of universal health care now!"

With a less than optimistic view, Jacobs (2004) suggests a number of imminent considerations affecting the social environment in the United States over the next decade. These include: home ownership, public transportation, family preservation, day care, public health, education, advancement in science, innovations affecting social-economic development, governmental powers, and the impact of taxation. In subsequent chapters, many of these topics will be examined in some depth.

When contemplating larger scale or structural change, it is helpful to conceptualize the social environment as a myriad of interrelated and interdependent **social systems**. Parsons (1951) portrays a system as a set of well-ordered, interrelated, and interdependent parts that share properties. Social systems may be a family, a group or larger system, an organization, a community, a state, a nation, or a world order. Higher-order systems such as society, community, and organizations are called **macro-level systems**. Individuals, families, and groups are considered **micro-level systems**. Although each system is intrinsically complete, each relates to other systems or may constitute a subsystem of other social sets.

In social work education and practice, the relationships between large, macro-level systems and the client are major considerations (Siu, 1991). Rules and policies of organizations oppress various segments of our population. Segregation and poverty found throughout many of our communities are destructive forces. Lack of employment and the absence of health insurance for millions of low-income families in the United States are societal-level problems with implications for nearly all Americans. Unfortunately, social service agencies often hire social workers to work exclusively with micro-level social systems, particularly individuals and families, with little organizational or administrative commitment given to macro-level system concerns.

This book is devoted to providing a broader, more comprehensive look at tactics and strategies for addressing the complex problems of our day. It describes specific life-cycle phases in relationship to macro-level system concerns and examples. The information provided here is intended to supplement and complement traditional readings in human behavior and the social environment that concentrate on micro-level systems involving casework, family therapy, and group work.

Each of the following chapters highlights a selected social theory for analyzing macro-level issues. The chapters also provide case examples and illustrations stressing organizational, community, policy, and/or legislative concerns. These anecdotal materials are included to help social workers intervene with a client system during a specific developmental phase. Each "Time to Think!" section provides appropriate macro considerations for the generalist social worker to examine.

Although social workers engaging in macro-level practice must also understand micro-level practice (Netting, Kettner, & McMurtry, 2004), the emphasis here is directed toward the macro level. Our goal is to have students think big! We encourage students to expand their thoughts about social work practice to national and international levels while examining the developmental issues of infants, preschool and elementary school children, and adolescents, as well as young, middle-aged, and older adults.

THEORY: ECOLOGICAL-SYSTEMS MODEL

A dominant theoretical approach for viewing human behavior in the social environment is the **ecological-systems model** (Germain, 1979). This model emphasizes the adaptive fit of human beings to elements of the environment, often referred to as the **person in environment**. Here, "person" refers to the client system. The client system can be an individual, a family, a group, or a social organization. The environment is all-encompassing, including both micro- and macro-level systems, as well as resources required for sustenance. Common environmental elements include nuclear families or multigenerational clans, reference groups, the local community, a culture, a society or a nation, or an element of the international scene (Chetkow-Yanoov, 1992, pp. 7–8).

Using the ecological-systems model, the interface between people and their environment is conceptualized as bi-directional: human beings affect the environment and the environment affects individuals and groups. To look at either people or environments is insufficient. Instead, ecological theory focuses on the interaction between the two.

For a social worker, the challenge in using an ecological-systems orientation is to assess simultaneously the interrelated nature of the client, the client's situation, all relevant micro and macro social systems, and any other environmental factors. This presents a **holistic approach** to social work assessment and intervention.

AN INSTITUTIONAL VIEW OF SOCIAL WELFARE

Social welfare is a necessary thread in the fabric of social structure, and society has a responsibility for the plight and well-being of its members. Social welfare should have a role of equal significance with other social institutions in our society, including the family, economics, political arenas, religion, and education.

Our fundamental premise is that people have intrinsic worth and are basically well intentioned, but they face routine and complex needs and problems of employment, food, shelter, and health care. In addition, because society helps create and perpetuate such social problems as unemployment, lack of affordable housing, and insufficient medical care, society has a responsibility to help remedy oppressive social conditions. Therefore, the social welfare institution is important not only for supplying goods and services to help clients cope with daily living but also for creating economic, political, and social opportunities for clients in their communities and throughout their society. With this **institutional or primary view of social welfare**, social services and its programs are viewed as necessary for advancing intrinsic human worth and dignity and for promoting the active participation of consumers of services in decisions affecting their lives. Social welfare is one of society's first-line institutions for meeting human needs and identifying and nurturing the strengths and power of people.

From an institutional or primary view, a major function of the social welfare institution involves the sustainable development of social environments that support healthy, productive, and meaningful ways of living. Should this not be a basic human right? Meenaghan, Gibbons, and McNutt (2005) suggest "people are entitled, as human beings, to a functional and positive community environment in which to act and grow. This entitlement, directly tied to the social nature of people, can in turn contribute to an evolving sense of social good and cohesion in the larger social world" (p. 2). Perhaps the macro-level content and activities suggested in subsequent chapters may appear to take a liberal or social-change slant. Much as Hawkeye perceived the war, the perspective presented here is geared more toward social reform than individual treatment. This view is not meant, however, to deny the need for individual responsibility, self-determination, and therapeutic intervention. On the contrary, the goal is to promote awareness of social and environmental issues while giving due respect to each client's struggle, responsibility, and choice.

Although social change usually occurs gradually, transformation is achievable in organizations, communities, and societies, as well as globally—not only with individuals, families, and small groups. This suggests that poor people need not suffer continual oppression. Social conditions can improve when social workers and citizens form meaningful partnerships with economically disadvantaged people. It is important to know and believe that through these partnerships and collaborative endeavors, people can advocate at various levels for policies and programs that improve social-economic conditions and create opportunities.

Many factors can impact the ability to bring about broader, wide-sweeping change. War, catastrophe, economic crisis, widespread unemployment, demographic changes, and a shift in political ideology bringing about a more liberal or conservative trend have been cited as elements to consider when contemplating "public and professional sentiment concerning the importance of systemic, structural change" (Long, Tice, & Morrison, 2006, p. 16). Dependent upon social-historical context, there will be periods when progressive change with macro social systems seems more or less relevant and doable than at other times.

During the 1980s, Francis Fox Piven and Richard Cloward challenged social workers to educate and mobilize the traditionally alienated electorate to vote in national political elections. In reaction to President Reagan's attack on social welfare programs, Piven and Cloward (1982) proclaimed the existence of a new class war in America.

As it became evident that capitalists and corporate leaders were attempting to dismantle public relief and entitlement programs for the disadvantaged, Piven and Cloward advocated for political resistance and protest for and by the unemployed, unemployable, and working poor. Social workers and social work students sought ways to actively engage consumers of services in political discourse and action aimed at thwarting President Reagan's attack on the social welfare state. Political engagement included television appearances and voter registration drives. Social workers were encouraged to utilize innovative techniques to educate clients about politics and voter responsibilities. As a result of such efforts, federal legislation was passed to make voter registration easier.

Whether it was a reaction to conservatism or the result of outcries from social critics like Piven and Cloward or recognition of the need to advocate on behalf of the vulnerable, social workers became more politically active during the Reagan years (Ezell, 1993). Their involvement is evidenced by letters written to public officials, discussion of political issues, membership in politically active organizations, involvement in candidate elections, and attendance at political meetings.

The problem of poverty has been at the heart and core of social work. The poor constitute an isolated group of people in America who have been "systematically subjected to conditions that virtually eliminate all possibility of equal life chances" (Ewalt, 1994, p. 149). Social workers have a rich tradition of practice with the poor, as emphasized by Michael Harrington's *The Other America in the United States* (1963), which was a wake-up call to comfortable Americans who often failed to see distressed city and rural poor. When examining the behavior of clients who live in poverty, social workers must view their efforts in the context of our profession's long-standing commitment to promote social and economic justice.

It is important to remember that social workers were at the forefront of President Johnson's War on Poverty during the 1960s. Education, training, and employment programs during this era benefited many citizens. During the Nixon administration, social workers debated the merits of a guaranteed annual income for all Americans, even though such legislation was never enacted. Through the decades, irrespective of the president or political party in power, social work has championed the causes of the less fortunate. Social work's vow to help people in need, address social problems, and eradicate social-economic injustice continues to be a challenge during the twenty-first century and the presidency of George W. Bush. Many would argue that neoconservatism, the War on Terrorism, illegal immigration, and a movement toward privatization of human services have complicated the interplay between social work, politics, activism, and social change. Even a cursory analysis of President Bush's political base, in two razor-thin presidential victories, reveals sharp divisions in America in terms of gender, race, political ideology, urban/rural geographical distinctions, and religious attitudes (*Time*, 2004).

As a critique of our profession, some social workers would argue that more could have been done during the early years of George W. Bush's administration to challenge conservative forces urging reductions in spending for social issues and increased spending to support a War on Terrorism. Much like the movement supported by Piven and Cloward during the Reagan years, social work educators, students, and practitioners should have more diligently questioned President Bush's federal tax cuts, reductions in domestic spending, and the wide-scale diversion of funds from social programs for the buildup of military forces and homeland security. Today, conservatism, patriotism, capitalism, global dependency, and a reliance on rugged individualism reign as dominant beliefs in the United States. This is an important realization concerning the present as "forces [political and cultural] can and will affect how human service professions operate. In turn, operations within the human service professions will reinforce larger cultural and political processes" (Meenaghan, Kilty, & McNutt, 2004, p. 6).

APPROPRIATE VALUE ORIENTATION

Social workers must guard against a naive perception and interpretation of life. As the rich get richer, the efforts to secure scarce resources for the poor become increasingly competitive and complex. Low-income families are likely to report specific problem areas pertaining to needs for safe neighborhoods, child support, steady income, housing, jobs, and schools (Proctor, Vosler, & Sirles, 1993). So, to view a problem for assessment and intervention without considering factors such as social-economic status, race, gender, ethnicity, neighborhood, and other environmental conditions is to fail to appreciate the complexities of the problem. The value orientation for social workers is rooted in the National Association of Social Workers' (NASW) Code of Ethics (1996), which emphasizes a respect for the unique life experiences of individuals and groups with a commitment to client self-determination. However, for social workers to profess to know the true feelings of any client in need would be a fallacy. The gut-level feeling of oppression or need is unique for each person and client. As a result, the goal is to respond in a nonjudgmental fashion and to attempt to grasp the situation of each client or client group.

To emphasize this point, a colleague had students perform a simple exercise. He asked each student to hold his or her breath as long as possible. Then, in the complete silence of the classroom, the professor instructed students to breathe as needed. Next, students described thoughts and feelings while holding their breath. Did any two students experience exactly the same sensation? How important did that next breath of air become? Did students think of much of anything other than that next breath?

This exercise focuses on the often desperate nature of human problems. In the struggle to attain the basics of life, consumers of our services typically focus on relieving the stress and pain resulting from their immediate, presenting circumstances. If clients face life-threatening needs, when is it appropriate or helpful to raise or contemplate macro-level issues in the helping process?

Arguably, one of the most distinguishing characteristics of social work as a helping profession is the commitment to pursue both macro- and micro-level issues simultaneously and with equal fervor. This is referred to as a **unified approach** and is manifested in the ability of social work practitioners to grapple with power, oppression, and matters of social justice while working in the confines of clinic-oriented practices (Vodde & Gallant, 2002, p. 439).

CASE EXAMPLE | # Friendship House—Homelessness

Betty Johnson is a 21-year-old senior and social work major in a field placement at Friendship House, a shelter for homeless women and children in northern Kentucky. Betty grew up in a middle-class white family from the suburbs of Louisville. Her parents expressed concern about her career choice of social work. Her father's reluctance focused on low earnings, her mother's on safety. But Betty convinced them that social work was her calling.

Betty's first client was Dorothy McCoy, an 18-year-old single parent with two daughters, ages 3 and 2. This Appalachian mother and her children were homeless and without an income. Her husband, an alcoholic, had left the state to seek a new start. Unable to pay her rent, Dorothy lost her apartment in Oldtown, Kentucky, and was searching for housing. A victim of domestic violence, Dorothy is a homeless woman with minor children in an economically depressed area in northern Kentucky.

As Dorothy seated herself at Betty's desk, her first words to the social worker were, "How old are you and how many kids do you have?" Somewhat startled by this opening question, Betty disclosed that she was 21, unmarried, and had no children. Two worlds began to collide!

Disbelieving, Dorothy asked, "Where do you live?" and continued to confront the worker. "Everybody I know has been married at least once or has children by your age. . . . I may not have much, but I have been around and I know what is happening! . . . How are you going to help me?"

Betty Johnson is learning about a world she has not experienced. While Oldtown, Kentucky, has made great strides over the last decade with regard to urban development, it is known by many in the tri-state area as a tense and dangerous community. Sections of Oldtown are characterized by nude dancing establishments, bars, poor housing, and poverty. By contrast, areas of Oldtown overlooking the Ohio River have expensive homes and successful businesses. Dorothy McCoy has lived her entire life in the Oldtown slums. Across the bridge, the city of Cincinnati seems to promise there is more to life than poverty. For the past five years, Dorothy and her children survived on the small amount of money left after her husband's alcoholic needs were met. She had friends in Oldtown, most of whom lived in similar circumstances. Her only possessions—three suitcases full of clothes and a few furniture items—were stored with one of her neighborhood friends. Dorothy's goal was to find housing and work as soon as possible. Only minimum-wage service jobs in fast-food restaurants or room cleaning for cut-rate motels were available in Oldtown for unskilled people such as Dorothy. These settings provided no guarantee of a 40-hour workweek or regular working hours and lack health care benefits for Dorothy and her two young children. Child care presented an additional concern and expense. Public buses were Dorothy's only option for transportation to her job and child care. Locating housing, though her most pressing need, was only one of a complex pattern of concerns. Dorothy had already picked up the extensive paperwork required to apply for Temporary Assistance for Needy Families (TANF). Meanwhile, Betty was unsure how to respond to Dorothy's confrontational remarks. While Betty had been sensitized to cultural differences during her student field placement, she was not prepared for Dorothy's hostility. As Betty began to build a relationship with Dorothy and assess the situation, many problems surfaced. Dorothy had lived a very different lifestyle and grown up in a more affluent social environment than Betty. Her expectations concerning the future, employment, and housing also differed from Betty's understanding of life goals. Betty sensed that Dorothy's primary need was for a safe environment. Betty also began to realize that Dorothy was typical of women served at Friendship House and that many women in America face similar circumstances.

TIME TO THINK!

What macro-level issues come to light with this case? As a social worker, what kind of macro-level activities (e.g., social advocacy, program development, community assessment, collaboration, and social planning) should Betty consider in order to promote the kinds of structural changes that would benefit women and dependent children as presented in the case example? How does this client's neighborhood and social setting create barriers or present opportunities for Betty to explore? What kinds of community-based or national organizations, agencies, or associations would be useful with respect to collaboration? How and when can Betty begin to establish a relationship and partnership with Dorothy to examine and address macro-level considerations and concerns?

Scanning Macro Systems

Let's scan different social-system levels and condition ourselves to think about the relevance of larger social systems to this case. Given the information as we know it, what are some issues at the organizational, community, society, or global levels that Betty should consider? Beyond individual attributes and family circumstances, macro aspects of the social environment must be assessed.

Organizational Level When examining the client-in-environment situation, social workers must consider the full range of organizations that may assist the client. An obvious beginning would be the services offered by the social worker's agency. In this case, Friendship House can provide short-term emergency housing, food, clothing, and financial counseling to Dorothy. But understanding the organization involves more than a description of available programs. To ascertain the availability of resources to the client, the social worker must be familiar with the organizational structure and power bases, formal and informal, that are unique to the social service agency.

For example, the response of administrators of social work agencies may vary by client as they consider utilization of scarce resources on a case-by-case basis. This protects the organization from overcommitting funds on a purely categorical basis— that is, where benefit allotments are predetermined according to classification of need. Flexibility in distributing goods and services allows agencies to use discretion while maintaining reserves for emergencies.

continued

CASE EXAMPLE | *continued*

In a similar fashion, Betty will need to be cognizant of the social structure and politics of interacting with other social service agencies in northern Kentucky. For example, it is not unusual for social workers to call in favors from other social workers with whom they have cooperated in the past. It will be to Dorothy's benefit that Betty is known and respected at social service agencies that frequently interact with social workers at Friendship House. Betty needs to be aware of the dynamics of informal networking and its appropriate use in addressing clients' needs.

As the social worker continues to intervene, Betty may become aware of special arrangements through which apartment rental companies in the area offer subsidized or low-deposit housing for clients. Does Betty's agency partner or collaborate with local emergency shelters to provide abused women with services or benefits tailored for victims of domestic abuse? Sometimes, local churches offer temporary housing programs to assist single parents with children. Has any effort been made to create and maintain a current resource file describing housing options for clients like Dorothy?

What companies in the area would be willing to hire Dorothy? Are there day care facilities or other child care resources available? Contacts and knowledge of local employers and day care options are critical to improving Dorothy's situation. This information needs to be updated on a regular, if not daily, basis and be immediately accessible to the social worker.

An array of other social service organizations should also be considered. What kinds of resources are available at the local Salvation Army, food and clothing banks, public housing authority, women's centers, or the Cabinet of Human Resources? Can contact people at these organizations provide information and new ideas that will assist Dorothy? Have interorganizational clusters or planning groups been formed to assist professionals in cutting through red tape and promoting a concerted, meaningful, and timely provision of goods and services to clients? If so, how can a client like Dorothy be included in decisions that will affect her and her children in a direct and life-changing way? Helping one client become self-sufficient, find protection, and discover resources for growth and change is vital. But addressing the client's problem from a macro-level perspective as well may bring about or contribute to a process that will aid hundreds of women in similar circumstances.

Organizations, much like individuals, operate via social exchange (Blau, 1964). To improve Dorothy McCoy's situation, Betty Johnson will use her knowledge of local employers and day care options. It benefits the client for the social worker to nurture relationships with people in various community organizations. While social workers often adequately network with people at other social service agencies and organizations, the greater challenge is to build contacts with area businesses and other for-profit organizations.

An example of successful networking with business is a community-based convenience store's corporate sponsorship of Friendship House. Beyond the provision of food and hygiene products, this corporation donates time and expertise in connection with fund-raising, public relations, and special projects at this neighborhood agency. This company has also created an employment program for residents at Friendship House to assist clients in their search for jobs.

Community Level The community in which one resides often restricts what one can do in life. The availability of resources within the community can be an empowering or limiting factor for people.

What do we know about Dorothy's neighborhood? What stereotypes are associated with economically disadvantaged people from Appalachia living in urban areas in northern Kentucky? Does Dorothy have available a neighborhood/community-based support system? How do friends and neighbors influence her behavior? How can such a support system benefit Dorothy and her children?

Betty will want to become involved in local northern Kentucky housing coalitions like Housing Incorporated, a nonprofit organization. Its mission is to provide decent, affordable housing opportunities and to support families and individuals with very low income. As a result of this involvement, Betty will be more informed about community resources available to Dorothy and other clients facing similar situations. Each community, like each individual, has distinctive differences. Communities vary in size, affluence, and commitment to the less fortunate. As a social worker, Betty strives to gain stature and respect within the neighborhood and acquire the information necessary to be an effective practitioner.

To gain acceptance, it is important for Betty to be perceived as a sensitive, professional social worker in the communities in which she practices. If people in a community are convinced that Betty is knowledgeable and cares about their welfare, she has crossed a major social hurdle. Betty's positive participation in community functions (the downtown renovation project, the community mental health board, women's rights organizations, and the homeless coalition) will open doors for her in assessing the impact of the community on Dorothy's presenting situation.

In her role as a social worker, Betty must be a student of this new culture. To help Dorothy make sense of the complex pieces of her life, Betty needs an accurate sense of the community and its role in her client's life. At this point, Dorothy may be skeptical of Betty and unsure that she understands her situation. Building a base of trust and respect with Dorothy and in the community will be among Betty's first goals.

Societal Level In the classic work *Mind, Self, and Society* (1934), George Herbert Mead describes the relationship between oneself and the society in which one lives. A basic tenet of Mead's theory is that who we are is influenced by how others view us.

Given this premise, how does society view people like Dorothy? For example, popular media conservatives, such as Rush Limbaugh, often portray needy people as irresponsible and lazy—freeloaders looking for handouts! A powerful segment of our population seeks to curtail or eliminate programs and services for the poor and needy. The growing clamor demands that those who require help should "pull themselves up by

continued

CASE EXAMPLE | *continued*

their own bootstraps." Many citizens expect people like Dorothy to be self-sufficient and find ways to survive without assistance from government and social service agencies.

Where does such an ideology leave our client? Is emergency assistance more acceptable to the general population than institutionalized welfare programs? What are Dorothy's feelings about asking for aid?

Americans tend to think of the homeless in the United States as a "faceless group" (Hartman, 1989, p. 483). Such a view enables people to distance themselves from the problem. With the continuing misconception that homeless people are usually drunkards or irresponsible misfits, the societal crisis in housing is often seen in the United States as the private troubles of those who deserve their lot in life.

Dorothy and her children are not alone in their domestic plight. Many other American families face homelessness due to divorce, mental illness, physical limitations, substance abuse, and abandonment. But this does not cancel out the stigma that will confront Dorothy McCoy and challenge Betty Johnson. Long, Tice, and Morrison (2006, p. 206) state: "Social workers often hope to promote social justice—to help create a more equitable world." At a societal level, this involves the ability to work hand-in-hand with clients like Dorothy to promote opportunities, rights, and an evenhanded distribution of goods for consumers of our services.

International Level International issues directly affect the problems presented by Dorothy to Betty. Clients are an integral part of their environment, and the environment directly affects the person and the problem. Northern Kentucky is only a microcosm of the global village in which we all live.

In the greater Cincinnati area, Procter & Gamble, Kroger's, and Delta Airlines have home or regional offices. These businesses have strong international components and serve as major employers in—and influences upon—communities in northern Kentucky.

The Greater Cincinnati and Northern Kentucky Airport is located in northern Kentucky, only minutes from Dorothy's home. Construction projects there as well as

REFLECTION ON DIVERSITY: A VARIETY OF FORMS OF DIVERSITY

Human diversity takes many forms. In each chapter of this book, a section is devoted to a critical reflection of human diversity. Although the importance of diversity may seem obvious, the primary goal of each "Reflection on Diversity" section is to identify and highlight relationships between minority status(es) and power, rights, social control, access to opportunities, and the ability of clients to affect decisions.

Many social workers would see Dorothy's Appalachian roots, lack of language skills, values, and traditions as important factors in the presenting situation. Many also would agree that people from her region are frequently tourism and international commerce bring income and new vitality to the community. Companies and corporations come to the area and strategically secure space for access to the airport.

Negative actions on the part of mega-companies can bring disastrous results to a community. If Procter & Gamble were to leave the Cincinnati area, people in that city and northern Kentucky would be economically devastated. Betty needs to be alert to both national and international economic influences that impact clients.

Years ago, the Newport (Kentucky) Steel Company faced grave economic hardship due to a deteriorating international climate for the U.S. steel industry. Social workers must not underestimate the effect of changes and fluctuations in businesses that contribute to the local economy in significant ways. When people are displaced from employment, make salary concessions at work, or fear for their jobs, stress is created for individuals and families.

Conversely, when international enterprises move into communities, creating a flurry of jobs and bringing new monies into the area, booms often occur. In Georgetown, Kentucky, one hour away from Oldtown, Toyota operates a factory that provides hundreds of jobs, skilled and unskilled. In the age of multinational corporations and global interdependence, and global economic inequalities, social workers must be sensitive to national and international conditions that have direct or indirect consequences for clients (Braun, 1991).

Employment opportunities for Dorothy in Northern Kentucky are limited. Economically, this geographical area, like many regions of our country, has experienced trying times. For Betty's clients, global outsourcing of products and jobs to reduce labor costs has contributed to both fewer and lower-paying jobs. Betty is keenly aware of the impact of outsourcing and downsizing initiatives for people on her caseload. Employers across the nation often restructure their labor forces in an effort to eliminate paid positions. In some cases, employees are asked to assume duties and responsibilities for what previously constituted two or more jobs. Even with beginning-level jobs, the complexity and multitask nature of reconstituted employment can be overwhelming for clients like Dorothy and undermine success.

stereotyped and discriminated against in unique and observable ways. Limited access to housing and discriminatory employment practices have often presented obstacles to those with regional dialects. Yet, it is important to realize that Dorothy also faces barriers as a result of her status as a single mother, a woman, and a victim of domestic violence.

The beliefs, values, language, and traditions of Appalachian culture are relevant considerations represented in the case example. However, being a young woman with small children is also a powerful factor. As a single parent with limited education, Dorothy's work experience is minimal. She is also responsible for providing and caring for her children. Limitations concerning child care and employability are directly related to societal, community, and cultural attitudes and beliefs concerning the role of women in child rearing and paid employment. Often, minimal consideration is given in our society to the responsibilities, obligations, and duties of fathers. If Dorothy's husband were to express an interest in returning to the family, one could anticipate social pressures on Dorothy to accommodate such a request. Despite gender equity efforts, men still wield power over women in our society.

Dorothy is also a victim of domestic violence at the hands of an alcoholic. These circumstances require attention and action. How do the needs of Dorothy and her children differ from those of other homeless mothers and children? Victimization can take many forms. How does each form of victimization warrant special consideration with respect to power, rights, and social control for clients? For example, would you not argue that this mother and her children have a right to a safe and secure existence without threat of violence from Dorothy's husband? How might this be achieved?

Finally, are the identified types of diversity from this case example interrelated? Are the limiting and restrictive effects of each status discernible? What is the role of the client in articulating the power and influence of each problem? Do you believe that Dorothy would readily recognize these dimensions of human diversity and their consequences for herself and her children?

APPLYING A SOCIAL WORK FRAMEWORK: ECOLOGICAL SYSTEMS

Each chapter in this book uses a different social theory to analyze chapter content and case examples. In this chapter, a general ecological-systems approach has been introduced as an important perspective when examining human behavior in the social environment. An ecological-systems approach highlights the significance of relationships between clients and the various systems with which they interact on a daily basis. Schools, workplaces, churches, neighborhoods, social work agencies, and even countries are integral to the functioning of individuals, families, and groups of people. Many of these elements will be addressed in "Time to Think!" sections.

Effective assessment and intervention from a social work perspective require a keen awareness of the dynamic and changing social environment in which clients live and professionals practice. As an example, social workers must learn to contend with managed health and mental health care and the emergence of multidisciplinary intervention teams in America. **Managed health care** is a term used to describe the method by which insurance companies and funding sources implement policies and programs directed at containing costs of services, while attempting to maintain effective intervention. Managed health care often involves the establishment of **interdisciplinary group practices** of professional social workers, psychologists, counselors, nurses, psychiatrists, and physicians who join forces to create a corporate entity aimed at addressing client needs in an efficient and cost-effective manner.

The era of private practice is nearing an end. Fueled by the health care reform movement and federal changes in funding, interdisciplinary group practices have replaced the individual practitioner/physician model in the United States. Although overlap exists among various helping professionals relative to theoretical orientations and approaches for intervention, each profession is characterized by a distinct and special focus. For social workers, utilizing macro-level systems analysis during assessment and problem solving is essential. The inclusion of larger social systems is a unique aspect of professional social work to be shared with other professionals.

At Xavier University in Cincinnati, Ohio, the Social Work Program offers a team-taught Human Life Cycle II course examining a broad range of information from adolescence through older age. A social worker and a psychologist work together to impart substantive content and theories related to human growth and development.

The instructors in this course use contrasting styles and approaches. During class, they each stress their discipline's views of human behavior but are sensitive to the other's professional training and experience. In the classroom, with students as active participants, discussions and debates reflect the multidisciplinary workplace in which many social workers practice.

In such a contemporary practice environment, an explicit goal for each professional is to work for the greatest benefit of each client. Group practices are typically organized with a division of labor that matches client problems to the appropriate provider(s). Toward this end, social workers must be articulate advocates of a social work perspective in each multidisciplinary endeavor.

Tower (1994) suggests certain orientations for helping that are unique to social workers. One such orientation is that of a **consumer-centered approach** in intervention. When social workers view clients as consumers, they must also respect them as people who are actively involved, self-determined, and seeking control of their lives.

In an interdisciplinary intervention climate, one challenge for social workers is promoting among various team members a clear and unequivocal understanding of the active role of consumers of services (clients) in assessing their problems. As social workers, we enable our colleagues to view presenting problems as more than personal or family conflicts. It is our responsibility to interpret for others the potential benefits of macro-scale social change and political action for clients (Feld, 1991).

With respect to the case example involving Dorothy McCoy, the social worker constructs and advances with colleagues a complete picture that highlights the interface between client and environment. Dorothy's neighborhood and the subculture in Oldtown, Kentucky, are important elements for consideration. Opportunities for employment, day care, and affordable housing and the ability to deliver services in a concerted, timely fashion are critical components for women who are homeless with children. The future for Dorothy and her children is contingent upon many macro- and micro-level system factors, as well as upon Dorothy's motivation and will to succeed.

As a social worker, Betty Johnson will also need to be actively involved in any social changes or policy considerations that might relate to her client's case. Welfare reform initiatives, changes in Medicaid policies, housing legislation, TANF, and modifications in child support assistance programs are areas of potential importance to young mothers.

Dorothy McCoy and her children also have physical and mental health needs. The restructuring of services under managed care has broad implications for her and many other clients. Variables such as the number of health and mental health providers, accessibility and availability of providers, and the professional composition of provider groups will influence assessment and treatment decisions. Environment and resource issues are focal points for social workers involved in the managed care movement.

To address the client's immediate needs, Betty helped Dorothy to secure subsidized housing and TANF. Dorothy's desire, however, was to become fully employed and self-sufficient. With encouragement and support from Betty, Dorothy examined various job opportunities in the community. By networking with local businesses, Betty facilitated several interviews for Dorothy with promising employers. Dorothy and Betty also explored various day care and housing options. With each day, they became more knowledgeable about the available resources in Oldtown, northern Kentucky, and the Cincinnati area.

Suggested Activities

1. Some organizations offer programs and retreats for experiencing various subcultures and lifestyles. Consider taking an "urban plunge" or spending some time in an unfamiliar subculture, such as an Appalachian community. The ability to assess values, norms, and strengths in less-familiar areas is a valuable asset for social workers.
2. Many social work students volunteer time and energy to social causes prior to entering field placement. Homeless shelters and centers serving women are two examples of organizations that can sensitize students to the plight of special population groups. Identify social problems or population groups in need of student volunteers.
3. Share your insights with classmates concerning socioeconomic crises that exist in your hometown or a nearby community. Consider social and ethnic composition, economic promise, employment opportunities, and housing concerns. Identify local, state, or national influences on the disadvantaged in your geographical area. Consider joining a planning or governing group, board, or committee that could have a meaningful impact in improving the social environment.

References

Blau, P. (1964). *Exchange and power in social life*. New York: John Wiley.

Braun D. (1991). *The rich get richer*. Chicago: Nelson-Hall.

Chetkow-Yanoov, B. (1992). *Social work practice: A systems approach*. New York: Hawthorne Press.

Ewalt, P. (1994). Poverty matters. *Social Work, 39,* 149–151.

Ezell, M. (1993). The political activity of social workers: A post-Reagan update. *Journal of Sociology and Social Welfare, 10,* 81–97.

Feld, K. (1991). Advocacy heals. *Headlines, 2,* 11–16.

Germain, C. (1979). *Social work practice: People and environments.* New York: Columbia University Press.

Harrington, M. (1963). *The other America in the United States.* Baltimore: Penguin.

Hartman, A. (1989). Homelessness: Public issue and private trouble. *Social Work, 34,* 483–484.

Jacobs, J. (2004). *Dark age ahead.* New York: Random House.

Long, D., Tice, C., & Morrison, J. (2006). *Macro social work practice: A strengths perspective.* Belmont, CA: Thomson Brooks/Cole.

Martin, P., & O'Connor, G. (1989). *The social environment: Open system applications.* New York: Longman.

Mead, G. (1934). *Mind, self, and society.* New York: Doubleday.

Meenaghan, T., Gibbons, E., & McNutt, J. (2005). *Generalist practice in larger settings: Knowledge and skill concepts.* Chicago: Lyceum.

Meenaghan, T., Kilty, K., & McNutt, J. (2004). *Social policy analysis and practice.* Chicago: Lyceum.

Miley, K., O'Melia, M., & DuBois, B. (2001). *Generalist social work practice: An empowerment approach.* Boston: Allyn & Bacon.

National Association of Social Workers. (1996). *Code of ethics.* Washington, DC: NASW Press.

Netting, E., Kettner, P., & McMurtry, S. (2004). *Social work macro practice.* New York: Pearson Allyn & Bacon.

Parsons, T. (1951). *The social system.* New York: Free Press.

Piven, F., & Cloward, R. (1982). *The new class war: Reagan's attack on the welfare state and its consequences.* New York: Pantheon.

Proctor, E., Vosler, N., & Sirles, E. (1993). The social-environmental context of child clients: An empirical exploration. *Social Work, 38,* 256–262.

Siu, S. (1991). Providing opportunities for macro practice in direct service agencies: One undergraduate program's experience. *Arete, 16,* 146–151.

Time. (2004). How Bush pulled it off, *164*(20), 40.

Tower, K. (1994). Consumer-centered social work practice: Restoring client self-determination. *Social Work, 39,* 191–196.

Vodde, R., & Gallant, J. (2002). Bridging the gap between micro and macro practice: Large scale change and a unified model of narrative-deconstructive practice. *Journal of Social Work Education, 38,* 439–458.

2 CHAPTER | INFANCY

Eric Clapton's famous ballad "Tears in Heaven," an ode to his deceased son, expresses a grieving father's pain and sorrow. Four-year-old Conor Clapton died as the result of an accidental fall from an open hotel window in 1991. In the lyrics, Clapton addresses his lost son as he asks, "Would you know my name, if you saw me in heaven?"

Eric Clapton is known in the entertainment world as a survivor of drug addiction, alcoholism, and the loss of close musical colleagues Jimi Hendrix and Stevie Ray Vaughan, but he will probably best be remembered for "Tears in Heaven," "His Saddest Song" (*Newsweek,* 1992). The song is unique because Conor was his son, and the pain he expresses in these lyrics was vivid and personal to him.

The high probability of death for young children during the first years of life is a chilling social fact—a dreadful topic frequently avoided in everyday conversation. It seems unfair when the joy and excitement of human birth is clouded by the risk of infant death. Many infants die each year as a result of preventable conditions. Research indicates that low-income, minority status children under the age of three and lacking insurance are three to twelve times more likely to be without a source of health care and two to thirty times more likely to have unmet health care needs than their higher-income, white, and insured counterparts (Newacheck, Hung, Hochstein, & Halfon, 2002).

From a global perspective, it might be assumed that, with its medical resources, the United States fares well with respect to **infant mortality,** the deaths of infants under one year of age (measured per 1,000 live births). Based on 2004 estimates (see Table 2.1), the United States ranks 185th lowest out of 226 countries with respect to infant mortality (Central Intelligence Agency, 2005). Many Scandinavian, European, and Asian countries experience lower infantile mortality rates than those found in America. Within the United States, demographic and socioeconomic differences among various groups contribute directly to disturbing differentials in infant mortality rates. One of the most glaring factors in this inequality involves race and ethnicity.

In the United States, African-American infants die at a rate twice that of white infants. The three leading causes of infant death are congenital anomalies, disorders relating to short gestation and unspecified low birthweight, and Sudden Infant Death Syndrome (SIDS). "Cause-specific mortality rates varied considerably by race and Hispanic origin. For infants of black mothers, the IMR [Infant Mortality Rate] for low birthweight was nearly four times that for white mothers" (Mathews, Curtin, & MacDorman, 2000, pp. 1–2).

These types of differentials in infant mortality can be directly related to the availability of proper prenatal and postnatal care. Americans take great pride in being a country of advanced technology and knowledge. Yet, it is evident that many expectant mothers do not have equal access to life-saving prenatal care and education or medical technology. This is especially evident when considering race and ethnicity. Few would disagree with the premise that timely and widespread availability of "comprehensive prenatal care can promote healthier pregnancies by providing health behavior advice and early detection and treatment of maternal complications that influence the infant's subsequent health and survival" (Mathews, Curtin, & MacDorman, 2000, p. 5).

For many expectant mothers and children in the United States, the tragic reality is that health care and medical services remain either beyond their reach or are inadequate. As a result, infants born to economically disadvantaged parents are at a higher risk of life-threatening illnesses, disabling conditions, and death. Social work practice verifies this trend as social workers deal with premature and failure-to-thrive babies, Sudden Infant Death Syndrome, child abuse, and infants who dwell in accident-prone environments.

On a more positive note, the Healthy People 2010 government initiative targets at-risk population groups experiencing inadequate access to health care in the United States (U.S. Department of Health and Human Services, 2000). Additionally, there is evidence that America's community health centers may have an impact on reducing racial and ethnic disparities in the provision of prenatal services and birth outcomes. It has become evident that, "increasing first-trimester prenatal care use through perinatal care capacity may lead to further improvement in birth outcomes for the underserved" (Shi, Stevens, Wulu, Politzer, & Xu, 2004, p. 1881).

Social workers know that proper nutrition, prenatal care and education, medical care, and nurturing living conditions are fundamental to the survival and healthy development of children. When working with at-risk mothers and families, promoting and offering enabling services such as translation programs, transportation, family preservation services, and child care are critical elements.

TABLE 2.1 | RANK ORDER INFANT MORTALITY RATES OF SELECTED
COUNTRIES

Rank (from lowest)	Country	Infant Mortality Rate (deaths/1,000 live births)
226	Singapore	2.29
225	Sweden	2.77
224	Hong Kong	2.97
223	Japan	3.26
222	Iceland	3.31
221	Finland	3.57
220	Norway	3.70
216	Germany	4.16
215	France	4.26
214	Switzerland	4.39
212	Spain	4.42
210	Denmark	4.56
209	Austria	4.66
208	Belgium	4.68
207	Australia	4.69
206	Liechtenstein	4.70
199	United Kingdom	5.16
194	Greece	5.53
192	New Zealand	5.85
191	Aruba	5.89
189	Italy	5.94
187	Cuba	6.33
186	Taiwan	6.40
185	**United States**	**6.50**
183	Lithuania	6.89
182	Guam	6.94
181	Israel	7.03
180	Korea, South	7.09

Source: Based on 2004 estimated values and adapted from the Central Intelligence Agency (2005), *The World Factbook*, online at www.cia.gov/cia/publications/factbook/rankorder/2091rank.html. *The World Factbook* is public domain, and its information can be used without permission of the Central Intelligence Agency.

This chapter began with a tragic, true story that highlights the calamity of infant mortality and the need to address issues of prevention and maternal support. The miracle of the beginning of life and the examination of human life cycle phases that follow are the primary focus. Our goal is to use macro perspectives that move us toward more comprehensive solutions to social problems.

The grief of losing a child, like that experienced by Eric Clapton, is a far from uncommon event in the United States. However, less prestigious families seldom have the opportunity to tell about a child's death in major newspapers or magazines. Although many Americans shared the sadness at the accidental loss of Conor Clapton, few Americans hear of the thousands of children who die each year in the United States as a result of inadequate sustenance and lack of health care and medical services. How many children could be spared each year if prenatal and medical care existed for all in America?

THEORY: SOCIAL DISORGANIZATION

Problematic behavior can be conceptualized in a variety of ways. The tendency to assign responsibility to individuals for problems is frequently referred to as **personal blame.** When social phenomena and social change are viewed as producing unacceptable behavior, we engage in **system blame** (Eitzen & Zinn, 1994).

This chapter uses a **social disorganization theory** for viewing problems associated with infancy. This theory is only one of many social perspectives that could be applied to children in the first years of life. Because infants are dependent on other people and systems for their very survival, a social disorganization framework seems particularly appropriate for analyzing this developmental phase.

The previous chapter stated that social systems are comprised of various social elements, including social roles, groups, organizations, institutions (e.g., the family and the economic structure), communities, and states (Meenaghan & Washington, 1980, pp. 3–5). However, because of social or cultural advancements and changes, some systems change at slower or faster rates than others. Change results in disequilibrium and social disorganization within the social system and related systems.

An examination of early sociological thought is useful in understanding social disorganization theory. Sociologists August Comte and Herbert Spencer espoused an "organismic" interpretation of society and social structure. They proposed that society and social systems are analogous to biological organisms. Spencer suggests that in both societies and organisms:

1. Growth and development are major themes.
2. Increases in size result in increased differentiation and complexity.
3. Increase in differentiation of structure results in differentiation of function.
4. Parts of the whole are interrelated and interdependent, with a change in one part affecting other parts.

5. Each part of the whole is a social unit or organism itself.
6. While the whole can perish, the parts of the whole can live. (Turner, 1974, pp. 16–17)

Using what is defined in sociology as a **functionalist perspective**, Spencer and others promote social system equilibrium and stability. Instead of explaining social structures as static, passive, and unchanging, functionalists tend to stress survival of social units and their ability to produce a state of **homeostasis**, or balance for the whole and its various parts.

For functionalists, social disorganization, whether due to social change, conflict, or innovation, is often viewed as problematic or pathological, while social order and harmony are perceived as more desirable. For social work practice, this view often requires identifying which system(s) in a social structure is producing social disorganization.

As an example, early social scientists in the United States utilized a social disorganization framework to focus on the processes of industrialization and urbanization and their relationships to social dysfunction in larger cities. Indeed, one could trace the origins of sociology and the profession of social work in the United States to concerns over rapid social change and the emergence of social problems in Boston, New York City, Chicago, Los Angeles, and other large urban centers.

Fundamental to the functionalist perspective is the premise that social structures are organized and maintained by adherence to common ideologies, beliefs, expectations, and rules. This framework creates **social integration** in social units. When social disorganization begins to take place, these binding beliefs and rules are often challenged and may be discarded. According to Julian and Kornblum (1986), social disorganization can result in one of three conditions: normlessness, culture conflict, and breakdown. **Normlessness** refers to a state in which rules to guide behavior are not evident. **Culture conflict** involves the presence of contradictory rules with regard to acceptable behavior. **Breakdown** occurs when "obedience to a set of rules results in no reward or in punishment" (Julian & Kornblum, 1986, p. 13).

In summary, social disorganization theory focuses on the consequences that occur when a "social system, or some part or parts of it, becomes disorganized, with the result that the system operates less effectively" or malfunctions (McKee & Robertson, 1975, p. 14). Underlying most social disorganization is some form of rapid social change that frequently disturbs social norms and expectations and subsequently disrupts the social structure.

DEVELOPMENTAL ISSUES

Developmental literature examining infancy has traditionally focused on physiological and psychological maturation. Physical movement, nurturance, and learning to relate with others constitute fundamental tasks during the first two years of life.

From a sociological viewpoint, growth, maturation, and well-being during infancy are contingent upon the influence of various social systems. For infants, these systems would include caregivers—parents, family members, child care providers, and health care professionals—and social programs, courts, employers, and various societal institutions that have an impact on the life of an infant. Systemic changes or disturbances in one or more of these systems impact infants.

Whereas social workers often readily recognize the influence on clients of caregivers, the family, and employers, changes in society as a whole and in social institutions are not as obvious. In the following sections, we examine implications for infants by family, economic, and political institutions.

THE CHANGING FAMILY

We begin our examination of larger social systems by focusing on the American family. Recent research as well as popular media and political commentators have focused the attention of the nation upon the crises within the American family. Although it is important not to blame a single institution for societal decay, the transformation of the family has broad implications for all Americans, especially infants. Segalman and Himelson suggest:

> The lack of effective family life is one major factor in the creation of a dysfunctional society. This is true in any of the phases of modernization, whether it is in North America, or South America, Africa, Europe, or Asia. Family life appears to be the major element in the creation of what Durkheim called "social solidarity" where people are positively connected to each other. (1994, p. 56)

The family as an institution is not easy to define. Such definitions usually begin with procreation, the regulation of sexual behavior, and the care and socialization of children. The definition and functions of the family are frequently distorted by one's family experiences and adherence to cultural values.

For many years, social scientists conceptualized the family in terms of either an extended or nuclear unit. The **extended family** is commonly defined as several generations of relatives living in close physical proximity. Here aunts, uncles, grandparents, and cousins are active participants in the daily lives of parents and children. Today, this form of family is most often associated with agrarian societies and rural or economically isolated segments in the United States. A distinct advantage of this type of structure involves a familial division of labor for child rearing as well as broader social and material support for infants, children, and parents.

Conversely, the **nuclear family** is a more independent unit consisting of a couple and their dependent children living away from their relatives. The nuclear family in industrialized societies has greater geographical mobility. A benefit of the nuclear family includes its smaller size and adaptability to changing conditions. This family configuration is capable of acquiring more resources for its members as a result of its geographical flexibility, which gives increased accessibility to job opportunities. Moreover, in industrialized societies that afford participation of both parents in the labor force, there is an immediate need for more formalized day care arrangements for infants and children.

Many people would argue that over the years the definition of family has broadened in our society to include "single parents, biracial couples, blended families, unrelated individuals living cooperatives, and homosexual couples" (Crawford, 1999, p. 272). The current legal debate concerning gay marriage is an example of the changing definition of the family in the United States. Indeed, people with a homosexual orientation can form various types of family constellations. These include: lesbian or gay people with children from a previous heterosexual relationship(s), gay or lesbian couples defining each other as spouses and assuming family functions (including adoption, surrogacy, or artificial insemination), and the single person with a homosexual orientation who chooses to be a parent (Kenyon, Chong, Enkoff-Sage, Hill, Mays, & Rochelle, 2003). And, contrary to the misconceptions of many people, research suggests that children of gay or lesbian parents function well with respect to personal development, gender identity, and social relationships (see, for example, Patterson & Redding, 1996).

Clearly, rapid change in family patterns of the 2000s has begun to have an impact upon our perception of the American family. As new and alternative forms of parenting become more prevalent and divorce among couples with children remains widespread, the stereotypic image of the American family as a two-parent, heterosexual head of household has become outdated. It is evident that the institution of the family in America is undergoing change.

Infants in the United States are now born into a high-tech, fast-paced society that lacks a shared, single definition of family. The term **dual worker family** describes the situation in which both husband and wife are employed. Like single-parent families, dual-worker families often face the absence of supports from the workplace and other community resources that could enable spouses to better cope with being both a parent and a worker. Indeed, Moen and Yu (2000) found that having a supportive work environment and employer enhanced quality of life for both male and female workers. Conversely, their results indicated that job insecurity and a demanding job were associated with low quality of life for employees.

Although marriage in the United States is still predicated on the notion of love and commitment, parents often appear to perform more as an economic unit, working together to secure goods in the same physical dwelling, than as two people dedicated to sharing a life together based on mutual aspirations and affection. This can be very frustrating for each member of the family.

Warner (2005) suggests: "For real change to happen, we don't need more politicians sounding off about 'family values.' Neither do we need to pat the backs of working mothers, or 'reward' moms who stay at home, or 'valorize' motherhood, generally by acknowledging that it's 'the toughest job in the world.' We need solutions" (p. 48). Many social workers would propose that greater attention be given to identifying ways in which fathers can better serve as actual or potential resources for their children (Featherstone, 2003). Warner (2005) advocates for societal change in relationship to tax subsidies to encourage corporations to become family friendly, affordable child care, the creation of viable part-time work options for mothers, and tax relief to support working families.

Byng-Hall (1995) suggests that emotional attachments lie at the heart of family life. In order for infants to grow in a nurturing environment, the family needs to be an emotional unit. A secure family base is provided when a reliable network of attachment relationships are present. Regardless of the composition of the family unit, infants and children require relationships between caregiving adults that are "sufficiently collaborative" to ensure that infants sense care and security in their development (Byng-Hall, 1995, p. 45).

Daka-Mulwanda, Thornburg, Filbert, and Klein (1995) expand the concept of collaborative relationships to include the cooperation and coordination of services for infants and children. Infants and parents can best be served by the integration of federal and state government agencies with community-based services and organizations. This integration can be accomplished through shared philosophies, leadership, funding efforts, and pooling of resources.

One of child welfare's greatest challenges is to become family centered (Cole, 1995). How can social workers shift from a mentality of rescuing children to a philosophy of strengthening families? **Family preservation services,** a term often used to describe efforts by social service agencies to help keep families intact, has evoked mixed reactions and is sometimes criticized for risking endangerment of the child.

Cole (1995) suggests that early intervention toward producing stability and support for all families promotes their healthy development. Cole (1995, p.167) identifies the goals of family preservation services as

1. keeping children and families safe,
2. improving family functioning to avoid unnecessary placement of children, and
3. improving the placement process for children, with an emphasis on facilitating reunification of the family.

Recent research indicates that family preservation programs are most effective when services are appropriately targeted for special, at-risk population groups. The difficulty is "in knowing, a priori, which families are truly at imminent risk and having practice and research instruments that operationalize the concept" (Kirk & Griffith, 2004, p. 13). In practice, professionals have come to believe that "the term special population has come to mean virtually everyone. Workers can use practice wisdom to assist in defining who special populations are. Practice-inspired definitions should take into account such factors as general risk, legislation guide, and child vulnerability issues like age and ethnicity" (Denby & Curtis, 2003, p. 164).

The Adoption and Safe Families Act (ASFA) of 1997 was created with the intent of fast-tracking children from foster care to more permanent adoptive homes and discontinuing a long-standing practice of granting primacy to the rights of biological parents and family preservation (Stein, 2003). Even with the creation of the ASFA, the termination of parental legal rights in favor of "the best interests of the child" continues to be a complicated and burdensome endeavor. Extensive court delays, high caseloads for judges and social workers, lack of coordination between courts and child welfare agencies, and heavy court calendars severely hinder the timely and meaningful disposition of child custody cases (Hardin, 1998; Stein, 2003). As a consequence, many children continue to spend an appreciable amount of time in various forms of out-of-home care awaiting court decisions.

As suggested by Warner (2005), one of the more important problems challenging parents of infants in the United States is the need in this industrialized society for a more adequate child care system—in both quality and coverage. The increasing number of single parents and dual-wage-earner families has produced a structural demand for high-quality child care services, yet few industries and businesses provide child care options for their employees.

Relatives, often grandparents, and day care centers address part of the need for child care, but low-income and disadvantaged families often utilize family day care. **Family day care** can be defined as "providers, generally women, who take children into their own homes for a few hours to an entire day. It differs significantly from day care centers in size, personnel, curriculum, physical setting, and atmosphere" (Frankel, 1994, p. 550). Another common aspect of family day care involves in-home child care babysitters, predominantly relatives or neighbors. Full-time nannies generally are employed only by upper-income families.

While all fifty states have some form of regulation of family day care, there are excellent as well as disastrous examples to be found in public, private, and family day care. Frankel asks several important questions with regard to state licensing, certification, and registration requirements that monitor child care services:

1. Do regulation requirements promote quality family day care?
2. How are regulations enforced?
3. How does family day care come under regulation?
4. Are national standards necessary? (1994, p. 552)

Regulating the quality of family day care is complex, with macro system problems of staggering proportions. Generally, state governments serve as the major legislative bodies mandating regulatory behavior. States often struggle to enact legislation initiatives aimed at monitoring an increasingly diverse day care industry. State regulations can be effective in improving quality of care, but day care regulations also tend to undermine the availability and affordability of services. Additionally, enforcement of regulations is cumbersome, tricky, and expensive (Gormley, 1999).

If we are committed to family preservation services, how can child care services be delivered in a manner that strengthens the overall family? Carol Williams, former Associate Commissioner of the Federal Children's Bureau, places child care as a primary element in family preservation. "We see child care as a part of a hub, a network in the continuum of services in the community . . . critical places where families can be linked to other resources" (Carroad, 1994, p. 15). However, there are continuing concerns that supportive services in preservation programs are too brief to both stabilize and rehabilitate a family. Ultimately, the question becomes which goal is of uppermost importance—protection of the child or continuation of the family unit? In abusive situations, this question is paramount and requires input from many disciplines.

Based on our brief examination of the American family, several macro system insights for social workers intervening on behalf of infants have emerged. First, the definition of the family is undergoing a significant transformation. Second, while the structure of the family in the United States is changing, infants require safe and secure environments to help ensure proper nurture and growth. Finally, when appropriately targeted and delivered, family support and preservation services can protect and nurture infants. These services impact society both directly and indirectly. "If the family is absent, fragmented, dysfunctional, or powerless, then the socialization of its children will lead to weak, ineffectual, parasitic or antisocial adults" (Segalman & Himelson, 1994, p. 58).

THE CHANGING ECONOMY

Central to all of human experience and present-day society is the principle of work. From the time of simple hunting and gathering to today's industrial age, societies have organized to produce goods and services that provide sustenance, clothing, and shelter to those who participate. Parents provide for their offspring through the structure of work instituted by the social system in which they live. At the same time, socioeconomic inequality is created through the rewards available to workers. The degree to which parents provide for their children is contingent upon earning power in the socioeconomic system, whether it is the result of participation in the labor force or inheritance.

The U.S. work world is typically described in terms of its capitalistic philosophy, high-tech environment, and leadership in the global marketplace. With an unprecedented (some sevenfold) growth in the global economy in the last fifty years (Seipel, 2003) and the weakening of trade barriers, particularly between the United States and Latin America, the American economy and employment have truly become global. A global economy creates specific social-economic conditions and challenges for poorer citizens in the United States, especially single women with dependent children.

Polack (2004) contends that the new global economy facilitates the proliferation of sweatshop labor, inferior and unsafe working conditions, and inadequate living wages in third world countries. Exploitation of labor in developing countries exemplifies "unbridled, free market capitalism operating in the context of a glutted labor market, which is to say the wholesale exploitation of vulnerable peoples in the pursuit of maximizing profit" (pp. 285–286). Of course, women and child labor head the list of probable exploited groups of people. Keep in mind, "The list of multinational companies benefiting from sweatshop labor is very long and includes virtually every major retail supplier in the United States" (p. 285).

The financial circumstances of parents with infants are the major focus of this section. How do changes as a result of a global economy affect employment opportunities? How do working conditions in the United States impact young children? Who are the working poor and the poverty stricken? Who in America feels most keenly the brunt of weakening trade barriers and exploitation of foreign labor sources?

We need to be familiar with some of the language of corporate America in order to set the tone for our inquiry concerning current trends in the U.S. economy. The following tongue-in-cheek phrases and words were coined more than a decade ago in *Fortune* magazine's "Cliched Corporate Conversations from Hell." These sarcastic definitions were written in the vein of Abrose Bierce's *The Devil's Dictionary* (*Fortune*, 1995, p. 22).

Team Player	An employee who substitutes the thinking of the herd for his [or her] own good judgment.
Reengineering	The principal slogan of the Nineties, used to describe any and all corporate strategies.
Vision	Top management's heroic guess about the future, easily printed on mugs, T-shirts, posters, and calendar cards.
Paradigm Shift	A euphemism companies use when they realize the rest of their industry has expanded into Guangdong while they were invested in Orange County.
Restructuring	A simple plan instituted from above in which workers are right-sized, downsized, surplused, lateralized, or in the business jargon of days of yore, fired.
Empowerment	A magic wand management waves to help traumatized survivors of restructuring suddenly feel engaged, self managed, and in control of their futures and their lives.

The relationship between employment opportunities for clients with children and labor outsourcing to developing countries is a concern for all social workers. Changes in the economy affect more than profit taking and the value of one's investment portfolio; they directly impact the lives of poorer Americans. If parents are unable to find work, experience a decline in wages, or are displaced from the labor force, they will be forced to rely on welfare programs or to seek help from other sources.

Labor market factors are commonly cited by married women with children as reasons for entering welfare programs, whereas "widowed, divorced or separated women were more likely to cite family structure changes as reasons for entering welfare" (Leahy, Buss, & Quane, 1995, p. 41). Over 75 percent of the respondents in the study by Leahy and colleagues indicated that their ability to leave welfare was a result of increased earnings or increased earnings of a spouse. The research of Perry-Burney and Jennings (2003) suggests underemployment and unemployment, transportation, and child care as barriers to self-sufficiency for consumers of public assistance programs. Similarly, Pearlmutter and Bartle (2000) report that women believe jobs with a living wage and subsidized child care are significant factors in making a successful transition from welfare to work.

Many studies mistakenly identify divorce as the major cause of women's poverty. These "analyses fail to recognize that it is the visibility of women's unequal access to independent resources, primarily employment income, that divorce reveals" (Pulkingham, 1995, p. 7). Gender is an important consideration as it relates to employment, underemployment, and the ability to acquire a living wage to support a family in America.

Edin (1991) indicates that the economy strongly affects behavior. When parents, usually women, are pushed to participate in welfare programs, they will engage in whatever actions they deem economically necessary to provide for their children. They may conceal from their welfare worker both outside income and financial assistance from family members or the absent father.

In a narrative fashion, Jason DeParle (2004) chronicles six generations of the Samuel Caples family to examine the relationship between the family, politics, economic conditions, race, gender, and welfare in America. Beginning with life on the plantation in 1840 and concluding with our nation's current drive to end public welfare, DeParle describes a family's multigenerational struggle to lay claim to a better, more independent, and prosperous existence.

In his epilogue, DeParle (2004) suggests that recent welfare reform emphasizing the trading of welfare checks for pay stubs has produced minimal structural gain for those impoverished. "No matter how many double shifts Angie pulled, she couldn't close the growing gaps that increasingly define American life. The rising inequality has grown so familiar that it has lost its ability to startle. . . . [L]ower wage workers have vanished from a domestic agenda that's been dominated by a tax-cutting frenzy, mostly aimed at the same upper-income families who have enjoyed outsized gains" (DeParle, 2004, p. 327).

The research of Edin and DeParle illustrate how women who rely on public assistance to provide for children are both resilient and resourceful. The misfortunes of women with dependent children can be more complex than typically imagined. Yet, their resilience can run equally deep (DeParle, 2004, p. 325).

Readers are cautioned to resist the temptation to view economic opportunities for parents with children in a piecemeal or program-by-program manner over large-scale systemic change. It is often simpler to focus exclusively on specific policies and programs such as child support enforcement (Oellerich, Garfinkel, & Robins, 1991) or parental leave plans that benefit infants than it is to attack the core of economic oppression. Goldberg reminds us that "childhood poverty in this country ought to be setting off national alarms" (1995, p. 47). While programs like the Special Supplemental Feeding Program for Women, Infants, and Children (WIC) have been very successful in addressing nutritional needs of low-income pregnant women, infants, and children, "poverty reduction rather than WIC expansion must be our primary goal" (Goldberg, 1995, p. 47). How that is to be accomplished continues to puzzle administrators of the program. Though WIC is an excellent program, it serves only a small percentage of women and children eligible for services.

To summarize, poor families in America at this time live in a capitalistic and global economy that is characterized by service-oriented employment, a demand for highly skilled jobs, utilization of part-time workers, and the outsourcing of labor to developing countries. Our brief consideration of the economic institution reveals several factors influencing the ability of parents to provide for infants and children in the United States. Among these are the types of jobs present in the labor force, availability of living wage employment, corporate exploitation of foreign labor markets, global economic interdependence, and the systematic economic oppression of people based on ethnicity, race, and gender.

THE POLITICAL PROCESS

Do you vote? Are you able to name the U.S. senators from your state or the congressperson serving your district? Are you familiar with the various state senators and representatives charged with formulating laws in your state? Who are the leaders of your state and local executive branches, your governor, your mayor? Who are the judges that interpret and act upon law in various federal, state, and local jurisdictions?

If you had difficulty in answering these questions, you are not alone. Many Americans struggle in their attempt to understand the political system in the United States and to keep abreast of political trends and current legislation. Yet the political action of a society performs important functions. Political systems, through the establishment of government, enable societies to establish social control, develop norms and laws, produce economic security, set priorities, provide for the common good, and equip for defense from outside dangers. Moreover, votes on health and entitlement policies and programs benefiting infants and children often are determined by political ideologies and alliances.

In general, **politics** can be defined as "the process that determines which groups of people or individuals exercise power over others" (Tischler, 1990, p. 490). Weber (1958) describes power as the ability of one person or group to carry out their will over others. The stakes are high when a particular person, group, or party takes political office. Government leaders have power. Sanctioned by their position, which was acquired by election, coup, or appointment, government officials have the ability to make decisions that impact large numbers of people of all ages.

Political debate concerning social welfare over the last two decades has centered on curtailment of spending and promoting fiscal responsibility, state and local rights, the work ethic, self-sufficiency, a reduction in welfare rolls, and privatization of services (Long, 2000). In 2005, President George W. Bush went so far as to propose a restructuring and overhaul of the social security system toward the creation of individual investment accounts.

Women who are single parents, as well as infants and children relying on government assistance, are easy political prey. This is especially true when compared to powerful lobbyist groups and corporate heads and stockholders prospering from the global economy and governmental spending on a post-9/11 build up of the military-industrial complex. The fact that children do not vote is not lost upon those in elected offices.

Women with young, dependent children rarely are heard by politicians and have minimal political clout. In addition, research suggests that recipients of public assistance, such as mothers receiving Temporary Assistance to Needy Families, are often misled by the political language and verbiage surrounding social welfare as stated by politicians. When considering the perspective of consumers of services, Tickamyer, Henderson, White, and Tadlock (2000) found: "Much welfare reform rhetoric revolves around classification of poor people as deserving versus undeserving and responsible versus irresponsible. . . . [It was] the women's allegiance to their families, especially their children that took precedence over most other considerations, including employment" (pp. 184–185).

One of the more important challenges for social workers involves promoting the voices and perspectives of consumers of services in policy development, legislative initiatives, and social planning. This commitment was reflected in the National Association of Social Workers' 2003 national campaign of "Preserving rights. Strengthening voices."

Unfortunately, powerful people often enjoy disproportional "access to information supporting their positions, develop an inside track to decision makers and power brokers, and approach planning in a sophisticated and savvy manner. People in power are adept at using behind-the-scenes means of persuading others to adopt their point of view" (Long, Tice, & Morrison, 2006, p. 148). Overcoming these unfair advantages is formidable and often requires a convincing and concerted effort among consumers, professionals, and other interested parties.

Our brief glimpse into the political system in America is intended to raise awareness of the crucial role of governmental leaders. Support for social programs benefiting infants correlates closely with the beliefs and priorities of individuals, groups, or parties in political power. As political winds change direction, government support for young children often shifts. It is important for social workers to analyze and participate in the political environment in which they practice. The social worker-client relationship is immersed in politics whenever the executive branch enforces the law, a legislative branch makes laws, or the judicial system interprets them.

| CASE EXAMPLE | # COMMUNITY INTERVENTION FOR MOTHERS AND INFANTS |

Mrs. Clara Sherman, a 36-year-old African-American woman, is the newly appointed executive director of Help Me Grow, located in a large city in the western United States. Help Me Grow is an organization specializing in preventative and early intervention services for at-risk infants and mothers. Clara received her Master of Social Work degree in 1995 with a concentration in clinical social work. She has worked at Help Me Grow for the past six years, first as a social worker and then as a supervisor of social workers.

While in graduate school, Clara also completed several courses in supervision and administration. Her faculty advisor was aware of research indicating the increasing number of MSW graduates entering supervisory positions (Skidmore, 1995), so she recommended these courses in anticipation of Clara's entry into an administrative position at the agency. Since graduation, Clara has continued to develop her knowledge base and skills in administration through graduate course work and specialized workshops. Every two years, Clara's state requires thirty clock hours of continuing education for license renewal. Help Me Grow has paid for and supported Clara's participation in workshops and conferences. Much of her continuing education has focused on social work administration.

In her new position at Help Me Grow, Clara is very involved in coordinating and supervising pediatric services and referrals for high-risk, low-income mothers and infants. Clara has assumed a leadership role in advocating for early detection and screening programs, the effective monitoring of growth and development of infants, preventive health care, psychosocial intervention, and prenatal and pediatric care clinics. Under her leadership, Help Me Grow developed a comprehensive and user-friendly information and referral system linking at-risk mothers and infants to a variety of organizations and professionals (e.g., social workers, nurses, pediatricians, and health care specialists).

As a new director, Clara faces many challenges. Last year, under her direction, the social work staff at Help Me Grow (two MSWs and two BSWs) conducted a comprehensive needs assessment for the service area. One goal of the assessment was to identify population groups within the purview of the agency that were not being served or were being underserved. Findings indicated that a growing number of women in the community were diagnosed with severe mental illness. Many of the respondents in this study who were mothers of infants needed services and case management from Help Me Grow. These women had little knowledge in the areas of nutrition, developmental milestones, and practical information regarding the care of infants.

The suburban area served by Help Me Grow is characterized by both economic and urban decline. The relocation of a major transportation center, the revitalization of the nearby downtown business district, and an increasing crime rate have resulted in suburban flight by longtime residents of the neighborhood. Those remaining have fallen even lower on the poverty scale. In addition, the national trend toward deinstitutionalization of people with mental disabilities has made this section of the city a haven for people experiencing mental illness who live alone.

Coincidentally, the Help Me Grow needs assessment and a recent community plan assessment completed by the local mental health association produced similar results in describing a profile of women and infants requiring prenatal and pediatric services. The profile of women in need of Help Me Grow assistance highlighted several characteristics: most were in their early twenties, predominantly white, living in some form of private housing. They had been hospitalized on average two times during the last five years and continue to receive psychotropic medication. They were marginally employed, and were involved in romantic relationships but remained unmarried. A large percentage of this group was enrolled in some form of case management funded by the county mental health association. Clara and the social work staff convinced the governing board of directors of Help Me Grow that this segment of the community is being underserved and will require special programming. While empathetic, the Help Me Grow board is concerned about public cutbacks in funding.

Time to Think!

In this case example, Clara Sherman is a social worker performing an administrative role in macro practice. She is exerting organizational leadership by identifying and articulating future directions whereby her agency can address a community need (Brody & Nair, 1995). Clara's client system comprises a specific population of women and infants. What macro-level issues are raised here? How should they be prioritized? Does Clara's employment as a social work administrator impose an increased need to assess and utilize macro-level systems? If so, why?

Macro Systems and Women With Severe Mental Illness and Their Infants

As previously emphasized, a major focus of this book involves the inclusion of macro systems and issues for assessing problems in social work practice. Our intent is to demonstrate how this emphasis transcends the specific role in which a social worker is employed. In the following sections, consider the organizational, community, societal, and global factors that could facilitate or inhibit the creation of special prenatal and pediatric programming for women with severe mental illnesses.

Organizational Level As the chief administrator at Help Me Grow, Clara Sherman is active in planning, coordinating, and evaluating various aspects of organizational life to help her agency define and achieve its goals. Thus, she has a clear vision of Help Me Grow's mission and objectives. Clara knows the structure of Help Me Grow, where the locus of power is located, the resources available, and how internal processes operate. Clara has thoroughly analyzed the strengths and limitations of her own organization for providing pediatric care.

Clara has also benefited from her experience in providing direct service to women and infants at Help Me Grow. Over the years, as a case manager and later as a social work administrator, Clara has collected information from and nurtured contacts with

continued

many important social service organizations. These included the local mental health center, the county mental health association and board, the local chapter of the National Association for the Mentally Ill (NAMI), children's services, many local health care providers, the county commissioner's office, city hall, and various advocacy and crisis centers for women.

Clara firmly believes that successful program development at Help Me Grow aimed at providing service for women with severe mental illness will require input and a collaborative effort from many, if not all, of the aforementioned organizations. For Clara and her staff, contacting key individuals and organizing meetings to assess common interests and goals for developing a program of intervention with this population will be essential. Clara is well aware of the financial hardships currently facing social service organizations and is realistic as she considers the ability of funding sources to finance new programs.

In her quest to appraise the willingness of various organizations to pursue prenatal and pediatric services for women with severe mental illness, Clara has not forgotten the perspective of the consumer and the importance of client input in all phases and aspects of social work practice. Whether it represents individual clients or organized associations of clients, the voice of the consumer in assessing problems and planning interventions is imperative. Clients with severe mental illness are strongly empowered when they take actions that improve their own life situations.

By regular study of research and practice literature, Clara is aware that gender differences exist when assessing viable social networks for people with severe mental illness. Walsh (1994) suggests that men with severe mental illness are more likely to participate in task-oriented and recreational organizations like the YMCA, the community center, and clubs, whereas women with severe mental illness are more likely to remain with relatives and nontask-oriented friends in neighborhoods and social groups. Clara also knows that there are many ways that clients can become involved and participate in social planning at her organization: consumer meetings, advisory boards, consumer support groups, board membership surveys, and participation in research (Long, Tice, & Morrison, 2006). This information is particularly important when considering how to shape the form and structure of any prenatal or pediatric program designed for women with severe mental illness.

Community Level Help Me Grow is located in a community experiencing rapid social change. Once a thriving suburb, the area is now characterized by low-income housing, high unemployment, and increasing crime. Many of these changes can be attributed to an economic downturn in this part of the city. A major airport serving the western half of the United States was closed and relocated outside of town. Meanwhile, city officials have spent millions of dollars to modernize the adjacent downtown business district, climaxed by new major league baseball and football stadiums, with little attention directed toward the community served by Help Me Grow.

For businesses that have remained in the community, vandalism, theft, and other forms of crime have become the norm. As an example, local pizza franchises no longer deliver and after dark require customers to pick up pizza orders via drive-through windows. This is intended to protect employees and customers from theft and physical harm.

Because rent is cheap, single parents as well as other people struggling financially have become residents in the community. Help Me Grow and other social service agencies have seen their client rolls and waiting lists climb as the community has become increasingly impoverished.

Fortunately, a stalwart faction in the community has been an ecumenical coalition of local congregations. Consistent with the findings of Cnaan, Sinha, and McGrew (2004), this religious coalition, along with many individual congregations, has worked to establish and support a variety of community-based social services. It is clear to Clara and other professionals that congregations "and their members have [an] intimate understanding of the changing needs of people in the community" (Cnaan, Sinha, & McGrew, 2004, p. 57). They have refurbished houses, held fund-raising activities, and provided informal care that brings together individuals for social support and accomplishment of simple tasks. They have developed support groups, including a group for parents with infants. Congregations have served an important function in the community by providing stability and an increased sense of security.

It is important to note that faith-based initiatives have become a prevalent means offered to solve America's social ills in communities. For President George W. Bush, faith-based organizations (FBOs) became a significant component in his domestic agenda. Solomon states: "As governor of Texas, Bush implemented Charitable Choice aggressively, promoted an ambitious legislative agenda designed to free FBOs from government red tape, and lent personal support to two controversial programs: Teen Challenge International U.S.A. and the InnerChange Freedom Initiative" (2003, p. 27). As president, George W. Bush has acted to reduce governmental responsibility for the poor and sought to promote a national faith-based policy. Such an agenda is fraught with difficulties, including the role of religion in public life, the constitutional separation of church and state, equal treatment of religions, and the influence of the faith-factor for client self-determination (Solomon, 2003, p. 22).

Gainful employment for her clients is one of Clara's greatest concerns. Clients repeatedly express their desire to work. However, with the recent relocation of the airport and jobs being lost to cheap labor overseas, employment is increasingly difficult to find. The city lacks an effective system of transportation for consumers of social services. This is a real and identifiable barrier to employment (see, for example, Blumenberg, 2000). Fulfilling work aspirations for women with severe mental challenges who are attempting to nurture infant children is particularly demanding. Successful job placement is a time-consuming endeavor requiring a careful assessment of the strengths of each client and realistic employment opportunities for the severely mentally disabled in the community (Tice, 1994).

Societal Level How do politicians in the United States view women who seek economic assistance for their infant children? Tickamyer, Henderson, White, and

continued

Tadlock (2000) suggest that efforts toward welfare reform "emphasize the carrot of making work pay and providing programs to enhance employability or the stick of time limits and sanctions for failure to adhere to social and program rules, norms, and values" (p. 176). For many social workers, recent events appear to reveal a dark time in U.S. history as politicians and legislative representatives work at reestablishing their definition of traditional family values and seek to overemphasize individual responsibility in social policy.

Yet many Americans fully accept a popular outlook that views women with infants on welfare as social parasites. This noncaring attitude is sometimes taken to extremes. Years ago, former House Speaker Newt Gingrich advocated for the return of orphanages for needy children as well as the severing of parental rights if parents were unable to nurture and provide for their children. Myths and stereotypes continue to abound in the United States regarding people with mental illness. Such people are often viewed as dangerous and a threat to society (Davis, 1991). These negative images serve to further discriminate and obstruct housing and employment opportunities for the mentally ill.

As she considers establishing a prenatal and pediatric program serving economically deprived women with mental illness, Clara joins forces with other professionals in finding ways to educate society to the plight of both the mentally ill and poor women with dependent children. Though many people will be empathetic toward helping small children, they may still regard the mothers of those children with suspicion and anger. Unfortunately, there are those who believe that mental illness is either an evasive diagnosis or a disease that can only be treated by hospitalization.

The passage of the Americans with Disabilities Act of 1990 (ADA) signaled monumental federal legislation mandating action to eliminate discrimination against individuals with disabilities. The stigma of mental illness, however, makes funding and promoting of programs all the more difficult. Clara will assess the implications of the ADA for her agency and determine if any ADA service mandates apply to mothers and infants being served at Help Me Grow. These mandates have particular significance regarding any future programs for clients diagnosed as severely mentally ill.

Clara's involvement with PACE, the NASW's political action committee, allows her to be informed of new legislation relevant to mentally ill women with young children. She can then be proactive in sharing her concerns with legislators and advocating for her agency's clientele. Therapy and medications need to be available to these clients who lack health coverage. Clara meets monthly with her local representative from the state legislature to share insights that will open up employment opportunities for mothers experiencing mental illness.

International Level The American welfare state has been and is in crisis as a result of current trends in the global economy (Karger, 1991). Corporations, forced to vie for profits in a highly competitive world marketplace, implement policies emphasizing efficiency and economic viability. These policies spur plant shutdowns, industrial reorganization, and the implementation of advanced technology.

To assist corporations in becoming more profitable, the government often curtails taxes and creates economic incentives to make capital available to corporations for investment. These forms of government support of business and industry fall under the classification of **corporate welfare.** The net economic outgrowth of these subsidies are increased government debt and a reduction in welfare spending.

People seeking employment in this economic environment see long-term employees being replaced by part-time, temporary, outsourced, and lower-paid workers. Even as a member of a professional, managerial, or technical group, an unemployed person may become a participant in a floating population of workers moving from job to job in pursuit of better salary and benefits, with little personal attachment or stake in her or his current employment.

For Clara, these types of employment practices are very familiar. In working with low-income mothers with infants, Clara sees a national trend toward reducing welfare services and benefits. Not only are the available jobs low paying and temporary, but Clara's clients compete with high school and college students for these service-oriented positions. The reality is that "cutbacks and or termination of programs and entitlements reduce our capacity as professionals to help those we serve" (Ramos & Briar-Lawson, 2004, p. 364).

It is important to realize that at the economic heart of globalization is "the expansion of markets so that investors can maximize profits by finding the cheapest labor with few labor and environmental restrictions" (Ramos & Briar-Lawson, 2004, p. 362). As such, globalization directly contributes to poverty and inequality worldwide through corporate exploitation of labor and natural resources.

As a social worker, Clara sees many of her clients unable to meet their needs through fair wage employment with health care benefits. Although she realizes that many infants in other parts of the world do not receive nutrition, medical care, and various forms of support of the quality provided in the United States, means of survival and standards of living are relative concepts. Clara's quest is to determine how to provide the best prenatal and pediatric care possible for expectant mothers and infants, using American standards. Comprehensive and equitable provision of care is important in order to save the lives of infants and because the United States is often seen as setting standards for desirable quality of care for children across the globe.

REFLECTION ON DIVERSITY: USING AN ASSORTMENT OF LENSES

An asset for any social worker is the ability to view diversity through multiple lenses. Perhaps this would clarify for the wearer the disadvantages that exist for one with a disability or one who is discriminated against on the basis of race, gender, ethnicity, sexual orientation, or age.

In social work practice, professionals must continually work to sharpen their abilities to visualize and understand various forms of diversity. Other factors provide guidance in selecting the appropriate lens: environmental conditions, presenting problems, and consumer self-determination, among others.

As an example, citing the high rate of black infant mortality early in this chapter might be seen as viewing through a racial lens a problem that is found in all groups. However, research is clear in describing the high risk of death for African-American infants in the United States.

Others argue that infants with Hawaiian and American Indian mothers also experience a high risk of death in our society. Or, given a growing Hispanic/Latino population in the United States, why not focus on the variation in infant mortality rates for babies of Puerto Rican mothers (7.8 per 1,000) as compared with those of Cuban mothers (3.6 per 1,000) or Mexican mothers (5.6 per 1,000) (see, Mathews, Curtin, & MacDorman, 2000). Although each of these constitutes a valid consideration, relevance to consumers and the presenting situation will be major determinants in deciding the pertinence and use of information.

Earlier in this chapter, we briefly examined a growing body of literature describing women receiving public assistance and their views concerning work and welfare (Blumenberg, 2000; Pearlmutter & Bartle, 2000; Perry-Burney & Jennings, 2003). These readings require the reader to try to apply a lens for viewing public assistance and work from the perspective of single women with young children. Do you own such a pair of glasses? If so, are you wearing an updated prescription?

As an aid to the profession of social work, *Affilia* is a journal explicitly dedicated to issues of gender and women. Diversity-based professional publications assist readers in sharpening their knowledge and outlook with respect to a range of issues affecting specific population groups.

In the case example, Clara Sherman has become adept at both separately and simultaneously wearing diversity lenses. She has diligently worked to develop her skills and knowledge in areas where discrimination occurs. In her role as a social worker, Clara is personally and professionally challenged to envision life with a severe mental disability. Learning from consumers, educational forums, and experiential opportunities increase her awareness of the needs and difficulties encountered by clients. Because appreciation and understanding of human diversity is a dynamic and ever-changing quest, Clara knows the effort to see and understand life through the eyes of other people constitutes more of a commitment and process than an outcome.

APPLYING A SOCIAL WORK FRAMEWORK: SOCIAL DISORGANIZATION THEORY

At the beginning of this chapter, a social disorganization perspective was introduced. Fundamental to an understanding of social disorganization theory is the premise that a social structure is comprised of various systems that are interrelated and interdependent. When change occurs in one system, changes take place in other parts of the whole. From this orientation, social structures, much like human organisms, strive to survive and establish a sense of balance or homeostasis.

In our case example, Clara Sherman stays abreast of modifications in other systems that could impact her agency. Over the years, it has become increasingly apparent to Clara that changes occurring at all social levels have affected life at Help Me Grow. Several of the more significant societal revolutions include a high divorce rate and the rapid growth of the single-parent family in the United States, a restructuring of corporate America and the American workforce in a global economy, and the recent political turn toward less government with greater emphasis on individual responsibility. Within the neighborhood served by Help Me Grow, a high rate of unemployment and underemployment has resulted in increased poverty and a rise in demand for social services.

Using a social disorganization perspective, Figueira-McDonough concludes that when communities experience high rates of poverty they "will have high levels of social disorganization in the domains of work, family, and community detachment" (1995, p. 63). Changes in the economy, family structure, politics, education, and religion impact Help Me Grow. What meaning will these changes have upon the agency's efforts to service mentally ill mothers? While Clara is uncertain as to which of them functions as the motor propelling social disorganization, she strives to understand the significance of these changing institutions.

When assessing organizational life from a social disorganization perspective, Clara has learned that Help Me Grow does not operate in a vacuum. A swing of the political pendulum, a turn in the economy, or a twist in family structures will influence the functioning of Clara's agency and the lives of her clients. At times, Clara's job seems overwhelming as she tries to keep up to date and knowledgeable about a dynamic and changing social environment.

SUGGESTED ACTIVITIES

1. Using a discussion group format, examine issues related to day care for infants in America. What five factors would influence your decision to place a child in day care? How many day care facilities are available within a three-mile radius of your home? From whom would you learn about the reputations of these providers? What are the difficulties and expenses associated with enrollment?

2. Contact the officer of a local labor union to observe a meeting, rally, or gathering. Are unemployment, outsourcing of the labor force, or corporate welfare referred to directly or obliquely? What union programs are family friendly and responsive to the health and welfare of young children?
3. Observe a city council meeting in your hometown or a legislative assembly session. If this is impractical, you may choose to watch a congressional session on C-Span via cable television. Analyze the political rhetoric and identify the group of people or constituency each member appeals to or represents. Would you consider the speaker to be in support of social policies and programs for families and children? Why or why not?
4. When you next make a phone call to an airline or a customer service representative, ask the employee for his or her physical location. In what country are they answering your request? How does this impact employment opportunities?

REFERENCES

Blumenberg, E. (2000). Moving welfare participants to work: Women, transportation, and welfare reform. *Affilia, 15*, 259–277.

Brody, R., & Nair, M. (1995). *Macro practice: A generalist approach*. Wheaton, IL: Gregory.

Byng-Hall, J. (1995). Creating a secure family base: Some implications of attachment theory for family therapy. *Family Process, 34*, 45–58.

Carroad, D. (1994). Key child care and other federal programs for infants and toddlers. *Children Today, 23*, 14–36.

Central Intelligence Agency. (2005). *The World Factbook*. Online at www.cia.gov/cia/publications/factbook/rankorder/2091rank.html.

Cnaan, R., Sinha, J., & McGrew, C. (2004). Congregations as social service providers: Services, capacity, culture and organizational behavior. *Administration in Social Work, 28*, 47–68.

Cole, E. (1995). Becoming family centered: Child welfare's challenge. *Families in Society, 76*, 163–172.

Crawford, J. (1999). Co-parent adoptions by same-sex couples: From loophole to law. *Families in Society, 80*, 271–278.

Daka-Mulwanda, V., Thornburg, K., Filbert, L., & Klein, T. (1995). Collaboration of services for children and families: A synthesis of recent research and recommendations. *Family Relations, 44*, 219–223.

Davis, S. (1991). An overview: Are mentally ill people really more dangerous? *Social Work, 36*, 174–180.

DeParle, J. (2004). *American dream: Three women, ten kids, and a nation's drive to end welfare*. New York: Viking Press.

Denby, R., & Curtis, C. (2003). Why special populations are not the target of family preservation services: A case for program reform. *Journal of Sociology and Social Welfare, 30*, 149–174.

Edin, K. (1991). Surviving the welfare system: How AFDC recipients make ends meet in Chicago. *Social Problems, 38*, 462–474.

Eitzer, D., & Zinn, M. (1994). *Social problems*. Boston: Allyn & Bacon.

Featherstone, B. (2003). Taking fathers seriously. *British Journal of Social Work, 33*, 239–254.

Figueira-McDonough, J. (1995). Community organization and the underclass: Exploring new practice directions. *Social Service Review, 69,* 57–85.

Fortune. (1995). Cliched corporate conversations from hell, *131,* 22.

Frankel, A. (1994). Family day care in the United States. *Families in Society, 75,* 550–560.

Goldberg, P. (1995). Poverty and nutrition: If Steinbeck were alive today. *Families in Society, 76,* 46–49.

Gormley, W. (1999). Regulating child care quality. *Annals of the American Academy of Political and Social Science, 563,* 116–129.

Hardin, M. (1998). Child protection cases in a unified family court. *Family Law Quarterly, 32,* 147–199.

Havighurst, R. (1952). *Developmental tasks and children.* New York: McKay.

Julian, J., & Kornblum, Q. (1986). *Social problems.* Englewood Cliffs, NJ: Prentice-Hall.

Karger, H. (1991). The global economy and the American welfare state. *Journal of Sociology and Social Welfare, 18,* 3–20.

Kenyon, G., Chong, K., Enkoff-Sage, M., Hill, C., Mays, C., & Rochelle, L. (2003). Public adoption by gay and lesbian parents in North Carolina: Policy and practice. *Families in Society, 84,* 571–575.

Kirk, R., & Griffith, D. (2004). Intensive family preservation services: Demonstrating placement prevention using event history analysis. *Social Work Research, 28,* 5–17.

Leahy, P., Buss, T., & Quane, J. (1995). Time on welfare: Why do people enter and leave the system? *American Journal of Economics and Sociology, 54,* 33–46.

Long, D. (2000). Welfare reform: A social work perspective for assessing success. *Journal of Sociology and Social Welfare, 27,* 61–78.

Long, D., Tice, C., & Morrison, J. (2006). *Macro social work practice: A strengths perspective.* Belmont, CA: Thomson Brooks/Cole.

McKee, M., & Robertson, I. (1975). *Social problems.* New York: Random House.

Mathews, T., Curtin, S., & MacDorman, M. (2000). Infant mortality statistics from the 1998 period linked birth/infant death data set. *National Vital Statistics Reports, 48,* 1–26.

Meenaghan, T., & Washington, R. (1980). *Social policy and social welfare: Structure and applications.* New York: Free Press.

Moen, P., & Yu, Y. (2000). Effective work/life strategies: Working couples, work conditions, gender, and life quality. *Social Problems, 47,* 291–326.

Newacheck, P., Hung, Y., Hochstein, M., & Halfon, N. (2002). Access to health care for disadvantaged young children. *Journal of Early Intervention, 25,* 1–11.

Newsweek. (1992). His saddest song, March 23, 52–53.

Oellerich, D., Garfinkel, I., & Robins, P. (1991). Private child support: Current and potential impacts. *Journal of Sociology and Social Welfare, 18,* 3–20.

Patterson, C., & Redding, R. (1996). Lesbian and gay families with children: Implications of social science research for policy. *Journal of Social Issues, 52,* 29–51.

Pearlmutter, S., & Bartle, E. (2000). Supporting the move from welfare to work: What women say. *Affilia, 15,* 153–173.

Perry-Burney, G., & Jennings, A. (2003). Welfare to what? A policy agenda. *Journal of Health and Social Policy, 16,* 85–99.

Polack, R. (2004). Social justice and the global economy: New challenges for social work in the 21st century. *Social Work, 49,* 281–290.

Pulkingham, J. (1995). Investigating the financial circumstances of separated and divorced parents: Implications for family law reform. *Canadian Public Policy, 21,* 1–19.

Ramos, B., & Briar-Lawson, K. (2004). Globalization and international social work. In A. Sallee (Ed.), *Social work and social welfare: An introduction* (pp. 356–378). Peosta, IA: Eddie Bowers.

Segalman, R., & Himelson, A. (1994). The family: Past, present, and future. *International Journal of World Peace, 11,* 51–64.

Seipel, M. (2003). Global poverty: No longer an untouchable problem. *International Social Work, 46,* 191–207.

Shi, L., Stevens, G., Wulu, J., Politzer, R., & Xu, J. (2004). America's health centers: Reducing racial and ethnic disparities in perinatal care and birth outcomes. *Health Services Research, 39,* 1881–1902.

Skidmore, R. (1995). *Social work administration: Dynamic management and human relationships.* Boston: Allyn & Bacon.

Solomon, L. (2003). *In God we trust?* New York: Lexington Books.

Stein, T. (2003). The Adoption and Safe Families Act: How Congress overlooks available data and ignores systemic obstacles in its pursuit of political goals. *Children and Youth Services Review, 25,* 669–682.

Tice, C. (1994). A community's response to supported employment: Implications for social work practice. *Social Work, 39,* 728–735.

Tickamyer, A., Henderson, D., White, J., & Tadlock, B. (2000). Voice of welfare reform: Bureaucratic rationality versus the perceptions of welfare participants. *Affilia, 15,* 173–193.

Tischler, H. (1990). *Introduction to sociology.* New York: Holt, Rinehart & Winston.

Turner, J. (1974). *The structure of sociological theory.* Homewood, IL: Dorsey Press.

U.S. Department of Health and Human Services. (2000). *Healthy people 2010: Understanding and improving health,* 2nd ed. Washington, DC: U.S. Government Printing Office.

Walsh, J. (1994). Gender differences in the social networks of persons with severe mental illness. *Affilia, 9,* 247–268.

Warner, J. (2005). Family. *Newsweek,* February 21, 42–49.

Weber, M. (1958). Class, status, and party. In H. Gerth & C. Mills (Eds.), *Max Weber: Essays in sociology.* New York: Oxford University Press.

PRESCHOOL CHILDREN

A mischievous-looking boy with tousled blonde hair pulls his wagon down the sidewalk. He is wearing bib overalls, tennis shoes, and a striped shirt. He greets his next-door neighbor with a cheerful "Good morning, Mr. Wilson." Mr. Wilson cautiously replies and hides behind his newspaper. In the background Mrs. Mitchell, searching for her son, calls, "Dennis! Dennis!"

Here is the profile of a familiar preschooler—Dennis the Menace of television, cartoon, and movie fame. Dennis Mitchell is a lovable and curious preschooler with a penchant for getting into trouble. Though without malice, Dennis has a propensity for making mischief at the most inopportune time. Mr. Wilson, the temperamental next door neighbor, is often the recipient of Dennis' misbehaviors.

From a developmental perspective, Dennis is experiencing a new and trying period. Now mobile and less confined to his home, Dennis has begun to express a sense of self, revealing how he views himself in relationship to other people. Dennis has begun the process of developing his own attitudes, beliefs, and behaviors, and he tests them in various ways, especially with Mr. and Mrs. Wilson.

The image Dennis presents is that of an energetic, playful, and active little boy. His parents are portrayed as reserved, conservative, and faithful to work, family, and home. Given these descriptions, one is left to wonder at the origin of Dennis' troublemaking antics. Is this child's behavior typical of most preschoolers? Does Dennis have a personality flaw or conduct disorder? Can his disposition be attributed to his exposure to others in particular social settings? Are we seeing a combination of psychological, behavioral, and social factors?

In examining self-image, two considerations are noteworthy. First, what is the role of **inborn directedness** (biological and genetic predispositions and determinants) in the development of self? Second, how important is social interaction for the development of self? **Acquisition after birth** is a term that encompasses all social and environmental factors influencing one's self-concept. From a macro-system perspective, our primary interest concerns the influence of various social systems on the emergence of a child's perception of self.

How do we conceptualize the full meaning of "acquisition after birth" in relationship to the development of self? When considering the complexity of human growth and development, we look for the locus of control. When exposed to different ideas and behaviors, are children able to use intelligence and moral insight to choose between right and wrong or appropriate versus inappropriate behavior? **An internal locus of control** implies that humans are active, assertive beings in the socialization process and are in command of their own actions. Conversely, when children are viewed as passive creatures and highly vulnerable to the influence of others, an **external locus of control** is evident.

Preschool children are engaged in the process of developing internal mechanisms of control. "Internal expectancies are probably based on a history of learning experiences where variations in one's behavior were followed by predictable variations in reinforcement consequences" (Feld & Radin, 1982, p. 267). Feld and Radin suggest that children who are consistently rewarded for compliant behavior by parents and/or significant others develop internal expectancies defining such behavior as desirable. Conversely, when children receive responses to behaviors that are inconsistent or unpredictable, the locus of control becomes more external and the behavior of the child becomes more directly linked to immediate consequences.

Because Dennis the Menace is a fictional character, his self-concept is clearly the result of the writer's pen. In real life, however, how a child views herself or himself is a combination of both inborn directedness and the acquisition of many factors after birth. But when considering where control lies, it is apparent that children are especially vulnerable to information and influence exerted by parents and significant others, as well as television, movies, music, video games, and other influential media.

To compound matters, children are exposed to conflicting messages. Some grow up under joint custody agreements and may find themselves spending extended periods of time in more than one household. Preschool children have little to say in choosing their parents, siblings, playmates, day care arrangements, or neighborhood. Even though parents are conscientious and assertive in influencing their children's socialization, court orders, employment, and other socioeconomic factors limit choices and restrict parental options for child rearing.

In cartoons, television, and movies, Dennis may confirm the impression that some children are born with a predisposition to oppositional, defiant, and troublesome behavior whereas other children are inherently obedient and sensitive to the wishes of others. When Mr. Wilson says "That Dennis!" is he condemning Dennis's actions or expressing discouragement with this young-ster's personality and lack of internal control?

As social workers, we are challenged to reframe our view of the develop-ment of preschoolers using a macro-level approach. George Homans (1950), in his classic *The Human Group*, studied factory life and street-gang influence, as well as an entire New England community, to examine individuals and their re-lationships with social groupings of various sizes. In assessing the actions of preschoolers, individually or collectively, one gains insight by studying the in-fluence of neighborhood, groups, preschools, television, and other related macro-level social systems. Measuring the effect of social forces on a child's self-concept and behavior is a complex process. The understanding of social determinants as well as psychological and genetic factors in explaining human behavior is a major challenge in social work practice.

THEORY: SYMBOLIC INTERACTIONISM

Forte (2004) asserts: "Symbolic interactionism provides an ideal conceptual framework for social work theorizing and practice" (p. 391). More specifically, he notes the merits of symbolic interaction for assessment and analysis of the effects of social systems of varied sizes. Forte suggests that symbolic interac-tionism has, over the years, yielded a variety of concepts, terms, issues, and processes of significant use and relevance to social workers. "These include the self, identity, social membership, communication, change, diversity, social ac-tion, justice, and the healthy society" (p. 391).

Symbolic interactionism is a helpful orientation in examining preschool children. This theory is particularly useful in understanding the world of preschoolers. Because preschoolers are immersed in the development of self, symbolic interaction provides valuable constructs for analyzing this dynamic human process.

Many social work students characterize symbolic interaction by the famil-iar adage: I am not who I think I am, and I am not who you think I am, but I am who I think you think I am. This concise, enigmatic sentence captures the essence of Cooley's (1909) **looking-glass self,** a perspective that describes how individuals derive a sense of self through interaction with other people.

As interpreted by Cooley, the self is a social product developed through social interaction. The looking-glass self begins early and continues to be an important determinant, not only during childhood but also throughout life. Key elements in the looking-glass self include social interaction, social com-parison, reflective appraisals, and self-judgment. When assessing the self-definition of a particular child or adult, sources and forms of social interaction and social comparison (e.g., the use of symbols, gestures, and language) are important considerations.

Each of us develops a sense of self based on presumed judgments of signif-icant others (Cooley, 1909). First, through **social comparison** human beings attempt to cognitively understand how their actions appear to others. Next, they receive feedback as to how others have judged or evaluated their behav-iors, often referred to as **reflective appraisals**. Finally, individuals make an analysis and judgment of their own behavior based on their perceptions of the feedback provided by others.

George Herbert Mead, a student of Cooley often credited as an originator in the application of symbolic interactionism, built upon his mentor's work. Mead (1934) gave special attention to specifying a definition of the self and analyzing the origin of the self in childhood.

Mead conceptualized self in terms of two distinct parts, the "I" and the "me." Similar to inborn directedness, the I refers to the spontaneous, biological part of the self that is free from control of others. The "I" is the unique and distinctive side of the self. Conversely, the **me** is the social part of self, obtained through socialization with individuals, family, friends, school, and other social entities.

With regard to the development of self, Mead, a pioneer in the study of human development, identified three stages. First, children imitate the behavior of other people, a preparatory stage. Second, children develop the ability to play specific social roles whereby they are able not only to imitate behavior but also to fulfill role expectations using appropriate language and action. Finally, through games children learn rules that teach appropriate versus inappropriate behavior among various players.

Through participation in games, children demonstrate the ability to **take the role of the other,** to envision the expectations of each role in a social system as well as general rules for behaving. As an example, a preschooler playing "Simon Says" learns that there are different expectations for each position (leader and follower), along with a general set of rules for playing the game. Mead extended this logic, asserting that through social comparison children learn broader definitions concerning societal positions, rules, and expectations.

Using symbolic interactionism, people can be compared to players in a game. They "interact in ways that, depending on the course of the interaction, create, maintain, and change the rules of the game" (Turner, 1974, p. 178). From this perspective, human beings are viewed at a more interpersonal level as active participants in both interpreting and changing the social world. Whereas other sociological theories propose that social systems have an existence separate from participants, "interactionists remind us that the educational system, the family, the political system and indeed all of society's institutions are ultimately created, maintained, and changed by people interacting with one another" (Tischler, 1990, p. 25).

DEVELOPMENTAL ISSUES

The preschool period extends from 3–6 years of age. Topics typically explored in life-span development literature examining preschool children include personality development, gender-role acquisition, play, peer groups, differential socialization of girls and boys, parent-child relationships, preschool facilities, and child care. The focal point of research in the preschool age group has been the relationship between the child and the primary caretaker, traditionally the mother.

The interactionist tenet states that preschool children establish a sense of self and learn appropriate ways of acting in a social system through social interaction. It allows us to identify and examine important macro-level factors with regard to the socialization of preschoolers. In this chapter, we consider the development of preschoolers as related to the detachment of fathers, parental coalitions, children parenting children, day care centers, television, toys, play, and racism. Each topic is framed in macro-level terms, as a societal trend or a function of the changing American family.

Detached Fatherhood

As of 2003, over 10 million children in the United States lived in one-parent family groups maintained by mothers (U.S. Department of Commerce, 2003). This figure raises important questions concerning the relevance of fatherhood. Early in his administration, President George W. Bush declared responsible fatherhood as a priority for the nation's domestic agenda. Many agree that "children have the most to gain when living in close association with two parents who are actively involved with the child's development, education, and overall well-being" (Slayton, 1993, p. 24).

When divorced, separated, and never-married fathers do not or are unable to assume responsibility for supporting their children financially, psychologically, or socially, children are penalized. If a father is absent or disengaged, both the child's emotional development and financial security are jeopardized.

The issue of fatherhood goes beyond providing basic economic and emotional security required for child growth and development. While establishing paternity—as well as the child's rights and entitlements—is an important first step, children require more from parents than the meeting of basic human needs. Thoughtful and consistent input from parental figures promotes a clearer understanding of age-appropriate behaviors. The child also begins to comprehend that there are societal regulations that govern our actions. Every child benefits from contact with a legally and morally responsible father.

Life without a father is a "leading cause of the decline in the well-being of children . . . the engine driving our most urgent social problems, from crime to adolescent pregnancy to domestic violence" (Blankenhorn, 1995, p. 6). Blankenhorn further suggests that children in today's society are confused as to what it means to be a man and a father. "Men are increasingly viewed as superfluous to family life: either expendable or part of the problem. Masculinity itself often is treated with suspicion, and even hostility, in our cultural discourse" (Blankenhorn, 1995, p. 6).

Preschool children look to mothers and fathers, as well as significant others, for feedback regarding the appropriateness of their actions. These individuals become **agents for socialization** imparting to children various values and ideals defining a sense of right and wrong for a particular social structure. In this sense, what is normal for a child is dictated by the reactions and feedback from those people interacting closely with the child. Family members and significant others serve to link macro-level community and societal expectations with a child's notion of normality. For example, a child reared in a family where drug culture is the norm will assume that those activities are normal and expected behaviors.

Noncustodial fathers can contribute to the well-being and stability of their children in a number of ways. In addition to economic support, it is important for fathers to maintain regular contact and interaction with their children, provide emotional support and compassion, participate in setting boundaries and disciplinary actions, serve as positive role models, and commit to long-term relationships with their offspring (Hamer, 2001; Strug & Wilmore-Schaeffer, 2003). Social workers know the significance of broadening the opportunities for fathers to participate and become involved in the lives of their children beyond the role as breadwinner. Kost (2001) suggests that fathers can be instrumental in helping children learn how to form and develop interpersonal bonds, generate confidence, and make good decisions.

Unfortunately, "too many fathers are demeaned, demoralized, and disenfranchised after divorce in ways that make it difficult for them to maintain close relationships with their own children" (Nielsen, 1999, p. 139). Societal beliefs and attitudes concerning divorce, custody, and gender-based parenting styles can create obstacles for fathers wishing to establish or maintain close and enduring relationships with children after separation or divorce. Mothers play a meaningful role in encouraging and influencing healthy relationships between noncustodial fathers and children.

The United States is a society comprised of many cultures. When a child's parents are not married or live separate lives, the child may be exposed to very different **cultural values**—prescribed ways of behaving manifested in language, thinking, and expression. Lum (1995) reminds us that: "To identify a unique set of values for all ethnic minorities or to claim that all cultures have common values misidentifies the multidimensional levels of culture." It becomes necessary to "strive to differentiate the particular cultural context when addressing the broad theme of cultural values" in early childhood socialization (Lum, 1995, p. 63).

PARENTAL COALITION

Parental coalition occurs when parents successfully form a bond or union for collaboration and coordination about decisions affecting their children. A strong coalition provides uniform rather than mixed messages for children. Research suggests that children benefit most when "parents share the same ideas about a child's need for control and guidance." To accomplish this unified approach requires a conscious effort, clear communication, and intentional compromise (Mc Hale, Crouter, Mc Guire, & Updegraff, 1995, p. 126).

Parental coalitions can be established in a variety of family contexts, including divorced, blended, and poverty-stricken families. Those coalitions may be facilitated by public and private programs. Hashima and Amato (1994) suggest the provision of child care from outside the family as a viable societal consideration for reducing problematic behaviors between parents. When parents in poverty have assistance in caring for their children, they are less stressed and more amicable, yielding a more supportive and affectionate family environment.

Increases in single parenthood, typically family groups maintained by a mother as well as custodial grandparents serving as parents, teen parenthood, and gay/lesbian parenting demand the coordination of all adults performing parental duties. Friends, grandparents, and companions must provide a united front or be the source of conflicting messages and expectations for children in their care. For children's welfare, steady, positive reinforcement, defining acceptable behavior over unacceptable behavior, creates structure and consistency in life. Juby and Rycraft (2004) suggest that family stability and preservation is optimized when families possess a sound sense of inner locus of control and surround themselves with support systems.

In the case of the single parent, demands placed on the preschooler must be steady, dependable, and understandable. Though a preschool child is parented predominantly by one adult, there is no assurance of consistency or clarity to the child of social expectations and norms.

For example, a single parent, weary and overwhelmed from a full day of work, may fail to establish boundaries for her or his child. At times, it may seem easier for an exhausted parent to allow the preschooler to disobey a rule or throw a temper tantrum than to generate the energy to intervene. Hilton and Desrochers (2002) summarize: "the pressures inherent in raising a child alone, combined with too few resources for coping with role demands, are disruptive to both parenting and parental control . . . children in single-parent families appear to respond to these deficits with disruptive behaviors" (p. 13).

To assist parents, many communities offer an array of supportive services. Presented under various auspices, these programs provide parents with a forum for expressing mutual support and exchange of ideas. Typically, meetings are held at night, with care provided for children. These types of arrangements are particularly important because many "single mothers face the dual stresses of poverty and working outside the home without sufficient supports" (Kesner & McKenry, 2001, p. 142).

WHEN CHILDREN PARENT

Unfortunately, many times children assume the role of parent in caring for younger siblings. Parenting by children often occurs out of necessity and/or default. The result is psychological and physical stress for the children involved. When older siblings assume parental responsibilities, their social-emotional needs and educational goals are compromised for the sake of their sisters and brothers.

Children rearing children contributes to difficulties in "forging a workable and coherent identity" as well as perils and "costs of slipping, of saying or doing the wrong thing, or making the wrong choice" (Halpern, 1995, p. 131). Basically, children who assume responsibilities in rearing siblings take on a role they are not intellectually or emotionally prepared to handle. For the most part, it is neither reasonable nor prudent to expect children to shoulder the duties associated with nurturing and socializing younger sisters or brothers to the expectations and rules associated with family life and society at large.

Parenting is a complicated and demanding role for adults; even older children lack the skills and maturity to feed, nurture, and protect their siblings. Zigler and Hall (2000) point out: "the repertoire of care-giving skills that are adequate at one stage of a child's development might not suffice as the child matures" (p. 183). The presence of a responsible adult is a particular concern for rearing preschoolers as "parents are the most important agents of socialization during early childhood" (p. 92).

CHILD CARE OPTIONS

Whereas in Chapter 2 we examined in-home care options, here we explore the use of child care centers for preschoolers. Most children in day care centers are 3 or 4 years old. Nearly a third of children served by supplemental care arrangements are placed in day care facilities (Zigler & Hall, 2000, p. 118–119).

Advantages of day care centers are their stability and public accountability. Approximately half of the day care centers in the United States operate for profit. The majority are small, single-center enterprises. Compared to other child care arrangements, child care centers usually have staff with child development training who introduce educational materials, offer full day care, and provide structured play time with peers (Clarke-Stewart, Gruber, & Fitzgerald, 1994).

Not surprisingly, the performance of children in day care can be linked directly to the behavior of caregivers (Clarke-Stewart, Gruber, & Fitzgerald, 1994, p. 12). Children tend to imitate actions of teachers, and they quickly learn to incorporate into their repertoire the language, habits, and mannerisms of day care staff members.

When educational programs exist in day care, children tend to spend more time engaged in complex and constructive play. Conversely, when children are left with unstructured playtime with other children and the ratio of adults to children is low, the classroom climate is likely to be less cooperative and more negative. Thus, the key to obtaining high-quality care appears to be "the teacher's degree of attention to, interest, and engagement in the activity of the child" (Thyssen, 1995, p. 91).

Day care centers also have their deficits. They can be noisy, bustling places that overlook the individual needs of the child (Zigler & Lang, 1991). Day care centers can also be expensive, with those families most in need of child care being least able to afford their services (Edelman, 1989).

Child care providers and day care centers are pivotal players in a child's world. A caregiver's activities are not one-dimensional; they include attending to the physical needs of the child as well as creating a rich environment for learning and development (Phillips & Whitebook, 1990, p. 132). The care of younger children and children with special needs requires an even greater output of energy. Unfortunately, as more women have joined the workforce and as single parenthood has contributed to an unprecedented need, the public sponsorship of day care programs has been grossly inadequate.

"Deciding who is responsible for child care is not like deciding to buy a pair of shoes on some Saturday in November. The decision requires far more than a mere statement of preference, because many complex influences affect the issue" (Deutsch, 1983, p. 10). Selecting an appropriate day care center or child care provider reflects a choice and an assertion concerning personal behavior, family practices, religious views, and individual attitudes. The discreet child care shopper will ask: Are these the kind of people I want to instruct my child? Will the teachers and children at this day care center be a positive influence on my child? Will the day care staff communicate openly with me concerning my child's developmental needs in order to provide a coordinated team effort in socialization? Or, will my child return home with language, ideas, and values I find to be unacceptable?

Social workers are often called upon to assist parents in locating appropriate child care facilities. Various centers are maintained by state and local departments of welfare in low-income areas. Family agencies are frequently resources for referrals to centers and individuals providing quality care. Among standards set by care centers should be employee background checks, safety and emergency plans, close professional contact with children and parents, adherence to public health standards, low teacher-student ratios, and an open-door visitation policy. Parents should be able to read and review a mission statement or have articulated to them a philosophy that guides child care activities. A positive image in the community and recommendations by those families who have used the child care program are usually reliable yardsticks. Community leaders and helping professionals may also be valuable in assisting parents in choosing safe, high-quality day care providers.

The National Association for the Education of Young Children (NAEYC) establishes guidelines for child care centers and "provides recommendations regarding child-adult ratios and caregiver education" (Burchinal, Howes, & Kontos, 2002, p. 89). As one might expect, child-adult ratios are sensitive to the age of children, with older children needing less adult supervision.

When considering the quality of child care, Burchinal, Howes, and Kontos (2002) suggest that parents and policy makers may want to consider the characteristics of caregivers. For example, the caretaker's education, licensing, and training may be as important a consideration for parents as adult-child ratios. The authors also advise that care needs to be taken in generalizing findings from one setting (e.g., child care homes) to another setting (e.g., child care centers) (p. 102).

PRESCHOOLERS AND TELEVISION

Parents often reveal that their most restful time is when their preschooler is watching television. It has been evident for some time that nearly every household in America has at least one television (Palmer, 1988). It is also clear that an appreciable number of preschoolers watch an excessive amount of television, two to four hours per day (Warren, 2003). Commercial, cable, and public broadcasting systems provide most of the programming. Cable and satellite access allow a growing share of households to receive programs originating from countries around the world.

Public broadcasting programs like *Sesame Street* and *Mister Rogers' Neighborhood* have been traditionally well received by children, parents, foundations, corporations, and public television organizations (Palmer, 1988). Yet, public television is so underfunded that repeat programming continues to be the norm. In public broadcasting, due in great part to limited resources, a well-conceived and organized children's program schedule remains unattainable, and the situation is unlikely to improve. Over the years, attacks on federal and state subsidies for public broadcasting have reduced governmental support for public television.

With regard to commercial television programming, children are viewed by television executives as active and viable economic consumers. Parents feel pressure to allow children to view popular television shows and cartoons and purchase program-related clothes, toys, and products. Kline suggests that programs

> are not scripted as moral parables or even innocent amusements. Character fiction must serve the marketing functions of introducing a new range of personalities into children's culture, orientating children to this product line, creating a sense of excitement about these characters, and ultimately leading children to want to use those characters in play. Most of the new children's television animations have been created explicitly for selling a new line of licensed goods. It is simply not sufficient for a program to be popular with kids (1993, p. 280).

Preschoolers and younger children of school age watching television and DVDs and playing video games represent not only exploitable but formative minds. One of the dangers is "the child's lack of ability to relate actions, motives and consequences . . . they may simply imitate the action that they see" on television (Van Evra, 1990, p. 82). An even greater concern arises when children view programs intended for an adult audience. If parents do not assume an active role in selecting, monitoring, and discussing programs, children may be left to bear the full brunt of commercial television's advertising, influence, and control.

Social workers are advised to make "a careful examination of television and its effects," particularly in relation to child welfare and government regulation of television (Lazar, 1994, p. 72). Social workers should be advocates for television without exploitation, joining with other professional associations and consumer action groups. An example of such an opportunity involves advocating for legislation, policies, and practices that promote technological capabilities to block television stations and programming. Blocking devices and program rating systems allow parents to make informed decisions concerning the appropriateness of each program for their child and to exercise control over the availability of programs showing disturbing or age-inappropriate material.

Parents quickly learn the persuasiveness of television commercials upon their children when they bring home from the grocery a generic brand of cereal instead of a highly advertised one in its well-known box. Children frequently ask parents to buy breakfast cereals based on television hype, the prizes inside the box, and/or the nature of the box itself. The reader may recall a long-eared rabbit's famous proclamation "Trix are for kids!" or may be familiar with specific brand names of cereals like Fruity Pebbles and Coco Pebbles, taken from popular cartoon characters. Other companies create likable fictional characters such as Captain Crunch to encourage children to request their product.

In an experiment designed to analyze the influence of food commercials on the food preferences of preschoolers, Borzekowski and Robinson (2001) report that multiple exposures to commercials had an immediate and appreciable effect. The study reported of the sample: "In the past week 19 (49%) children had requested a food item advertised on TV and 22 (57%) had requested to go to a store or restaurant advertised on TV" (p. 44). Also, an emerging literature suggests an association between viewing TV and obesity among low-income preschool children (Dennison, Erb, & Jenkins, 2002).

Regarding television programming for children, "Socially, the problem seems to be that we once saw a special vision of human possibility in television and now that vision appears to have been pushed aside for the sake of business" (Schneider, 1987, p. 4). Schneider further suggests that children should not view television in isolation. Parental guidance of preschool children's television viewing is important and can take three forms: restrictive mediation, instructive mediation, and co-viewing (Warren, 2003). **Restrictive mediation** establishes and enforces parental rules governing appropriate content and time limits for viewing television. **Instructive mediation** involves parents and families watching television programming and commercials together. Television content is discussed and translated, and children can be encouraged by parents to comment about and reflect upon what is seen. **Co-viewing** is more passive in nature and lacks purposeful discussion of program content.

Consider the potential effects of television with regard to gender stereotyping, particularly for girls. Preschool girls are often portrayed in passive, submissive roles. Girls are presented as clever and pretty, but dependent, whereas boys are viewed as energetic, strong, and decisive. Powell and Abels (2002) state: "some change in portrayal of sex-roles to a preschool audience is happening through Teletubbies and Barney & Friends. However, this change is mostly opening up accepted behavior for boys, while sex-roles are primarily reinforced for girls" (p. 14). Given these findings, it is particularly important for parents to debunk gender-related media characterizations and role expectations.

Research also suggests interesting differences in viewing television and videos according to type of residency. When comparing urban and suburban children, suburban preschoolers were found to be more likely to spend time outdoors, visit the library, attend summer camp, and have books read to them than their city counterparts. School-age urban children were more likely to watch television or videos than children living in suburbia (Damore, 2002).

A considerable amount of research has been conducted on the ill effects of television commercials on children, but TV advertising "has certain benefits for the child and family" (Schneider, 1987, p. 73). Advertising can prompt children to enter into conversations with adults concerning consumerism and the value and nature of various products. Children can be guided to develop and articulate judgment about television and advertised products, so that they eventually learn to take responsibility for their viewing decisions and buying habits. Ultimately, television can be a positive influence in the emergence of the child's self if parents assist their child in recognizing a diversity of choice and in acquiring the ability to reject or accept programming and products based on their individuality and interests, as well as the family's values.

Finally, television can be a powerful ally in promoting the welfare of children and in raising awareness of children's rights. As an example, Oprah Winfrey's documentary *Scared Silent: Exposing and Ending Child Abuse* was aired simultaneously on the CBS and NBC television networks, as well as on the Public Broadcasting Service, with ABC providing a rebroadcast. The National Child Abuse Hotline received over 112,000 calls in the five days following the airing of this documentary (Rowe, 1992). Many of the phone calls were from young children. Oprah's informative presentation demonstrates the power of television to reach out to children in need and to influence their view of the appropriateness of behaviors of other people.

RACISM AND CHILD DEVELOPMENT

How children interact with people of different races and creeds is influenced by many factors including family, friends, caretakers, religious instruction, and popular media.

> The parents are the first members of the larger society in the life of the child. They are members of a social network that may or may not be a part of the social mainstream. They bring their particular skills and the social network attitudes, values, and ways to the task of child care and rearing. Because of the extreme dependency of the child and the important role of the caretaker, the attitudes, values, and ways of the caretaker greatly influence those of the young child. This allows the caretaker to mediate the child's experiences—to give them meaning and to establish their relative importance. (Comer, 1989, pp. 17–18)

Although much has been written about gender identification during the preschool years, psychological development of children around the age of 3 also permits children to begin to differentiate people on the basis of race and ethnicity and to experience the effects of racism. In the preschool years, children develop positive or negative responses about their racial status as well as that of other racial groups. Children learn about racial differences and culture from their parents and the social situations to which they are exposed. Primarily through play, preschoolers can begin to appreciate and celebrate human differences based upon language, skin color, traditions, and customs

(Littlejohn-Blake, 2002). Parents are given the onerous task of helping their children to understand and appreciate human diversity and to show them that the error in thinking is with the person who displays racial antagonism (Comer, 1989, pp. 18–19).

In preparing children to deal with the issue of race and ethnic diversity, the appropriate language and concepts for describing racial diversity are important. The words, terms, phrases, and expressions that children hear others use help to form their perceptions and views about racial groups. Even though parents, adults, and helping professionals may struggle with identifying and using appropriate language in addressing racial differences (Brill, 1995), parents have the responsibility of defining appropriate and acceptable behavior in this domain for their children. Research conducted by Bernstein, Zimmerman, Werner-Wilson, and Vosburg (2000) suggests "children can profit when conversations about race and ethnicity are conducted in a structured format that acknowledges and accepts differences between groups" (p. 190). Unfortunately, children too frequently encounter negative language about race and ethnicity that is then incorporated into their vocabulary. This leads to misperceptions and stereotypes concerning racial groups that ultimately lay the foundation for racial discrimination.

In July 1995, President Clinton recommended to Congress and our country the reestablishment of formal relationships with Vietnam. This, of course, triggered negative reactions from many Americans. Memories and emotions associated with an undeclared war, an impoverished and war-ridden Asian country, and loss of human life were rekindled. Regardless of one's position concerning the normalization of relationships with Vietnam, the president's declaration prompted public discourse and discussion focusing on America's history, Vietnam, and the Vietnamese people.

How would you react if a relative, friend, or neighbor were to make a negative remark about a person of another ethnic origin or race in the presence of your preschooler? To make no response would imply acceptance. An intellectual discussion of racism with the preschooler would serve little purpose. Parents routinely are placed in circumstances where they need to determine the best way to mediate negative and potentially destructive social experiences for their children.

Imagine how Dennis the Menace or the Mitchells would have reacted to the aforementioned racial situation. Do you recall Dennis ever having any friends or acquaintances who were people of color? How influential is the cartoonist in transmitting these values through her or his drawings? Are there some who seem to attempt to build tolerance and understanding through their art?

In a highly mobile and multicultural America, children will eventually interact with people representing diverse racial and ethnic backgrounds. What happens when children lack prior exposure to diverse populations? What obligations do parents have, even in isolated geographical areas, to teach their children about modern race relations, economic oppression, and lifestyle differences?

Although research by Demo and Hughes (1990) supports the basic premise that parents are important in providing race-related socialization to their children and that race-related messages are associated with racial identity, we should consider other potentially relevant factors. As an example, Sanders Thompson suggests that, for African-American children, racial socialization messages from adult family members other than parents were more numerous and had a stronger impact on racial identification than did parental messages (1994, p. 185). In considering the African-American family structure as an extended system, the actions, comments, and demeanor of nonparental adults in the household on the development of racial attitudes and identity appear particularly germane.

HELPING FAMILIES RAISE HEALTHY CHILDREN

A major focus of this chapter has been on the function of parents and family as agents of socialization for preschoolers. When social workers and teachers hear racial epithets or contemptuous remarks from preschoolers, it is important to examine the home environment. Parents serve as a vital bond for disseminating community and societal values influencing a child's development of self.

As suggested in Chapter 2, attitudes and orientations by parents and family can be assisted by social legislation and well-organized social programs (e.g., the Family Preservation Act and Head Start). Data collected over the last several decades clearly demonstrate "the economic value in preventing children's problems through investment early in their lives" (Scales & Brunk, 1990, p. 24). Various task forces "have showed us that programs like Head Start and good parental care really worked, and that they deserved significantly more investment than heretofore given" (Scales & Brunk, 1990, p. 24). Yet, when compared to other types of preschool programs, Head Start continues to be "placed at the low end of a continuum in terms of the amount of preschool intervention and . . . both short- and long-term benefits," suggesting the need for higher levels of funding (Caputo, 2003, p. 121).

Former Secretary of Health and Human Services Donna E. Shalala, responding to a report from the Advisory Committee on Head Start Quality and Expansion, remarked, "Nothing is more important than helping parents develop child-rearing skills that keep families together and help children grow up happy" (Shalala, 1994, p. 6). Although Head Start has been lauded as a highly successful program for improving the lives of many low-income children and their families, it also faces the challenge of becoming better equipped to serve the growing and diverse needs of American families. At a macro level, such expansion needs to include a broad social agenda that promotes comprehensive family services and seeks new, innovative ways to provide high-quality experiences for preschool children, regardless of the economic means of their family. This type of commitment requires prioritizing services for children and families in the national budget.

CASE EXAMPLE	FAMILY LIFE EDUCATION— THE RIVERA FAMILY

Keith Romero is a social worker in the family life education division of a three-county community action agency in rural northern California. A 44-year-old Hispanic-Latino American, Keith resides within the area. During the four years he has been employed by the agency, his primary role has been to lead parent effectiveness groups and to function as a liaison to the Head Start program, which is also a member of the county community action agency.

Referrals for Keith's groups routinely originate from Children's Services, the Head Start program, the local community mental health system, and various family service associations. Because of limited resources in the rural counties served, the referring agencies have formed an interagency cluster group to address common needs and concerns of children and families. Keith is an active member of this organization.

Prior to establishing a parenting group, Keith receives a social history of each parent interested in participating. Keith has worked closely with each of the referring agencies to construct a comprehensive assessment instrument that includes presenting problems as well as a detailed background of family and parent needs and resources. Following a review of the social history, Keith interviews a prospective group member to assess suitability for participation in a particular group.

Frequently parents seek admission into Keith's groups to deal with acting-out behaviors exhibited by their children. A typical scenario presents a child in trouble at home or at school, already involved with the court system. The parents are encouraged to seek and participate in individual and/or family intervention. Referrals to the parenting group frequently come via the school or courts.

Keith reviewed the application and social history of Juan and Jean Rivera requesting enrollment in a group for couples with preschoolers entitled "Enrichment and Boundaries for Our Youngsters." Juan and Jean have been married for five years and have one son, 4-year-old Billy. Juan is 41 years of age, Hispanic American, and a supervisor of work crews at a nearby winery. Jean is a 34-year-old white woman who works second shift as a nursing assistant at the local community hospital.

Billy's unacceptable language and defiance of authority caused Juan and Jean to seek professional help at a child guidance clinic. Recently, when Jean told Billy to go to bed prior to the end of his favorite television show, *The Simpsons*, Billy replied "This is bullshit!" and stomped up the stairs. Juan and Jean were stunned. Several similar instances of negative behavior at home and with friends led to the request to join a parenting group.

Following a careful review of the social history and an interview with Juan and Jean, Keith found that because of the parents' employment schedules Billy was with his mother during the day and with his dad in the evenings. While this arrangement eliminated day care, Billy's time was highly organized during the daytime with his mother but highly unstructured in the evenings with his dad.

Once or twice a week, Billy accompanied Juan to a local bar and grill to eat dinner, where they associated with winery employees after work. The atmosphere at the

continued

bar and grill was typical of an adult sports bar, with the game of the week being shown on large television screens. Juan looked forward to time at the bar and grill as a reward for hard work at the winery and at home. The language is usually coarse; people at the bar seldom realized that Billy was present.

During the other weeknights, Billy typically stayed home with his father and watched television. Juan sometimes joined his son but many times was busy around the house preparing dinner, doing minor repairs on the home, and completing domestic duties. Juan seldom monitored Billy's television viewing.

As a social worker, Keith saw marital and family dynamics and issues that require attention. He decided that Juan and Jean are appropriate for an educational group focusing on child enrichment and boundary setting. Comments by Juan and Jean during their interview suggest they were motivated, interested in topics regarding child rearing, and would be an asset to the group. Juan and Jean signed release-of-information forms allowing Keith and the referring family service social worker to communicate and monitor their progress.

Keith's groups usually explore parenting issues related to dual-income families, monitoring of television, enrichment activities, role modeling, parental coalitions, the influence of others, and appropriate boundary setting. In addition, racial and ethnic diversity in the group's membership could yield opportunities to discuss the development of healthy attitudes toward self and others, as well as other topics related to race and ethnicity.

Time to Think!

Although this chapter's case example features a social worker engaged in group work, Keith is also highly involved in community organization, especially the coordination and delivery of family preservation services. How will the consideration of macro-level influences enhance the effectiveness of group work practice? In what ways could Keith's group be seen as a microcosm of society? How effective is group work as an agent of socialization for parents? Are there community-level issues that could infringe upon service delivery at Keith's agency? How might Keith's group work become even more oriented toward macro-level change?

Macro Systems and the Rivera Family

In this chapter we have stressed the importance of parental figures in the socialization of preschoolers. Billy, like most children, looks to his parents for guidance and as models for behavior. With Billy's well-being and family preservation in mind, consider relevant organizational, community, societal, and global elements.

Organizational Level The Rivera family is fortunate that the rural area in which they live has a well-integrated network of social service organizations. The presence of a professional cluster group concentrating on family issues demonstrates both organizational and community commitment to family preservation. Typically, such groups are small, voluntary, and formed around common concerns and causes. Cluster groups emphasize interorganizational approaches and seek innovative ways to address specific client needs with limited resources.

By taking part in the cluster group, Keith and other social workers become more familiar with both the unique and the more common problems facing families across agencies as well as the availability of programs and resources. Although Billy does not currently attend a preschool or day care program, his parents may want to consider the merits of enrolling Billy in a preschool with an educational emphasis.

Through knowing the focus of programming at various preschool and day care programs, social workers can better assist clients like the Rivera family. By nurturing close relationships with various preschool programs and preschool directors, social workers encourage and assist preschools and Head Start programs to better address community needs.

While Keith lives in the community in which he practices, he may not be familiar with wineries or hospitals as workplaces. As a supervisor of winery workers, Juan associates and socializes with field and manual laborers. In his business, the supervisor is a friend and a confidant. Winery workers not only work together but drink together. Language is direct and often coarse. Their after-work conversations will provide insight for Keith into the true nature of some of their concerns.

Conversely, the hospital where Jean works constitutes a very structured workplace. Physicians, nurses, and nursing aides have well-defined roles and a planned regimen. Jean clocks in at 4 P.M. and clocks out at midnight five days a week. She rarely sees her colleagues outside of work and spends most of her daytime hours working at home and participating in planned activities with Billy. Billy experiences two very different parenting styles each workday. Interestingly, Juan and Jean's parenting methods reflect the interaction styles at their respective workplaces.

Community Level Juan and Jean live in a rural community in northern California, near Napa Valley. The people who live and work in this area come from varied backgrounds and represent numerous nationalities. While interracial marriage is not uncommon in the region, Billy has been confronted by some neighborhood children about being biracial. Billy has biracial buddies his age in the neighborhood, including Ricky, his best friend. This seems to be reassuring to both Billy and his parents.

Generally, members of this northern California area are hard-working and trustworthy people. Much like farmers of the Midwest, they believe in what Martinez-Brawley and Blundall (1991, p. 315) call "a fair and just world," where people take responsibility for themselves. Only when forces are deemed outside of a person's control is help acceptable.

Having this cultural insight, one might argue that Juan and Jean are clearly exceptions to the rule. Why did these parents seek help for Billy? Keith's experiences working in this geographical area concur with findings from research conducted by Martinez-Brawley and Blundall (1991, p. 318). They suggest that young children in

continued

farm areas are more likely to be seen as helpless; therefore, services for children are more acceptable and less stigmatizing. So, it is acceptable for Juan and Jean to seek help for Billy's acting-out behavior. Meanwhile, Keith and the other professionals in the cluster group assess and seek new ways to encourage families of children at-risk to come forward for help.

Keith finds the lack of community resources to be a major problem in group work. While the integration of social service programs and the presence of preschool and day care programs have already been highlighted as important factors, parents in Keith's groups frequently voice concerns related to the need for playgrounds, parks, pools, and community life for their children.

As a result, Keith has allocated an increasing portion of his time to community planning and projects aimed at enhancing local recreational opportunities and cultural life for families and youth. In the beginning, Keith felt hesitant to use agency time to attend these meetings and to serve on the Regional Recreation Board. But Keith knows that many of his clients need affordable and family-centered activities and programs in the community to assist in building and maintaining quality family relationships. Keith has become particularly interested in the work of Delgado (2000) describing how murals, playgrounds, and gardens can reflect community strengths and cultural heritage. He also has the support of his supervisor in developing these broader affiliations and participating in community-based projects intended to foster pride and empower the consumers of his services.

Societal Level As a social worker and lifelong resident of the state of California, Keith is keenly aware of the impact that changes in state or national priorities can bring to human services. When Ronald Reagan was governor, social services in Keith's community received low priority or were discontinued. It was not until the 1990s that the family life education division was able to offer group intervention to parents in Keith's county. California, like many other state governments, continues to grapple with economic and financial woes. The war on terrorism, a national trend toward privatization, and federal and state curtailment of social services have placed restrictions on program delivery and resulted in client waiting lists.

To date, Keith and his clients have successfully been able to advocate for the continuation of his family life education group work on the basis of productivity and cost effectiveness (Motenko et al., 1995). Keith has fully embraced the growing trend in social work practice emphasizing **evidence-based practice.** He embraces practice methods and techniques that have been shown to be effective, seeks every opportunity to evaluate his own practice, is committed to communicating the results of practice effectiveness in appropriate ways to others, and is dedicated to the evaluation of definable and **measurable outcomes** in social programming (see Briar, 1979; Yegidis & Weinbach, 2006).

Keith also makes a special effort to regularly attend workshops and conferences and review current research describing **best practices** concerning the delivery of family life education. With each family preservation group, Keith and his clients have conscientiously developed an evaluation plan, reviewed relevant data sources, standardized collection procedures, evaluated outcomes, and reported the efficacy of their work together (Neuman, 2003). Identifying and utilizing valid and reliable measures to evaluate practice effectiveness is one of Keith's priorities as a social work practitioner. Administrators and funding sources have responded favorably to these evaluative and accountability efforts.

Like Juan and Jean, several other people in the groups have expressed concerns over the influence of television and video games on children. In the rural area where Keith practices, people who cannot receive cable television acquire satellite dishes with a myriad of channels. Television is a vivid connection to the outside world. Rural as well as urban children are bombarded daily with its images.

Familiar with research on this subject, Keith is interested in assessing the impact of television on children in rural areas and in his community in particular. Toward this end, Keith started discussing research possibilities and potential funding sources with his supervisor and a colleague at the agency. Because rural residents tend to be more physically and socially isolated, Keith and his clients are interested in examining parental control and mediation over both the amount of television and the content of programs watched by younger children.

Keith plans to engage the consumers of his services as active participants in the research process. This is termed **participatory research** (Finn & Jacobson, 2003). Clients will be viewed as co-investigators and members of the research team. They will be afforded opportunities to use their knowledge and experience concerning children and television to affect decisions in the various steps of the research process.

Keith is also considering forming a group of parents interested in exploring and discussing the impact of television on children in the community. Several people in Keith's groups saw the issue as an opportunity to explore policies, practices, or mechanisms aimed at regulating television programming for children.

International Level The Rivera family lives in "wine country." The international marketplace for wine and wine products has a direct bearing on this, the biggest industry in the valley. Both social workers and clients realize that if the wine industry were to suffer a setback, there would be widespread ramifications for the local economy and residents.

For example, each year new investors from around the world enter vineyard ownership in the valley. What has been traditionally a family-owned and managed industry has gradually become an international venture. Foreign investors see the wine industry as chic and trendy. But with each new owner come new policies and employment turnover.

Typical of California, the members of this community represent a wide array of nationalities. Migrants from Mexico make up much of the population of this region. For Keith and other social workers, this means becoming acquainted with customs and values that have their origin in other lands. Attitudes and behaviors of clients can

continued

often be connected to practices derived from other countries. Social workers are continually educating themselves to the meaning of human behavior from a cultural perspective.

Keith is aware, for example, that in Hispanic-Latino families the father is often the decision maker and disciplinarian (Lum, 1992, p. 179). And while commitment by Juan to the helping process is crucial for Billy's sake, Juan also serves as an example to other Hispanic American males that engaging in formalized helping is acceptable.

Finally, tourism is a factor to be considered. Northern California ranks as one of the most popular destinations for travel internationally. Each year, many tourists pass through this three-county area on their vacation travels, and wineries and other local businesses and jurisdictions rely on revenues generated by tourists. When tourism suffers, businesses, local governments, and citizens feel the consequences. Although the negative impact of September 11 on travel has diminished, residents of Northern California are aware of the potential consequences of terrorism, fuel costs, and international relations on commerce. Employment, the funding of social services, and community development also are deeply impacted by such national and global events.

REFLECTION ON DIVERSITY: THE IMPORTANCE OF PLAY

As suggested earlier in this chapter, "A preschooler's primary means of learning is through play" (Littlejohn-Blake, 2002, 96J). The use of toys is an important element in providing children with early information and insight as to the expectations, values, beliefs, and norms of any particular social grouping, community, or society. Consider the messages being sent by either an organized or impromptu "show and tell" among preschoolers. The sharing of a toy by a child can be revealing with respect to social class, accessibility of play, and cultural traditions, as well as racial-cultural bias (Rettig, 2002).

Toys can be conceptualized as **social objects**. While a can, a piece of wood, a dog, or any article can be viewed as a social object, it is via "interaction we call attention to it, name it, and attach legitimate lines of behavior to it" (Allen, 2005, p. 240). Social objects, along with symbols and signs, constitute the basic tools for constructing human interaction, social reality, and a sense of one's self.

For preschoolers, toys may include balls, dolls, action figures, bikes, drawing kits, musical instruments, picture books, board games, and in recent years, electronic devices. A child's favorite toy or choice of toys can reflect cultural preference, family values, purchasing power, and as suggested above, a tendency to behave in a predictable way.

Levin and Lobo (2000) suggest that families and preschools consider promoting an appreciation of cultural values and diversity with children through intentional and meaningful play. Ethnic, racial, and cultural diversity can be explored through examination and discussion of story books and tapes, drawings and paintings, photographs, recorded music, food items, and a variety of commonplace toys. If "play is a means by which societies communicate cultural values to children," then parents and adults in positions of authority need to be intentional and deliberate in evaluating the attention, meaning, and credibility given to toys and various forms of play. An appreciation of the influence of toys and play, positive and negative, seems particularly germane when considering the thoughts and expectations of preschoolers regarding racial, ethnic, gender, and physical distinctions among those with whom they interact.

APPLYING A SOCIAL WORK FRAMEWORK: SYMBOLIC INTERACTION

In our case example, we begin to see how one child's identity is being shaped through human interaction. Billy has begun to take the role of significant others, assimilate language and gestures, and become aware of certain rules of society (Allen, 2005, p. 245). His father and mother, the workers at the bar and grill, his neighborhood friends, and television each have an impact in shaping Billy's verbal communication, sense of self, and perspective on right and wrong.

A warning bell sounded for Juan and Jean concerning Billy's development. Fortunately, they answered the call by seeking professional help. Through participation in Keith's group, Billy's parents learned new techniques to monitor and control input from others in Billy's life. In group intervention, Juan and Jean gained insight into role-modeling for their son. The group assisted Juan and Jean in becoming aware of and reflecting upon their parenting styles and the type of experiences most beneficial for Billy.

Thus, Juan has reevaluated the wisdom of exposing Billy to the neighborhood bar and grill as well as to the company of other wine workers. It is clear that Billy's language echoes what he has heard, whether from acquaintances or television. Also, parents must decide what their preschool child should see on television. If, as symbolic interactionists believe, children develop a sense of self through social comparison and the appraisals of others, Jean and Juan must decide who they want to serve as role models for Billy.

Billy is fortunate that he has two parents unified in their commitment to do whatever is best for him, in seeking professional assistance, and in examining their parenting goals and methods. Strong parental cooperation in the helping process is an invaluable asset.

With regard to macro-level social work, Keith is using group work to assess community needs and priorities. He knows that preschools, recreational facilities, forums for discussing race relations, family preservation services, play, toys, and the impact of television are powerful influences affecting preschoolers in his community. As a result, Keith is active in the multiagency cluster group and works with professional colleagues in research and policy analysis aimed at assessing these important issues.

SUGGESTED ACTIVITIES

1. Reserve a Saturday morning for watching cartoons on television. Identify products (e.g., toys and games) being marketed in programming and commercials. Give special attention to the depiction of women and men, of girls and boys. What messages are being transmitted to young children?

2. Ask friends and acquaintances about day care centers in your neighborhood. Ask them to rank the top three day care providers, listing the strengths of each. Do any of these day care centers promote learning about cultural diversity? If so, how do children celebrate human diversity through play or instruction? If you visit such a center, look for posters, drawings, indications of awareness of a global village.

3. Practice being an active listener to racial or ethnic phrases, statements, and jokes that have negative connotations. Were children present when you heard these comments being made? Discuss with a classmate of a race or ethnicity other than your own how these comments might influence children and their perceptions of people of diverse color or culture.

REFERENCES

Allen, K. (2005). *Explorations in classical sociological theory: Seeing the social world.* Thousand Oaks, CA: Pine Forge Press.

Bernstein, J., Zimmerman, T., Werner-Wilson, R., & Vosbur, J. (2000). Preschool children's classification skills and a multicultural education intervention to promote acceptance of ethnic diversity. *Journal of Research in Childhood Education, 14,* 181–192.

Blankenhorn, D. (1995). Life without father. *USA Weekend,* February 24–26, 6–7.

Borzekowski, D., & Robinson, T. (2001). The 30-second effect: An experiment revealing the impact of television commercials on food preferences of preschoolers. *Journal of the American Dietetic Association, 101,* 42–46.

Briar, S. (1979). Incorporating research into education for clinical practice: Toward a clinical science in social work. *Sourcebook in research utilization,* 13–133. New York: Council on Social Work Education.

Brill, N. (1995). *Working with people.* White Plains, NY: Longman.

Burchinal, M., Howes, C., & Kontos, S. (2002). Structural predictors of child care quality in child care homes. *Early Childhood Research Quarterly, 17,* 87–105.

Caputo, R. (2003). Head start, other preschool programs, and life success in a youth cohort. *Journal of Sociology and Social Welfare, 30,* 105–126.

Clarke-Stewart, K., Gruber, C., & Fitzgerald, L. (1994). *Children at home and in day care.* Hillsdale, NJ: Erlbaum.

Comer, J. (1989). Racism and the education of young children. In F. Rust & L. Williams (Eds.), *The care and education of young children.* New York: Teachers College Press.

Cooley, C. (1909). *Social organization.* New York: Scribner's.

Damore, D. (2002). Preschool and school-age activities: Comparison of urban and suburban populations. *Journal of Community Health, 27,* 203–211.

Delgado, M. (2000). *Community social work practice in an urban context.* New York: Oxford University Press.

Demo, D., & Hughes, M. (1990). Socialization and racial identity among Black Americans. *Social Psychology Quarterly, 53,* 364–374.

Dennison, B., Erb, T., & Jenkins, P. (2002). Television viewing and television in bedroom associated with overweight risk among low-income preschool children. *Pediatrics, 109,* 1028–1035.

Deutsch, F. (1983). *Child services on behalf of children.* Monterey, CA: Brooks/Cole.

Edelman, M. (1989). Economic issues related to child care and early childhood education. In F. Rust & L. Williams (Eds.), *The care and education of young children.* New York: Teachers College Press.

Feld, S., & Radin, N. (1982). *Social psychology for social work and the mental health professions.* New York: Columbia University Press.

Finn, J., & Jacobson, M. (2003). *Just practice: A social justice approach to social work.* Peosta, IA: Eddie Bowers.

Forte, J. (2004). Symbolic interactionism and social work: A forgotten legacy, Part 1. *Families in Society, 85,* 391–400.

Halpern, R. (1995). Children on the edge: An essay review. *Social Service Review, 69,* 131–151.

Hamer, J. (2001). *What it means to be daddy: Fatherhood for Black men living away from their children.* New York: Columbia University Press.

Hashima, P., & Amato, P. (1994). Poverty, social support, and parental behavior. *Child Development, 65,* 394–403.

Hilton, J., & Desrochers, S. (2002). Children's behavior problems in single-parent and married-parent families. *Journal of Divorce and Remarriage, 37,* 13–36.

Homans, G. (1950). *The human group.* New York: Harcourt Brace Jovanovich.

Juby, C., & Rycraft, J. (2004). Family preservation strategies for families in poverty. *Families in Society, 84,* 581–587.

Kesner, J., & McKenry, P. (2001). Single parenthood and social competence in children of color. *Families in Society, 82,* 135–143.

Kline, S. (1993). *Out of the garden.* New York: Verso.

Kost, K. (2001). The function of fathers: What poor men say about fatherhood. *Families in Society, 37,* 499–508.

Lazar, B. (1994). Under the influence: An analysis of children's television regulation. *Social Work, 39,* 67–74.

Levin, D., & Lobo, B. (2000). Learning about the world through play. *Scholastic Early Childhood Today, 15,* 189–199.

Littlejohn-Blake, S. (2002). Learning about cultural diversity at the preschool level. *Childhood Education, 79,* 96J.

Lum, D. (1992). *Social work practice and people of color.* Pacific Grove, CA: Brooks/Cole.

Lum, D. (1995). Cultural values and minority people of color. *Journal of Sociology and Social Welfare, 12,* 59–74.

Martinez-Brawley, E., & Blundall, J. (1991). Whom shall we help? Farm families' beliefs and attitudes about need and services. *Social Work, 36,* 315–321.

McHale, S., Crouter, A., McGuire, S., & Updegraff, K. (1995). Congruence between mothers' and fathers' differential treatment of siblings: Links with family relations and children's well-being. *Child Development, 66,* 116–128.

Mead, G. (1934). *Mind, self and society.* New York: Doubleday.

Motenko, A., et al. (1995). Privatization and cutbacks: Social work and client impressions of service delivery in Massachusetts. *Social Work, 40,* 456–463.

Neuman, K. (2003). Developing a comprehensive outcomes management program: A ten-step process. *Administration in Social Work, 27,* 5–23.

Nielsen, L. (1999). Demeaning, demoralizing, and disenfranchising divorced dads: A review of the literature. *Journal of Divorce and Remarriage, 31,* 139–177.

Palmer, E. (1988). *Television and America's children.* New York: Oxford University Press.

Phillips, D., & Whitebook, M. (1990). The child care provider: Pivotal player in the child's world. In S. Chehrazi (Ed.), *Psychosocial issues in day care.* Washington, DC: American Psychiatric Press.

Powell, K., & Abels, A. (2002). Sex-role stereotypes in TV programs aimed at the preschool audience: An analysis of Teletubbies and Barney & Friends. *Women and Language, 25,* 14–22.

Rettig, M. (2002). Cultural diversity and play from an ecological perspective. *Children and Schools, 24,* 189–199.

Rowe, P. (1992). Child abuse telecast floods national hotline. *Children Today, 21,* 11.

Sanders Thompson, V. (1994). Socialization to race and its relationship to racial identification among African Americans. *Journal of Black Psychology, 20,* 175–188.

Scales, P., & Brunk, B. (1990). Keeping children on top of the states' policy agendas. *Child Welfare, 69,* 23–32.

Schneider, C. (1987). *Children's television.* Chicago: NTC Business Books.

Shalala, D. (1994). Remarks by Donna E. Shalala. *Children Today, 22,* 6.

Slayton, A. (1993). First things first: Paternity and child support for nonmarital children. *Children Today, 22,* 22–24.

Strug, D., & Wilmore-Schaeffer, R. (2003). Fathers in the social work literature: Policy and practice implications. *Families in Society, 84,* 503–511.

Thyssen, S. (1995). Care for children in day care centers. *Child and Youth Care Forum, 24,* 91–106.

Tischler, H. (1990). *Introduction to sociology.* New York: Holt, Rinehart & Winston.

Turner, J. (1974). *The structure of sociological theory.* Homewood, IL: Dorsey Press.

U.S. Department of Census (2003). *America's families and living arrangements.* Retrieved from http//:www.census.gov/population/www/socdemo/hh-fam/cps2003.html, on May 4, 2005.

Van Evra, J. (1990). *Television and child development.* Hillsdale, NJ: Erlbaum.

Warren, R. (2003). Parental mediation of preschool children's television viewing. *Journal of Broadcasting and Electronic Media, 47,* 394–417.

Yegidis, B., & Weinbach, R. (2006). *Research methods for social workers.* New York: Pearson Allyn & Bacon.

Zigler, E., & Hall, N. (2000). *Child development and social policy: Theory and applications.* New York: McGraw Hill.

Zigler, E., & Lang, M. (1991). *Child care choices.* New York: Free Press.

CHILDREN OF SCHOOL AGE

In the mid-1980s, Ryan White, a 13-year-old student from Kokomo, Indiana, who had been diagnosed with AIDS, captured the attention of a nation. His efforts to stay in school and to inform a fearful public about AIDS were not his first crusades. Having been diagnosed with hemophilia soon after birth, Ryan depicts his life as "growing up different," in *Ryan White: My Own Story:*

> Most hemophiliacs look like me—small and skinny with knobby knees and elbows from all the times our joints got swollen from bleeds. Me, I look at myself in the mirror and figure, small but tough. But I guess a lot of people, my grandparents included, think we hemophiliacs don't look like we're built to last. Before Factor VIII, we didn't. Doctors told Mom that a severe hemophiliac like me could only expect to live maybe to age fourteen or fifteen. In between, he'd spend a lot of time being rushed to the emergency room whenever he got a bump or a scrape. (1991, p. 16)

A contaminated batch of Factor VIII, the blood-clotting agent designed to save the lives of hemophiliacs, infected Ryan with AIDS. Even though Ryan frequently experienced prejudicial treatment as a result of hemophilia, his greatest challenges came from discrimination as a result of AIDS.

Ryan White shared a universal desire of school-age children. In *People Weekly*'s cover story, Ryan stated, "All I wanted was to go to school and fit in" (Friedman, 1988, p. 89). "Fitting in" for a 13-year-old hemophiliac with AIDS was not an easy task in Kokomo, Indiana. "Because Ryan's diagnosis was one of the first in Indiana, fear and panic among parents caused a battle in the school district [that] split the community." Ryan's mother, Jeanne, added: "They didn't know what to do about AIDS. They didn't want it involved in their lives" (SerVaas, 1988, p. 54).

Western school administrators cited a lack of policy and guidelines from the State Board of Health as the reason they denied Ryan the right to attend school. The possibility of infection of other children became an emotional flashpoint. With encouragement and support from his mother, Ryan became the first student in the United States to protest being barred from school as a result of AIDS.

Jeanne White immediately took Ryan's case to court. The Whites argued that the Western school system's actions constituted discrimination against a handicapped child. Unfortunately, the court system responded with bureaucratic delay. Meanwhile, summer break was nearing an end and fall classes were about to begin at Western.

On the day he became a seventh-grader, Ryan participated in school by using a two-way phone hookup between home and classroom. Because the likelihood of Ryan attending school was bleak, Jeanne felt that if the school was willing to offer this arrangement, they should try it. Ryan responded, "I don't want to be treated worse than other kids, but I don't want to be treated better either. I just wanted to be the same. . . . It stinks. . . . I wanted to say, it sucks" (White & Cunningham, 1991, pp. 82–83).

As time passed, a Howard County health official and an expert from the Indiana State Board of Health agreed that Ryan's condition was not a threat to other students and that he belonged in school. Although the Western school system appeared unyielding, pressure from media reports and the refusal of Western's appeal by the state of Indiana cleared the way for Ryan's eventual return to school. A separate water fountain and a private toilet were included in the numerous conditions of his attendance.

Upon reentering school, Ryan was met by protest from a concerned citizens group, the removal of over 20 children from junior high, and a spirit of social isolation. Ryan soon learned that being at school could be almost as lonely as being at home. After a bullet was fired into the White home, Ryan and his family relocated to Cicero, Indiana, and a more understanding and friendly school environment.

Ryan White's story is offered both as testimony to the courage of this young man and as an example of how students with special needs and disabilities are confronted by discriminatory acts within school systems. Ryan became a casualty of AIDS through hemophilia, but many children with other forms of physical, learning, and developmental disabilities routinely encounter insensitive and ill-informed educational, legal, and social systems.

As we look at macro systems affecting elementary school children, let Ryan White's story serve as a reminder that social acceptance is a prerequisite for learning. An enhanced educational environment requires a climate in which children will be welcomed and valued, regardless of their differences.

THEORY: NORMALIZATION

"Social work is more than a science, because the profession is value oriented" (Kilty & Meenaghan, 1995, p. 445). Social work operates under an inherently political context. As social workers contemplate the use of various theoretical orientations for research and practice, larger societal forces such as political conservatism have "pushed for a testing of interventions and theories" (Kilty & Meenaghan, 1995, p. 445). The micro aspects of social work have resulted in a proliferation of theories and research addressing the effectiveness of individual and family interventions instead of efforts directed toward the definition of problems and conditions afflicting different groups of people in our society. Hence, in social work practice, it becomes imperative to "select goals [and implement strategies] that focus on groups and risk as well as those that focus on individuals and needs" (Meenaghan, Kilty, & McNutt, 2004, p. 18).

By way of avoiding the "micro trap" that characterized the 1980s and 1990s, the macro concept of normalization provides a broader thesis. First written in 1959 into Danish law for regulating services for the mentally retarded, **normalization** can be defined as promoting an existence for clients as close to normal as possible (Bank-Mikkelsen, 1969). Wolfensberger describes normalization in human services as providing clients access to culturally valued behaviors and activities and suggests, "in as many aspects of a person's functioning as possible, the human manager will aspire to elicit and maintain behaviors and appearances that come as close to being normative as circumstances and the person's behavioral potential permit" (1972, p. 28). "Normative" is defined in relationship to typical or conventional actions.

Some people believe normalization is more value judgment than theory. Normalization in our view is helpful in conceptualizing research questions and macro-level assessment in social work practice. Wolfensberger warns:

> The normalization principle as stated is deceptively simple. Many individuals will agree to it wholeheartedly while lacking awareness of even the most immediate and major corollaries and implications. Indeed, many human managers endorse the principle readily while engaging in practices quite opposed to it—without being aware of this discordance until the implications are spelled out. (1972, p. 29)

THE APPLICABILITY OF NORMALIZATION FOR DIFFERENT SYSTEM LEVELS

Normalization is an analytical principle applicable for assessment and change with individuals, families, schools, work settings, service agencies, and neighborhoods, as well as laws and the government (Wolfensberger, 1972). Normalization maximizes **mainstreaming,** as it advocates keeping the client in the larger group. The converse of mainstreaming is **segregated service,** whereby people with similar disabilities are segregated.

Following the logic of normalization, clients achieve integration when they experience culturally valued lives. Residence in a normal community, age-appropriate types of social interaction, and typical utilization of community resources are examples of normative participation. Availability of public transportation, places of worship, hospitals, schools, stores, recreational facilities, and job placements are essential. "Integration is only meaningful if it is social integration, i.e., if it involves social interaction and acceptance, and not merely physical presence" (Wolfensberger, 1972, p. 48).

In the United States, Wolfensberger's ideas concerning normalization can readily be seen in relationship to the Disabled People's Movement quest for self-determination and empowerment. Members of the disability community have increasingly sought culturally valued lives and "to exert control in their lives and, as a function of such actions, to become empowered to do so to a greater extent" (Wehmeyer, 2004, p. 23).

PHYSICAL INTEGRATION

Programs and services for physical integration should be community based and "absorbed into the prevailing social, economic, educational, etc. systems," not isolated or segregated within an organization or community (Wolfensberger, 1972, p. 48). Services should also be physically and socially accessible to clients, including being in close proximity to transportation routes and systems.

In many respects, physical integration involves a complete package. For example, one could centrally locate social service programs in the county courthouse, near other services, businesses, and transportation routes, but relegate social services to the basement, with inconvenient and inferior office facilities. Or, consider administrative decisions at schools that squeeze social work, tutoring, and educational enrichment programs into former janitor rooms or storage spaces. In each of these cases, clients are physically part of the mainstream but are still perceived as different and inferior.

SOCIAL INTEGRATION

Beyond physical integration, social workers are especially interested in assessing the social integration of services and programs. Social integration is affected by how both clients and others perceive the actual services and facilities. Labels, language, and symbols associated with people, sites, and facilities are important in promoting culturally valued social programs and in building a desired perception of social services.

As mentioned earlier, a goal of social work intervention is to build a positive image for client services. Consider, for example, your reaction when you see a smaller than normal yellow school bus. Do you look at this type of bus differently? Why? Could it be because you know that students with developmental disabilities use this kind of bus?

Similarly, imagine the keen disappointment when students find out that they have been placed in regular classes, while their friends are in advanced classes. They receive a clear message about academic status and promise.

ENHANCING SOCIAL IMAGES AND PERSONAL COMPETENCIES

In subsequent publications, Wolfensberger (1983) proposes that professionals should work to promote socially valued roles and to improve life conditions for clients. He suggests an emphasis on the strengthening of clients' social images, or their perceived value in the eyes of others, and enhancement of their competencies.

> In our society, image enhancement and competency enhancement can be assumed to be generally reciprocally reinforcing, both positively and negatively. That is, a person who is competency-impaired is highly at risk of becoming seen and interpreted as of low value, thus suffering image-impairment; a person who is impaired in social image is apt to be responded to by others in ways that impair/reduce his/her competency. Both processes work equally in the reverse direction; that is a person whose social image is positively valued is apt to be provided with experiences, expectancies, and other life conditions which generally will also increase his/her competencies, and a person who is highly competent is also more apt to be imaged positively. (Wolfensberger, 1983, p. 236)

Thus, whether through physical setting, the use of language and symbols, activities and programming, relationships, or the groupings of clients, social workers should approach helping from the standpoint of valuing people in both word and action. Following the principles of normalization, if fifth graders at a particular school typically go to football games on Friday nights, sit in a certain section of bleachers at home games, and wear school colors, then participation by clients in this type of culturally valued event should be supported.

A caveat: As social work students, you may not be familiar with normalization as a fundamental educational theory. Yet, it may present a more appropriate basic framework for considering macro issues than other orientations presented in the social work literature. Kilty and Meenaghan's (1995) proposition appears worthy of consideration. They submit that the conceptualization of social work problems and process is influenced by the current sociopolitical context. With a political agenda of recent decades that stresses individual responsibility, normalization is a theory often opposed or rarely considered to be usable except as the law demands.

Promoting Inclusion

Normalization provides the theoretical underpinning for the contemporary notion of inclusion. **Inclusion** "urges schools, neighborhoods, and communities to welcome and value everyone, regardless of differences. . . . Inclusion is a lifelong goal that crosses all environments and social settings where people without disabilities learn, work, live, and play (Renzaglia, Karvonen, Drasgow, & Stoxen, 2003, p. 140).

Social workers encourage inclusion by helping to create, develop, and sustain social systems that are accessible and inviting to all people. More specifically, social organizations and settings should provide a diverse spectrum of people with the ability to maximize their abilities and take control over their lives. People with disabilities should be afforded the opportunity to experience an existence similar to people without disabilities.

For school-age children, inclusion as a philosophical premise is particularly pertinent to the various aspects associated with education, after school activities, worship, play, and recreation. As stated by Ryan White, children want to be treated the same as their peers, not better or worse than others. In inclusive settings, the community and professionals work together in an enthusiastic fashion to provide coordinated and integrated programming, services, and support so that people with disabilities are valued, and possess the same rights and opportunities as others.

DEVELOPMENTAL ISSUES

Several aspects of human development of children between the ages of six and eleven are examined in this chapter. Psychological, intellectual, and moral growth are dominant themes during middle childhood. Socially, a key developmental issue involves entry into formalized education. At age six, most children experience life in primary school: riding school buses, following instructions by teachers, experiencing the limits of a classroom, and a structured academic curricula. Relationships with their peers and orientation to playground rules are all opportunities for growth.

The particular school a child attends will depend on several factors. Generally, children attend school in the geographical area in which they live. Unless the district is trying to achieve racial desegregation, public school systems will typically assign students to the elementary school nearest their home. Notable exceptions would include participation in magnet and charter schools. In the case of private or parochial school education, a child's acceptance is frequently contingent upon ability to pay and the passing of screening tests.

Real estate agents attest that among the first questions prospective home buyers ask are those regarding location and quality of schools for their children. Schools ranking high on academic achievement indicators are almost always located in more affluent and higher-priced housing areas. Our school systems reflect a segregated society—not solely on the basis of race but also as a reflection of socioeconomic class.

During the 1960s and in the midst of landmark U.S. Supreme Court decisions ordering the end of racially segregated school systems in major cities in the United States, the term "white flight" was coined. **White flight** refers to the movement of Caucasians from city to suburban areas, often to escape racially desegregated school systems.

"Suburban flight" better describes contemporary relocation patterns of residents in relationship to formalized primary and secondary education. **Suburban flight** occurs when upwardly mobile people, regardless of race, move from cities to more affluent school districts located in the suburbs in their quest for a higher-quality education for their children. The prerequisite for suburban flight is having the money for more expensive housing.

SCHOOLS AT RISK

Before addressing the issue of students at risk, let's examine the problem of schools at risk. Montgomery and Rossi (1994) suggest that some schools—with negative milieus and limited resources—put students in jeopardy as a result of the poor quality of the school environment.

Other schools provide a multitude of administrative and supportive services to complement traditional classroom experiences. Extracurricular events, counseling services, athletics, clubs, and active parent-teacher associations help provide a full and balanced school climate that permeates every aspect of the educational program and teacher-student relationships.

Unfortunately, not all schools can afford auxiliary services and activities. Indeed, "researchers increasingly conceptualize poor educational performance as the outcome of a process of **disengagement** that may begin as early as a child's entry into school" (Montgomery & Rossi, 1994, p. 12). If students do not identify with various school-sponsored programs and activities, the risk of poor academic performance and of dropping out is increased.

Montgomery and Rossi further recommend that schools engage in **investment behavior,** whereby school officials "encourage student involvement in academic and extracurricular activities by stimulating students' interests, increasing their personal resources, and rewarding their efforts" (1994, p. 12). The inability or unwillingness of a school district to finance education, however, often precludes investment behavior. In the case of economically disadvantaged school systems, investment opportunities for poor children may be very limited and supply little encouragement to students to persevere in school.

Investment behavior also involves recruiting and maintaining high-quality and dedicated teachers, staff, and school administrators. The impact of social support from teachers and staff on academic success should not be underestimated. Teachers influence students in many ways, including their sense of belonging and attachment to a school (Brewster & Bowen, 2004). When encouraged by teachers, students are given a special reason to attend and participate in classroom and extracurricular activities.

Progressive, inclusive-oriented instruction is costly. Initiating and sustaining an inclusive educational setting for children typically involves

- the pairing of special education and general education teachers,
- the use of paraprofessionals,
- modifications in instructional materials and delivery of curriculum content,
- collaborative lesson planning and special attention given to grading,
- behavior management,
- classroom rules,
- and contacting parents. (Amerman & Fleres, 2003)

These responsibilities require school systems to educate and train administrators, teachers, school social workers, counselors, and paraprofessionals in techniques and modes of instruction designed to optimize the success of each and every student in the classroom.

Later in this chapter, you will read about the No Child Left Behind Act (NCLB) of 2002 as a major policy initiative intended to identify at-risk students and schools. While recognition of academic difficulties is an important element in education, the ability to provide resources and support for inclusive-oriented instruction is also vital. Without appropriate funding, school systems, administrators, parents, and professionals can feel helpless in their pursuit of quality instruction.

STUDENTS AT RISK

According to Magrisso:

> The young child's positive growth and development are reliant upon his (her) effective movement between spheres of influence—the environments of school, home and neighborhood . . . the school's vision of the at-risk child is framed within an epidemiological model—one that attributes problematic characteristics to the child, and that the child brings from the home into the school. (1992, p. 26)

However, it may be more appropriate to assess students at risk by observing the relationships that exist between schools and students. Students are often first identified as being at risk by their classroom behavior and lack of achievement. Rather than perceiving the student as having a problem, a dynamic social history involves assessment of teacher, classroom, and school expectations in relationship to student performance.

As an example, when a student who is severely visually impaired attends a school that relies heavily upon classroom lecture, note taking, and paper-pencil essay testing, why is the student at risk? In part, the student's visual impairment limits her or his note-taking and essay-writing abilities. But classroom expectations also serve to place the student at risk. If the visually impaired student was required to use audio recorders for note taking and all examinations were oral, a pupil might even have an academic advantage.

Students at risk may be affected by various factors such as living circumstances, social-economic class, and disability. As an example, Nash (2002) examined neighborhood characteristics (e.g., social control, crime, and peer culture) as predictors of a sense of school coherence (functioning) and educational success. Based upon his results, Nash concludes that future research examining at-risk students should adopt a more comprehensive approach and be expanded in scope to include neighborhood factors.

It is clear from the existing literature that the presence of a variety of sources of social support (e.g., friends, teachers, and healthy adults) can optimize educational outcomes for at-risk students (Rosenfeld, Richman, & Bowen, 2000). The role of the social worker is often to "enhance support provided by adult caretakers, teachers, and peers by working with community and school resources to develop caretaker and school involvement programs" (Rosenfeld & Richman, 2003, p. 82).

TRADITIONAL RESPONSES TO STUDENTS AT RISK

Assessing organizational response by school systems to the task of educating at-risk students reveals wide variations. The challenge for many schools is to provide a quality education for a diverse academic and socioeconomic student population. How can educational programs be designed to enhance opportunities for at-risk students without lowering the level of social acceptance and the students' ability to fit in? Historically, the traditional reaction to student diversity involved "various systems of sorting and selecting students into more homogeneous learning groups" (Legters & McDill, 1994, p. 24).

Legters and McDill (1994, pp. 24–25) provide examples of sorting and selecting methods used in schools during past decades. They included:

Grouping/tracking   separating students into distinct academic streams— college preparation, vocational, and general.

Retention   keeping students back as a result of failing to reach required levels of achievement.

Special education   placing low-achieving students into special programs designated for the physically disabled and mentally challenged.

Pull-out programs   removing students from their regular class twenty to forty minutes per day for small-group remedial instruction.

"In practice, however, the research evidence available suggests that these strategies add few benefits and often may do more to limit than to increase learning opportunities" (Legters & McDill, 1994, p. 25). Additionally, sorting and selecting programs by definition obstructed students' abilities to fit in, feel accepted, and maintain involvement in socially valued experiences.

INDIVIDUALS WITH DISABILITIES EDUCATION ACT

The Individuals with Disabilities Education Act (IDEA) of 1997 clearly embraces the concept of inclusion in education. This federal legislation mandates that "students with disabilities be educated with their non-disabled counterparts in the least restrictive environment" (Amerman & Fleres, 2003, p. 66). Irrespective of their disability, students are to be considered first for inclusion in a general, regular classroom. Upon completion of an Individualized Education Plan or Program (IEP) with parent and staff input, student placement in a general education classroom with any needed supplementary aids or services constitutes the first option. If placement in a general education classroom is not appropriate, schools are required to explain and document why a student cannot be educated in such a manner. Inclusion and IDEA advance the notion that "every child should be an equally valued member of the school culture. Children with disabilities benefit from learning in a regular classroom, while their peers benefit from being exposed to children with a diversity of talents and temperaments" (Dybvik, 2004, p. 42).

Application of the IDEA is a complex undertaking. Consider that there are over thirty distinct eligibility categories and subcategories for special education services alone (e.g., learning disabilities and autism) (Sailor & Roger, 2005). Completing IEPs and providing for the least restrictive environment for the education of students with various types of disabilities is a formidable task. Yet, "today more than 95 percent of students with physical, emotional, learning, cognitive, visual, and hearing disabilities receive some or all of their education in regular classrooms. As of 2000–01, . . . 47 percent of students with disabilities spent at least 80 percent of their school day in the general-education classroom, up from 31 percent in 1988–89" (Dybvik, 2004, p. 42).

However, Sailor and Roger (2005) provide a few words of caution with respect to the implementation of principles of inclusion and IDEA. They state, "students with IEPs (individualized education program) who cannot function in various components of the classroom curriculum often find themselves at tables, usually in the back of the classroom, with paraprofessionals who, in a one-on-one approach, work with them on 'something else'" (p. 504). These practices bear a striking similarity to the previously noted "pull out" programs. Though not removed from the classroom, students with disabilities can become "pulled away" from other students inside the physical confines of the classroom.

Dybvik (2004) provides several helpful suggestions to facilitate the successful achievement of inclusion and enactment of the IDEA in school systems. For example, school officials should not be content with the mere physical presence of students with disabilities in the classroom. Teachers, staff, administrators, and paraprofessionals need to be provided with appropriate education and training to implement the principles and intent of the IDEA. The integrity of the educational curriculum and learning process needs to be maintained. IEPs should be tailored to the unique needs of students. Unfortunately, much too often, IEPs are written in a boilerplate fashion and fail to recognize the unique needs, qualities, and strengths of students. Wraparound programs in some communities are an attempt to fulfill these special needs.

The No Child Left Behind Act

With broad, bipartisan support from Congress, in January 2002 President George W. Bush signed into law the No Child Left Behind Act (NCLB). Although since the 1980s many states had been developing and refining measures and reporting mechanisms to evaluate public education, the NCLB has been touted by many politicians as a monumental achievement in mandating performance accountability in schools across the nation (Peterson, 2005).

Few people would disagree with the general premise of including every child in the delivery of a public education. The reported goals of the NCLB are to ensure that all children have an opportunity to attain a high-quality education and reach minimum standards of proficiency on state academic achievement standards and assessments (Cochran-Smith, 2005). More specifically, states are required to "prepare and disseminate an annual state report card . . . at the beginning of the 2002–03 school year" (Christie, 2005, p. 341). State report cards are mandated to include the following information:

- achievement information on state assessments in reading, language arts, and mathematics;
- achievement data on statewide assessments broken down by student groups (e.g., race, disability);
- 2-year trend data by subject area and grade level;
- comparison data comparing achievement levels to achievement goals by groups of students;
- state indicators determining adequate yearly progress;
- the percentage of students not tested by student grouping;
- high school graduation rates by student group;

- indicators of attendance or matriculation for elementary and middle school levels;
- performance of schools with respect to adequate yearly progress; and
- information on teacher qualifications and percentages of classes not taught by "highly qualified" teachers. (Christie, 2005, p. 341)

Given the magnitude of the reporting requirements, it is not surprising that some people have suggested that this bill should have been renamed the "no child left untested act" or the "no psychometrician left unemployed act" (Cochran-Smith, 2005, p. 99). Indeed, because of the largely unfunded nature of this wide-sweeping federal mandate, many states have struggled to meet reporting standards. "By November 2004, nearly half the states appeared to report on all indicators at the state, district, and school levels, and several states were very close to meeting all requirements. By contrast, in March 2003, just three states reported on all indicators or even had policies in place" (Christie, 2005, p. 342).

NCLB has faced criticism on several fronts. For example, differentiating teachers may be artificial because "highly qualified doesn't necessarily mean good. It means the teacher took the right number of subject-area courses in college and is teaching only those subjects" (Houston, 2005, p. 469). Others contend that the NCLB does little to facilitate connections between parents and schools (Truman, 2004). Convincingly, Cochran-Smith (2005) confronts the very assumptions underlying the NCLB. She suggests that proponents of the NCLB assert: "A highly coercive accountability system, based on competitive pressure and including public shaming and punishments for failure, will improve schooling for disadvantaged students without the improvement of school capacity, increases in resources, and major investments in programs" (p. 102).

Parental management of school choice has certainly become more complicated as a result of the NCLB. For many parents, particularly those with low-income or in rural areas, it can be very difficult to switch their child from a failing school to a more desirable alternative. Neild suggests, "in districts with few good school options for students, there are limits to parents' ability to find a school that represents a substantial improvement over the school their child already attends" (2005, p. 270).

Even when parents are able to gather critical information concerning quality of education and are capable of negotiating application processes for changing schools, a key consideration "surrounding the choice provisions of NCLB is whether families in affected schools will decide to exercise the choice option, what kinds of alternatives will be available, and on what basis families will choose to leave or stay at a child's current school" (Neild, 2005, p. 271).

STRATEGIES FOR STUDENTS AT RISK AND STUDENTS WITH DISABILITIES

Biklen argues that before significant alterations are made in school programs for students with disabling conditions and at-risk students, "how we in this society think about disabilities must change, and change dramatically"(1985, p. 174). Toward this end, Biklen identifies five broad important principles for influencing fuller inclusion of disabled and at-risk students in schools.

PRINCIPLE 1: EQUITY REQUIRES AN INSTITUTIONAL COMMITMENT.

In order for equity to occur for people with disabilities, integration cannot be viewed as experimental. School systems and state departments of education must mandate and guarantee integration. For students with disabilities this means that any accommodations that facilitate learning are seen as normal by school administrators, teacher, parents, and students.

PRINCIPLE 2: ACTIVISM, RIGHTS, AND EQUITY, NOT PITY, COMPASSION, AND BENEVOLENCE, WILL FOSTER THE EMERGENCE OF INTEGRATION.

As a society, we must move beyond a charity mentality where students with disabilities and those at-risk are pitied. A more productive approach views students having special needs with high regard and channeling energies into activities aimed at securing a quality education.

PRINCIPLE 3: NORMALIZATION MUST BECOME PART OF EVERYDAY LIFE.

Students with disabilities and at-risk in schools need to be treated as normally as possible. This requires broad-based support in communities and nationally.

PRINCIPLE 4: WORKING WITH PEOPLE WITH DISABILITIES IS IMPORTANT.

Recognition and support for the value and dedication required of these staff people should be an intrinsic part of the mission of each school district. Stereotypes and myths abound with regard to students with disabilities. Negative attitudes toward students with any form of disability need to be eliminated.

PRINCIPLE 5: THE SUCCESS OF INTEGRATION THROUGHOUT SOCIETY WILL BE DETERMINED BY OUR COMMITMENT TO IT.

Consensus building that promotes the integration of students in schools is crucial. Without a general value or belief in support of integration, success will be weak and inconsistent. (Biklen, 1985, pp. 175–186)

As a social work student, you may already be assessing how avidly schools embrace Biklen's five principles. However, they are not offered as quick fixes. Securing human rights for any group is likely to be more of a process than a product. Given the overall complexity of the public educational system, characterized by independent school districts, school boards, and superintendents, any major overhaul or reshaping of education in the United States is bound to be a difficult and time-consuming undertaking.

COMMUNITY, SCHOOL, AGENCY, AND PARENT PARTNERSHIPS

Creating successful collaborations among schools, agencies, businesses, and parents in communities can create exciting possibilities as schools organize to maximize their potentials. By joining forces, these entities are forming successful partnerships across our nation to better serve and support educational programs for all children through sharing information, generating support, and combining resources (Sanders, 2001).

Collaborative community projects and programs don't have to be expensive or grandiose to be effective, but they do involve commitment, energy, and time. "The beauty of these groups is that community members are developing the capacity to deal together with difficult problems that no individual parent could solve alone" (Winter, 1994, p. 13). Collaborative efforts can be insightful in defining problems and can serve as forums for assessing community interest and organizing community support for sociopolitical action.

Sanders (2001) collected data describing school-community partnerships from over 400 schools in the United States. Findings from her research identify specific barriers and obstacles in forming partnership programs. For example, successfully involving families, students, and community members in participation is often difficult. Identifying community partners and finding sufficient time to approach business and community leaders can be formidable challenges. Other considerations include the availability of leadership, adequate funding, the ability to effectively communicate across population groups, and forming a shared focus.

Dupper (1993) points out that social workers often play significant roles in implementing and sustaining school-community collaborations. He suggests that social workers bring insights about interpersonal relationships, knowledge of community resources and leaders, and understanding of complex organizations to the school setting and thus, "are in a strategic position to develop and nurture collaborative efforts between schools, businesses, and social service agencies in local communities" (Dupper, 1993, pp. 37–38).

While membership in community-based family-school-agency collaborative partnerships would appear particularly relevant for school social workers, support for these types of projects needs to be broad based both within the profession of social work and across helping professions. Frey and Dupper (2005) suggest that school social workers are beginning "to move away from specialist-oriented services to comprehensive general programmatic approaches" (p. 33). Because school social workers contend and work with managed care and services that are provided in the context of community delivery systems, it is time for "school social workers and other practitioners working in schools . . . [to be] viewed as mental health practitioners working in an overall system of care aimed at serving a predefined population of children and adolescents" (Franklin, 2000, p. 6). However, it is impractical to conceptualize or rely upon school social workers as specialists capable of creating or developing school-community partnerships without broad support and help.

Picture, for a moment, a crowded conference room at a school district's administrative office building. School administrators, board members, parents, teachers, representatives from city council and the county commissioners' offices, the city police chief, local business leaders, and social workers from various child service organizations are meeting to examine the topic of children and school absenteeism, suspension, and expulsion. Several members hold political power. Some members control community resources, and others provide important insights concerning the needs of at-risk children in school. Parents express growing anxiety and a desire to share their ideas about this problem. By working together, the collaborative hopes to better understand school absenteeism in their community and eventually to pursue viable programs and interventions concentrating on changes at the organizational, community, and societal levels.

THE EARLY SCHOOL SCENE—SOCIAL POLICY AND SOCIAL CHANGE

A major thrust of macro-level change in social work practice is the identification of groups experiencing structural oppression and organizing clients for action to improve the social environment (Long, 1995, p. 48). The school environment includes assessment and monitoring of relevant policies and procedures established by school administrators, psychologists, staff members, and teachers—especially those policies that impact students at risk. Long (1995) also stresses the importance of parental input at the policy-setting level. Only through an intimate, working knowledge of school policies and procedures as well as of various state and federal laws can clients and social workers challenge local and state school systems to better provide for the academic needs of children at risk.

Social change is often manifested by program development and/or the enactment of social legislation. Social workers must be knowledgeable about the many voluntary associations (e.g., parent-teacher associations), special interest groups (e.g., child welfare councils), and clubs (e.g., music and athletic boosters) organized around student needs. These organizations can provide valuable information and serve as sources of power in advocating and lobbying for social legislation on behalf of students.

NATIONAL AND STATE DEPARTMENTS OF EDUCATION

Social workers and professional social work organizations play critical roles in shaping statewide and national agendas for programs addressing problems of children in schools. The participation of social workers in assessing and developing federal and state initiatives is important for several reasons. Social workers are frequently called upon to intervene with schoolchildren in need. Social workers are able to provide background and information for guiding program formation and development in the educational macro systems.

Social workers are not only skilled at program development and evaluation but they also excel in networking with various professional organizations. Federal and state initiatives focusing on school programming for children at risk require coordination and communication between various human service agencies, professional groups, and education departments. Social workers have the skills to facilitate the interface between practitioner and policymaker necessary for effective school-based services.

The influence of federal and state mandates for schoolchildren should not be minimized. Although school programs initiated at the state and federal level are commonly modified by school systems to meet local needs, state and/or federal support and resources often serve to prompt local action. For example, state and federal mandates often pressure communities to be more responsive to issues they are reluctant to address (Helper, 1989). National drug and sex education programs for students in middle childhood have been implemented by many local districts. Barrier-free codes and policies have made it possible for thousands of students who are physically challenged to participate at a near-normal level. Pressure from the federal government or state can provide impetus for convincing local school systems to pursue program development in these areas.

CASE EXAMPLE	COLLABORATIVE PLANNING AND ATTENTION-DEFICIT/HYPERACTIVITY DISORDER

Melissa Richardson is a school social worker with Hogan City Schools, a school system in a city of 150,000 residents located in southern Illinois. She serves grades one through six at the three city elementary schools. Family assessments, case management, parent counseling, and family support are her primary service responsibilities. In addition, she is frequently asked to assist with program development, training, and evaluation. She is often an advocate for families with children having special needs and is highly involved in community programs.

For the last three years, Melissa has developed a special interest in children with an attention-deficit/hyperactivity disorder (ADHD). When a student exhibits behaviors that might indicate a diagnosis of ADHD, the case is referred directly to Melissa. The three major factors indicating the diagnosis of ADHD involve inattention, impulsivity, and hyperactivity. Children with ADHD frequently have difficulty in organizing themselves for school tasks and projects. ADHD and other learning disabilities are frequently diagnosed during elementary school.

To her credit, Melissa's approach to working with children with ADHD has included both micro-level and macro-level components. Melissa is keenly aware of the unique stressors and challenges for children with ADHD and their families (McCleary, 2002). She has always thought of students with ADHD as a client group, not only as individuals. Melissa has been a leader in organizing parents of children with ADHD both for social support and for social action, and she is a founding member of the local ADHD Council. She is perceived in the community as an expert in understanding children with ADHD as well as a champion for their rights. Her assistance to teachers in devising new approaches to learning for these students is well known.

Two years ago, school officials, parents, and other area social workers, in cooperation with the local ADHD Council and under Melissa's leadership, formed a collaborative planning group called Assessing Attention Deficit Disorders (ATTEND). The timing of this venture was ideal. Because parents of children with ADHD felt anxious and depressed about their situation, they were highly motivated to take steps to assist their children. They began to request differential diagnoses for their children labeled "behavior problems." These individualized diagnostic plans provided detailed information about each child that could be translated into specific classroom strategies. Meanwhile, strong administrative leadership and support in the school system and community created an atmosphere of empowerment for parents of children with special needs. School and community officials openly encouraged an entrepreneurial spirit for building a collaborative approach for examining diverse issues related to ADHD. Examination of the organizational context of empowerment identified these factors as crucial in supporting the emergence of ATTEND (Gutierrez, GlenMaye, & DeLois, 1995).

Two themes appeared in the first two years: a general lack of awareness and knowledge concerning ADHD in the school system and community, and a general disdain for ADHD programming in the school expressed by both students and parents. Students with ADHD were too easily identified as a result of educational

continued

CASE EXAMPLE | *continued*

accommodations (e.g., classroom seating and assignment of a teacher's aide). Consequently, they often felt stigmatized by other students, teachers, and staff. This information was documented and used as the basis for a grant proposal requesting funding from the Hogan County Mental Health Board.

The Hogan County Mental Health Board agreed to fund a three-year pilot project to be administered by the ATTEND collaborative. The project had three purposes: first, to educate community residents, school employees, and area professionals and present to them the most recent research and information concerning ADHD; second, to fund a special interagency task force for assessing school and government policies and procedures affecting students with ADHD in the Hogan City School system; and finally, to conduct a needs assessment to identify the needs of families having children diagnosed with ADHD.

Melissa played an important role in securing this funding by actively facilitating parent participation in educational planning and linking families with resources in the community. Many phone calls and meetings with parents, school administrators, mental health board officials, and social workers at other agencies began the process. Her in-depth knowledge of community-based assets allowed her to strategize the plan and to network the appropriate agencies and personnel. Melissa's enthusiasm in working with children with ADHD energized parents and school staff members toward action. Including a program evaluation component in the grant proposal helped to secure funding for the project. Funding sources were particularly interested in learning how information associated with research outcomes would be used to improve policies, programs, and practices.

At a time when the Hogan County Mental Health Board and the Hogan City School System faced severe financial issues, Melissa and the members of ATTEND felt fortunate to be recipients of this pilot grant. The Hogan County Mental Health Board was persuaded to act favorably upon the ATTEND grant request because of its collaborative character: community agencies and schools would be working together (Carlson, Clark, & Marx, 1993). Mental health board members viewed the ATTEND proposal as an approach that emphasized coordination of services over duplication of efforts, resulting in more effective delivery of service to children with ADHD.

Time to Think!

Melissa Richardson, school social worker, was faced with a multitude of demands. She was involved in both macro and micro elements of social work practice in working with children with ADD. What conditions made macro-level assessment and intervention more appropriate for Melissa than for other social workers in practice with schoolchildren? Is there anything inherent in the role of school social worker that encourages a macro-level approach to problems? As suggested by Frey and Dupper (2005), is it advantageous or realistic for school social workers to downplay "a focus on individual, small group, and family work in favor of prevention and intervention efforts that affect large systems" (p. 42)? Or, should social workers approach their practice in a manner that reflects a **unified approach,** where credibility is given to both issues of power and social justice as well as to clinical work with individuals and families (Vodde & Gallant, 2002)?

Macro Systems and Children with ADHD

The client system described in this chapter is not an individual or family. Instead, children with ADHD in the Hogan City Schools and their families constitute the identified client system. As a result of the recent grant, the ATTEND collaborative's work has just begun. Acknowledging that assessment is an ongoing process, we examine this client system in terms of relevant organizational, community, societal, and international factors.

Organizational Level The Hogan City School System, the Hogan County Mental Health Board, and other related agencies appear open, flexible, and supportive of client-interagency collaboratives. Change does not appear problematic, and a spirit of cooperation apparently prevails.

However, as the ATTEND collaborative goes about its work, continued assessment of organizational climate will be imperative. Direct involvement in school policies and programming for students with ADHD could create organizational tension and turmoil within the school system. As ATTEND consults with faculty and staff and ultimately suggests policy and program changes to administrators, the organizational mood may shift. School is a vital part of a child's environment. If the collaborative project alienates the school, students could suffer the consequences. Ongoing assessment by the social worker of interrelationships among the school system and other key organizations (e.g., the funding source) is critical.

During the three years of the ATTEND organization, changes will occur. For example, as membership terms expire at the Hogan County Mental Health Board, new board members will begin service, each bringing additions to the agenda. Also, it is not unusual for directors and leaders at social service agencies and boards to be replaced. As fiscal cutbacks occur, schools and social service organizations often restructure or downsize. With modifications in parental involvement, the composition and thrust of the collaborative could drift. The school social worker will need to stay abreast of the many dynamics occurring within and among the key organizations involved in the ATTEND project.

Community Level The city of Hogan lies in rural southern Illinois. Although generally interested in the problems of schools and schoolchildren, residents of the area tend to be underinformed about school issues and frugal in their spending for school programs and student services.

continued

CASE EXAMPLE | *continued*

To increase community understanding of schoolchildren's learning problems, Melissa has considered publishing a community newsletter. Currently, discussions center on community acceptance of yet another newsletter because both the Hogan City Schools and the Hogan County Mental Health Board produce quarterly publications. One alternative would be to highlight various school-age problems in the Hogan City School, ADHD Council, and Mental Health Board newsletters. Those opposed to this idea cite editorial control issues and possible conflicts of interest. Another option involves purchasing cable time for educating the community about various elementary school issues.

Several ATTEND collaborative members proposed that a portion of their grant project monies be used to contract an independent consulting group to conduct research, examining the effectiveness of various newsletter and cable access options in educating the community. Previous research has demonstrated broad support citywide for mental health programs, children's services, and school issues, with the exception of the affluent suburban areas of West Landon Farms and Green Meadows. Some ATTEND committee members are also interested in targeting only West Landon Farms and Green Meadows for a newsletter or cable spots.

Despite high-profile efforts to inform, children with special needs are still viewed by many in the community as either "slow" or "retarded." Social workers and organizations like the ADHD Council remain dedicated to finding new ways to normalize the school experience and increase acceptance for their school-age clients.

Societal Level As a school social worker, Melissa has had a long-standing interest in working with children with disabilities, but not until she read about research on ADHD as conducted and supported by the National Institute of Mental Health (NIMH) did she become excited about working with this group of children. The more she learned about ADHD, the greater her appreciation for the support generated nationally by the NIMH.

When reviewing literature and research on ADHD, Melissa has identified several valuable resources. Jensen (2004) provides a useful overview of ADHD, citing common forms of treatments and the efficacy of stimulants. McCleary's (2002) article is a particularly helpful examination of parenting and ADHD. Thomas and Corcoran (2003) review literature on ADHD by theoretical framework and developmental state of the child. Through a cooperative agreement with a local university library, Melissa is able to effectively identify and obtain the most recent articles and books on ADHD from a variety of sources.

Living in a conservative corner of Illinois, Melissa feels the impact of the national movement where "education is undergoing scrutiny and assault by a powerful political movement guided by conservative activists" (Gianesin & Bonaker, 2003). In the last several years, distrust of public education and an emphasis on fiscal control and restraint have become increasingly evident. Parents are demanding increased involvement, greater choice in schools, and a reduction in bureaucratic overhead. Services and programs for children with special needs have come under increased scrutiny. Some taxpayers have begun to question the relevancy of ATTEND and the need for school social workers.

The conservative political aura across the nation has acted as a barrier for those advocating for programs and services for children with ADHD and their families, especially in Hogan City School District. Melissa has attempted to moderate the challenges presented by the conservative movement by listening carefully to various issues as they are presented and continuing to advocate for the rights and opportunities of children with ADHD.

International Level As a school social worker in a low-profile region of the United States, Melissa makes special efforts to keep abreast of the most recent findings in her field. To receive regular and up-to-date information about learning disabilities, ADHD, and other school-age problems, Melissa has become an avid user of the Internet. She belongs to several electronic distribution groups and regularly checks her e-mail for updates and information.

The World Wide Web allows for an international approach to information processing and management. Via her membership agreement at a local university library, Melissa can use web-based search tools to find the most recent literature. Confronted with a need for information or alternative strategies, Melissa can pose questions on two different electronic mailing lists to professionals around the world. She also belongs to one international discussion group devoted to ADHD. Melissa's Favorites bar on her browser is filled with websites providing valuable content on ADHD. If monies become available, Melissa hopes to develop her own website so that she can more efficiently share news and her electronic resources and links with local families interested in ADHD.

In assessing the use of information technology in social work practice, Melissa faces several decisions. She could spend hours each day sending and answering e-mails and searching for information. Although it is a bonus to be able to acquire needed information in a timely fashion, such capabilities can become time-consuming and take away from other professional activities. In addition, Melissa's students and families often prefer to send her an e-mail rather than call. Being able to access her accounts from home and on vacation only provides further temptation. Melissa has had to place firm limitations on her computer use and time.

Through the literature, Melissa has followed the efforts of social workers interested in promoting an international perspective for examining mental health services. In particular, she is interested in the many challenges faced by mental health professionals across the globe in providing programs and services and advocating for children with disabilities (Gerstein & Ægisdottir, 2005). Melissa hopes that by becoming familiar with the diverse needs of people and various mental health service delivery systems around the world, new ideas will emerge for enhancing and improving the quality of life for her clients.

REFLECTION ON DIVERSITY: THE ADAPTIVE PROCESS

At an early age, Ryan White was an advocate and educator. He sought to inform and enlighten classmates, teachers, administrators, and citizens in his community about the hopes and aspirations of a student with AIDS. Although Ryan was unaware of his role, he was the originator and the vanguard of what is now known as the Disability Rights Movement.

One of the most formidable challenges facing contemporary education at all levels involves overcoming prejudicial attitudes and discriminatory practices. Successful inclusion of students in school programs requires "a combination of information about disabilities and contact with people who are disabled" (DuBois & Miley, 2005, p. 338). Upfront and in person, Ryan White attempted to educate reluctant teachers, parents, and administrators about the social and emotional benefits associated with creating an enabling environment for students experiencing disabilities.

As a social worker, you will learn to challenge yourself and other professionals to "actively ask questions and to direct . . . energies toward allowing consumers [of services] to teach us, use their competencies, and acquire needed resources" (Green & Lee, 2002, p. 185). Learning from the experiential expertise of clients is particularly important with respect to human diversity. Professionals often rely upon readings, research, practice wisdom, and their own experiences to heighten their awareness of human diversity. Significantly, one of the most enlightening and useful sources of information is the client and caretaker.

Hardy-Desmond (2003) suggests that social workers approach practice with clients as an **adaptive process**. Social workers learn about clients through partnerships and reciprocal change. Hardy-Desmond identifies the key questions for professionals utilizing an adaptive process as:

- What information am I gaining (learning)?
- How am I changed by this information?
- How can I use this information effectively? (2003, p. 18)

Social workers, professionals, and citizens can learn from children with disabilities. Intentional use of the professional self in social work practice involves a commitment to self-awareness and an understanding of the views and social realities of consumers of services. "Cultural competence is a process of working with ALL people that acknowledges how their heritage, language, family, social experiences, backgrounds, locality, and a whole host of other factors impact how they perceive and experience the world" (Hardy-Desmond, 2004, p. 270).

In macro-oriented practice, social workers form partnerships with clients to promote a broader public awareness of the client's situation and circumstances. It is imperative that disability issues are seen as an "inequity in how an environment responds to and interprets human diversity" and not only as a personal problem in need of being fixed or cured (Gilson & DePoy, 2002, p. 156). This is why Ryan White's story provides such an important insight. People who define themselves as disabled can share their experiences and circumstances in the social environment in realistic and convincing ways.

APPLYING A SOCIAL WORK FRAMEWORK: NORMALIZATION

Schoolchildren with ADHD as well as those with other kinds of disabilities desperately want to be accepted by peers and teachers. They are often stigmatized by school programs and services that separate and label students with disabilities as "different." They are anxious to be seen as full participants in school, family, and society. The sensitive social worker will exert every skill and effort to normalize as many settings as possible for the client.

In our case example, Melissa has been a catalyst in developing a cooperative venture to examine how school systems can better educate children with ADHD. To avoid the labeling and stigmatizing of students with ADHD, teachers, administrators, parents, professionals, and others involved in the educational process need to be better informed about this particular disorder. In the Hogan community example, an examination of curricula, classroom practices, teaching styles, school policies and programs, and administrative decision making will be conducted by the ATTEND collaborative to identify mechanisms that will assure that, as much as possible, children with ADHD are afforded the same opportunities as other students.

Years of practice have left Melissa with vivid memories of the anger and disappointment of students when they are singled out by school officials. She has received phone calls from parents desperate in their search to find teachers and school programs amenable to the learning style and educational plight of their son or daughter. Melissa has seen the painful expressions on faces of students and parents when teachers and school administrators in individual educational plan (IEP) conferences have referred to students with ADHD as "lacking initiative," "troublemakers," or "lazy." Melissa knows that negative attitudes and behaviors directed toward people with mental disabilities must be minimized in order to attain normalization of service delivery.

Three years ago, Melissa came to the realization that battling for the rights of students with ADHD case by case, teacher by teacher, and school by school was inefficient and ineffective. Funding of the ATTEND collaborative was a milestone as it signaled an initial step in Hogan City toward acknowledging systemic responsibility and concern for the treatment of children with ADHD. As the school system in Hogan City begins the task of evaluation of the delivery of their educational programs, we are reminded of the real-life struggle of Ryan White and the many hurdles to be overcome by advocates for children with special needs in schools.

SUGGESTED ACTIVITIES

1. Interview a school administrator, inquiring about programming and accommodations for students with special needs. Ask about task forces and/or committees of the school district or community that address issues confronting students with disabilities and their parents. How do suspension and expulsion rules apply to emotionally impaired children? What kinds of services and programs are available?

2. When in your state's capital, arrange for a visit to the department of special education. Ask about pending or recent landmark legislation written to protect the rights of all students and those bills that are intended to normalize the classroom experience for students who have disabilities, physical or mental.

3. Access information from the World Wide Web using a search tool like InfoTrac®. Identify research articles describing a problem, program, or policy involving schoolchildren—for example, discipline codes. How do these apply to students with disabilities, particularly those with severe emotional impairment (SEI) who have anger issues, who are emotionally unstable, or who are sometimes combative? Attempt to locate an e-mail address or home page to receive additional information concerning your topic.

REFERENCES

Amerman, T., & Fleres, C. (2003). A winning combination: Collaboration in inclusion. *Academic Exchange Quarterly, 7* (3), 66–71.

Bank-Mikkelsen, N. (1969). A metropolitan area in Denmark: Copenhagen. In R. Kugel & W. Wolfensberger (Eds.), *Changing patterns in residential services for the mentally retarded.* Washington, DC: President's Committee on Mental Retardation.

Biklen, D. (1985). *Achieving the complete school.* New York: Teachers College Press.

Brewster, A., & Bowen, G. (2004). Teacher support and the school engagement of Latino middle and high school students at risk of school failure. *Child and Adolescent Social Work Journal, 21,* 47–67.

Carlson, S., Clark, J., & Marx, D. (1993). School and community resource collaboration. *School Social Work Journal, 17,* 47–49.

Christie, K. (2005). Stateline: Providing the facts. *Phi Delta Kappan, 86,* 341–342.

Cochran-Smith, M. (2005). No child left behind. *Journal of Teacher Education, 56,* 99–103.

DuBois, B., & Miley, K. (2005). *Social work: An empowering profession.* Boston: Pearson Allyn & Bacon.

Dupper, D. (1993). School-community collaboration: A description of a model program designed to prevent school dropouts. *School Social Work Journal, 18,* 33–39.

Dybvik, A. (2004). Autism and the inclusion mandate: What happens when children with severe disabilities like autism are taught in regular classrooms? *Education Next, 4,* 42–49.

Franklin, C. (2000). Predicting the future of school social work practice in the new millennium. *Social Work in Education, 22,* 3–7.

Frey, A., & Dupper, D. (2005). A broader conceptual approach to clinical practice for the 21st century. *Children and Schools, 27,* 33–44.

Friedman, J. (1988). The quiet victories of Ryan White. *People Weekly, 29,* 88–96.

Gerstein, L., & Ægisdottir, S. (2005). A trip around the world. *Journal of Mental Health Counseling, 27,* 95–103.

Gianesin, J., & Bonaker, P. (2003). Understanding conservative challenges to school social work and public education. *Children and Schools, 25,* 49–62.

Gilson, S., & DePoy, E. (2002). Theoretical approaches to disability content in social work education. *Journal of Social Work Education, 38,* 153–165.

Green, G., & Lee, M. (2002). The social construction of empowerment. In M. O'Melia & K. Miley (Eds.), *Pathways to power: Readings in contextual social work practice*. Boston: Allyn & Bacon.

Gutierrez, L., GlenMaye, L., & DeLois, K. (1995). The organizational context of empowerment practice: Implications for social work administration. *Social Work, 40*, 249–258.

Hardy-Desmond, S. (2004). Cultural competence. In A. Sallee (Ed.), *Social work and social welfare: An introduction*. Peosta, IL: Eddie Bowers.

Hardy-Desmond, S. (2003). *Social work practice innovation: The adaptive process*. Peosta, IL: Eddie Bowers.

Helper, J. (1989). Utilizing organizational theory to improve the effectiveness of implementing evaluation and intervention programs in elementary and secondary schools. *School Social Work Journal, 14*, 26–35.

Houston, P. (2005). Point of view—NCLB: Dreams and nightmares. *Phi Delta Kappan, 86*, 469–470.

Jensen, C. (2004). Medication for children with attention-deficit hyperactivity disorder. *Clinical Social Work Journal, 32*, 197–214.

Kilty, K., & Meenaghan, T. (1995). Social work and the convergence of politics and science. *Social Work, 40*, 445–453.

Legters, N. & McDill, E. (1994). Rising to the challenge: Emerging strategies for educating youth at risk. In R. Rossi (Ed.), *Schools and students at risk*. New York: Teachers College Press.

Long, D. (1995). Attention deficit disorder and case management: Infusing macro social work practice. *Journal of Sociology and Social Welfare, 12*, 45–55.

Magrisso, B. (1992). A case study consideration of role in relationship to an identified at-risk child. *School Social Work Journal, 17*, 25–37.

McCleary, L. (2002). Parenting adolescents with attention deficit hyperactivity disorder: Analysis of the literature for social work practice. *Health and Social Work, 27*, 285–292.

Meenaghan, T., Kilty, K., & McNutt, J. (2004). *Social policy analysis and practice*. Chicago: Lyceum.

Montgomery, A., & Rossi, R. (1994). Becoming at risk of failure in America's schools. In R. Rossi (Ed.), *Schools and students at risk*. New York: Teachers College Press.

Nash, J. (2002). Neighborhood effects on sense of school coherence and educational behavior in students at risk of school failure. *Children and School, 24*, 73–87.

Neild, R. (2005). Parent management of school choice in a large school district. *Urban Education, 40*, 270–297.

Peterson, P. (2005). The children left behind: NCLB is a giant step forward—but a mid-course correction is needed. *Education Next, 5*, 3.

Renzaglia, A., Karvonen, M., Drasgow, E., & Stoxen, C. (2003). Promoting a lifetime of inclusion. *Focus on Autism and Other Developmental Disabilities, 18*, 140–150.

Rosenfeld, L., & Richman, J. (2003). Social support and educational outcomes for students in out-of-home care. *Children and Schools, 25*, 69–86.

Rosenfeld, L., Richman, J., & Bowen, G. (2000). Social support networks and school outcomes: The centrality of the teacher. *Child and Adolescent Social Work Journal, 17*, 205–226.

Sailor, W., & Roger, B. (2005). Rethinking inclusion: Schoolwide applications. *Phi Delta Kappan, 86*, 503–509.

Sanders, M. (2001). The role of "community" in comprehensive school, family, and community partnership programs. *Elementary School Journal, 102,* 19–34.

SerVaas, C. (1988). The happier days for Ryan White. *Saturday Evening Post, 260,* 52–98.

Thomas, C., & Corcoran, J. (2003). Family approaches to attention deficit hyperactivity disorder: A review to guide school social work practice. *Children and Schools, 25,* 19–34.

Truman, C. (2004). No child left behind disconnects parents from schools. *Curriculum Review, 44,* 3.

Vodde, R., & Gallant, J. (2002). Bridging the gap between micro and macro practice: Large scale change and a unified model of narrative-deconstructive practice. *Journal of Social Work Education, 38,* 439–458.

Wehmeyer, M. (2004). Self-determination and the empowerment of people with disabilities. *American Rehabilitation, 28,* 22–29.

White, R., & Cunningham, A. (1991). *Ryan White: My own story.* New York: Dial.

Winter, M. (1994). Parent networks strengthen communities. *Children Today, 23,* 12–32.

Wolfensberger, W. (1972). *The principle of normalization in human services.* Toronto: National Institute on Mental Retardation.

Wolfensberger, W. (1983). Social role valorization: A proposed new term for the principle of normalization. *Mental Retardation, 21,* 234–239.

ADOLESCENCE

A teenage boy is hanging with his friends near a street corner. He sports a billed cap turned backward and tilted sideways. The tall, thin African American wears oversized baggy shorts that droop low, exposing his silk boxer shorts. His high top athletic shoes look new and expensive. A long chain hangs from his neck and accessorizes an XXXL Jay-Z shirt. The teen's appearance has a trendy look. Music booms from an adjacent automobile as the bass vibrates through the neighborhood. To passersby, the boy appears to be in animated conversation with his buddies. His peers know this teenager as an active member of hip-hop's "bling" culture.

Across the nation, "Hip-hop is officially happening. Once dismissed by corporate America as a niche musical genre with minimal buying power, hip-hop is now spreading its influence across a host of industries and brands are at last taking notice" (Devaney, 2004, p. 38). Approximately thirty years in the making, "it is estimated that two out of every 10 records sold in America is hip-hop, with 80 percent of its customers being White" (Chappell, 2005). Many teenagers attribute the origins of this trend in music to artists like Run-D.M.C., Salt-N-Pepa, Heavy D., Kool Moe Dee, and LL Cool J. However, the beginning of hip-hop can be traced back to the late 1970s and Jamaican immigrant Kool Herc, considered by many to be the founder of hip-hop music (Chappell, 2005). Contemporary hip-hop artists include 50 Cent, OutKast, and Eminem.

There is little doubt that for teenagers, particularly urban youth, hip-hop has become extremely popular. However, the meaning of hip-hop can vary as widely as each teenager's favorite artist. Hip-hop music is regarded by many adults as loud, annoying music that peddles violence, sex, anger, and profanity as a form of artistic expression. Advocates of hip-hop suggest that it "speaks about all issues of societal concern; politics, love, aberrance . . . hip-hop is a type of music that reflects the life that struggling people live, especially those whose existence is barely recognized . . . they (rappers) try hard to venture into people's consciousness" (Balesent, 2005, p. NA).

The sounds and images associated with the multibillion-dollar hip-hop culture and industry are harsh and disturbing. The related music and promotional materials "reflect the fantasies of the consumers of hip-hop culture. They are adolescent dream landscapes. The images depict a world of unlimited access to sex, drugs, cars, and money. . . . Masculinity is equated with toughness and power over women. Femininity is depicted as a fetishized female who is an available sex toy" (Javors, 2004, p. 42).

Adolescents are vulnerable, psychosocially and economically, to the "gangsta" mentality of self-indulgence, control, and violence. Listening to hip-hop, wearing Roc-A-Wear clothing, adopting an egocentric philosophy of "on the make and on the take," and fantasizing about life in terms of "hos" and "gangstas" is a peer-based reality for many teenagers in America. With the phenomenal development of electronics, its culture is rapidly spreading around the world. If only as a fantasy, it is fashionable in many circles for adolescents to be living the street life and an "in the hood" existence via hip-hop.

Parents commonly view hip-hop with fear and suspicion, even as they shell out large sums of money to support their children's purchases of hip-hop CDs, clothing, concert tickets, and memorabilia. It is a difficult position for parents. Teenagers yearn for social acceptance from their peers. Parents have a responsibility to monitor the activities of their children and to set appropriate boundaries concerning the use of language, respect for authority, and gender roles. Protests by parents over their teen's choice of music and clothes can be counterproductive. Being a critical though concerned parent may inadvertently push one's adolescent toward peer groups. If, for example, a teen is labeled as "gangsta," numerous unplanned consequences may occur. Stereotyping and labeling are likely results of affiliation with a counterculture or peer group (Rosenbaum & Prinsky, 1991).

This is not to suggest that the emergence of a hip-hop culture is necessarily a novel or unusual occurrence. During the 1960s, the Beatles captured the imaginations of teenagers with their long hair and unique rock and roll style. Kurt Cobain and Nirvana gave rise to the grunge movement among adolescent youth during the 1990s. Over the years, generations of teenagers have laid claim to a variety of rebellious musical groups and genres.

Basic to a social work approach is the understanding that an adolescent involved in hip-hop may not necessarily behave in an antisocial manner. Instead, the stereotype of a member of hip-hop or a rapper produces a social label that often imposes negative attributes upon the individual. In social work, professionals endeavor to recognize and reinforce the uniqueness and strengths inherent in each person and group of people and seek ways to combat the negative effects of social labels.

Do such movements have any redeeming qualities? In 2003, superstar Bow Wow performed a benefit concert in New York City to raise awareness and monies for Computers For Youth (CFY). Bow Wow elected, with production by HBO, to assist CFY in its effort to provide low-income, inner-city children and families with home computers and appropriate computer training. An avid computer user, Bow Wow chose to make a difference through technology by assisting "low-income students to become engaged learners and thereby succeed in school" (*PR Newswire*, 2003, p. NR). Bow Wow's efforts exemplify how stars from the hip-hop bling culture can partner with media outlets (HBO) and nonprofit organizations (CFY) to accentuate the importance of technological literacy, education, and information in the lives of adolescents.

Adults may be tempted to harshly judge the contemptuous ways of teenagers. Although they once experienced their own identity struggles, they are inclined to label counterculture adolescents as deviant. This chapter examines the consequences of negative labels for the adolescent. As we explore concepts and terms, consider the hip-hop culture's influence on youth. Is it without merit or value? How is the hip-hop experience any better or worse than the cultural influences of your days as a teenager?

THEORY: LABELING

In this chapter, we are less interested in why adolescents engage in actions that may be considered deviant and more concerned with the negative effects of social definitions and sanctions as influences on self-perception. What are the consequences "when certain official 'labelers' in a society (e.g., law enforcement officials or psychiatrists)" describe an adolescent or a group of adolescents as deviant (Traub & Little, 1975, p. 159)? **Labeling theory** enables us to focus upon the impact of punitive forces on adolescents.

Howard Becker describes the process of labeling: "The deviant is one to whom the label has successfully been applied; deviant behavior is behavior that people so label" (1963, p. 9). Labeling theorists stress the subjective nature of rules and societal reaction to rule-breaking behavior in defining deviance. Becker concludes "social groups create deviance by making the rules whose infraction constitutes deviance, and by applying those rules to particular people" (1963, p. 9).

Several important questions emerge as one considers the effect of labeling. What occurs when adolescents violate social norms or break rules? Does societal reaction vary based on the time, place, and person, as well as the social significance of the rule(s) violated? If so, who defines what is deviant? Once a label is used, how difficult is it to shed the unfavorable ones such as "punk," "delinquent," "druggie," or "major L (loser)"? Do negative labels contribute to future deviant behavior for adolescents in a manner that becomes a self-fulfilling prophecy?

Lemert (1951) provides valuable insight into these questions by distinguishing between primary and secondary deviance. **Primary deviance** describes individuals whose behavior is only occasionally deviant. The term

secondary deviance is reserved for more pervasive atypical behavior. At what point does the offender see self as a social outcast?

The transition from primary deviance to secondary deviance is a significant step. When primary deviance occurs, the social ramifications for those involved are minimal. A group of high school students are caught vandalizing a local park following an emotional soccer victory. While they are made to pay for damages and penalized by the school, the police department and school administrators believe the actions to be a one-time occurrence. The matter is handled privately with the teenagers and their parents.

Conversely, when adolescents, individually or as a group, are given the label of deviant and view themselves that way, the result is often social disgrace and isolation. A group of teenage girls sitting in a car in a parking lot are busted for getting high on marijuana. The police prosecute all involved in the incident. The word gets out that these teenagers are druggies and are probably involved in hard drugs as well. Soon, the teenage girls experience difficulties in developing friendships and associations with other students. Friends, teachers, and even family members maintain social distance from them. The girls soon find themselves hanging out and associating only with one another; they begin to perceive themselves as social misfits. They are becoming "outsiders" to the conventional world. Once labeled, can these girls shed their stigma as druggies and juvenile delinquents? Or will the negative sanctions and the stigma applied to them be overwhelming and fuel subsequent deviant acts?

"The critical variable in the study of deviance, then, is the social audience which eventually determines whether or not any episode of behavior or any class of episodes is labeled deviant" (Becker, 1964, p. 11). Becker further suggests that when community officials consider exerting control over the behavior of its members, many factors not directly related to the deviant act itself are weighed. These may include "the suspect's social class, his past record as an offender, the amount of remorse he manages to convey, and many similar concerns which take hold in the shifting moods of the community" (Becker, 1964, p. 11).

Adams, Robertson, Gray-Ray, and Ray (2003) suggest that labeling can come from both formal and informal sources. Agencies, parents, teachers, significant others, and peers contribute to the labeling process. Findings from Headley's research point to teachers and peers as especially important links or sources in attempting to predict teen involvement in delinquency.

In summary, the labeling perspective shifts the focus away from the offender to the attitudes of community or society toward the individual. As various developmental issues for adolescence are examined, it will be important to keep in mind the effect of being labeled as deviant. Our focal point will be the reaction of others and the application of labels as related to adolescent developmental issues.

DEVELOPMENTAL ISSUES

The literature on adolescence deals with a variety of topics, including rapid physical growth and maturation, sexuality, development of self-concept and self-esteem, rebellious behavior, substance abuse, career planning, and adolescent-parent relationships. Although not necessarily more difficult than other life stages, adolescence is characterized by the teenager's need for individuation. As the adolescent matures physically, she or he searches for a sense of self, often characterized by rebellion and movement away from parental figures toward peer-group affiliation.

Examining adolescent issues from a social work perspective involves searching out social forces that contribute to individual behaviors and actions. This examination does not negate the relevance of physiological and psychological components in the lives of teenagers. Instead, by highlighting social aspects of adolescent development, social workers can focus more clearly on the influence of various social systems, trends, and movements in assessing behaviors.

We must remind ourselves that adolescents are developing people. Even though some parents may have their moments of doubt, most adolescents transcend this phase and become responsible, productive citizens. Aronson, addressing the topic of "people who do crazy things" in *The Social Animal*, states:

> To my mind, it does not increase our understanding of human behavior to classify these people as psychotic. It is much more useful to try to understand the nature of the situation and the processes that were operating to produce the behavior. This leads us to Aronson's first law: "People who do crazy things are not necessarily crazy." (1972, p. 9)

Using Aronson's logic, we will focus on the social processes that can help explain the actions of adolescents, as opposed to entering into a dialogue regarding the eccentric nature of adolescent behaviors. Teenagers who do crazy things need not be crazy and should not be viewed that way. "At least one quarter of all adolescents are at high risk for engaging in dangerous behaviors that threaten their health and long-term prospects" (Carnegie Council on Adolescent Development, 1996, p. 4).

ADOLESCENT GIRLS

The perils of being young and female are many. Problems include dropping out of school, teenage pregnancy, substance use, and exposure to violence, particularly gang activities.

Unique to teenage girls is the threat of eating disorders. Bulimia—the urge to binge and purge—can be as serious and lethal as an addiction to cocaine. Anorexia is a problem of Western civilization. Bombarded by television and magazine images of thin, popular, successful women, many girls in puberty and adolescence become obsessed with weight and shape.

> They feel confident if they are losing weight and worthless and guilty if they are not. By the time the anorexia is full-blown, family members are terrified. They try everything to make their daughters eat—pleading, threatening, reasoning and tricking. But they fail because the one thing in life that anorexic girls can control is their eating. . . . Their thinness has become a source of power, a badge of honor. . . . Anorexia is a metaphor. It is a young woman's statement that she will become what the culture asks of its women, which is that they will be thin and nonthreatening. (Pipher, 1994, pp. 174–175)

The past several decades have been a time of intensified pressures for young women. More divorced families, chemical addiction, casual sex, and violence against women are factors that leave them vulnerable. Adolescent girls face unique and unparalleled pressures to be beautiful and sophisticated or suffer being labeled as undesirable. "America today limits girls' development, truncates their wholeness and leaves many of them traumatized" (Pipher, 1994, p. 12).

It is important to note that adolescents deal with transitions and difficulties in a variety of ways. Abrams (2003) suggests that expressions of distress tend to reflect an internalizing versus externalizing dichotomy, often characterized as "acting-in" versus "acting-out." **Acting-in** refers to the turning of stress inward (e.g., depression, suicide ideation, self-mutilation, and eating disorders). **Acting-out** involves behaviors and actions that reflect overt, outward displays of defiance (e.g., delinquency, fighting, substance abuse, and sexual risk taking). As a general rule, when confronted with challenges, adolescent girls tend to act-in, whereas boys are more likely to act-out. "However, young women's acting-out behaviors are beginning to parallel the importance of their acting-in tendencies, both in their prevalence and in their potential consequences" (Abrams, 2003, p. 141).

Furthermore, Abrams (2003) suggests sensitivity to a range of sociocultural variations in assessing how girls react to distress. Race, ethnicity, and social-economic status are important factors to consider. For example, Abrams says: "Counter to popular stereotypes, white young women are not the only ethnic group who are 'at-risk' of internalization problems. The literature shows that Hispanic females are most vulnerable to suicide risk and depression, and moderately at-risk for the development of eating disorders" (2003, p. 145). On the other hand, he says: "African-American young women are most vulnerable to being detained for delinquent conduct, and to engaging in fighting and risky sexual behavior" (2003, p. 146).

Differentiation between stereotypic labels and a preponderance of empirical evidence is vital in social work practice. It constitutes the difference between what people think they know and what research demonstrates. When assessing adolescent reactions to distress, low-income girls and teenage girls of color are at risk of acting-out behaviors. The degree to which these population groups become labeled as "troublemakers" as opposed to "teens in need of treatment" is in part socially determined. Access to caring others, legal services, and health care providers can assist teenagers in avoiding negative labels. As many helping professionals will attest, the less negative and harmful the descriptive adjectives laid upon young people, the better the prognosis for avoiding subsequent difficulties.

Girls in community-based residential settings (closed), predominantly low-income and African-American, appear to be particularly vulnerable and in need of professional intervention emphasizing minimal stigmatization. Ruffolo, Sarri, and Goodkind (2004) indicate that in their study this subpopulation "had significantly higher levels of depression, experienced more negative life events, reported more sexual abuse, more often had special education status, were more likely to come from families who received welfare, had more disruptions in living situations, exhibited more delinquent behavior, and used more negative coping behaviors" (p. 237). Beyond the psychological trauma and social disruption faced by these teenage girls, there are numerous obstacles to overcome in terms of labeling. Many middle-class teenagers believe that it is cruel and unfeeling to be asked to endure life without current, desirable fashions, jewelry, book bags, hair styling, etc. Imagine the negative reactions of others when they learn you live in residential placement, attend a special school, have a criminal record, or that your family has received welfare.

From this brief description, it can be seen that being young and female presents distinct challenges. Other factors such as race, ethnicity, delinquency, social-economic class, living circumstances (e.g., placement outside of the home), and sexual orientation can serve to complicate matters, accentuate any sense of being different, and contribute in unique ways to labeling processes.

Visualize for a moment the potential difficulties experienced by adolescent females "whose gender identity (appearance, behavior, and characteristics) differs from the gender stereotypes associated with their birth sex, or whose birth sex is indeterminate at birth," that is, a **transgender** person (Invik, Mills, & McCreary, 2005, p. 15). For purposes of definition, it is often helpful to differentiate transgendered people from transsexual people. **Transsexuals** typically identify more fully with the opposite gender and are likely to consider or undergo sex reassignment procedures or surgeries (Invik, Mills, & McCreary, 2005, p. 15). Consider how children and adolescents who do not fit expected sex and gender stereotypes face unique and distinct challenges that may be misunderstood; they are also mistakenly assumed to be similar to people who are gay, lesbian, or bisexual. As helping professionals, it is vital to educate ourselves and others as to the struggles and negative reaction of others associated with various forms of diversity and sexual identity.

Delinquent Behavior

Adolescents are known for their tendency to test boundaries and rules. We are aware that isolated incidents of delinquent behavior occur as a function of normal adolescent development (Kazdin, 1995). However, as noted in an earlier section in this chapter, there is frequently a distinction made between an occasional deviant act and pervasive behavior.

Imposing unrealistic restrictions on teenagers may constitute an invitation for problem behavior. Social control systems are then called upon to impose sanctions to help ensure that the deviant act will not recur. Labeling theory suggests, though, that sanctions levied against teenagers may create additional deviant behaviors. A deviant label given by any source may become difficult for a teenager to shake and may perpetuate subsequent delinquent acts.

An alternative approach, **deterrence theory**, contends "the threat or actual imposition of sanctions so elevates actors' perceptions of the risk of non-normative behavior that they will choose to avoid—or at a minimum to reduce the frequency of their participation in—such conduct" (Thomas & Bishop,

1984, p. 1223). Fundamental to the deterrence orientation is a belief that individuals are rational beings with the capacity for self-control and self-determination. Thomas and Bishop report the basic tenets of deterrence theory in terms of people who are

1. motivated by what will serve their best interest.
2. free to choose between alternative courses of action.
3. motivated to avoid deviant actions to the extent that timely and negative sanctions are a sure consequence of such behaviors. (p. 1228)

An interesting debate on the merits of labeling theory versus deterrence theory as opposing orientations for explaining the effect of social control on delinquent behavior has emerged over the past several decades (Sherman & Berk, 1984). While there is no consensus as to the merits of one approach over the other, a review of literature reveals several interesting considerations for social workers in assessing the potential impact of social sanctions and labeling of teens. For example, Horwitz and Wasserman (1979), analyzing longitudinal data with teenagers, report that the offender's motivation for committing a crime is a powerful predictor of future arrest. They also suggest that for first offenders the more severe the social reaction and social control, the higher the likelihood that adolescents will commit subsequent crimes.

Research indicates that the origin of negative sanctions is a primary consideration. Palamara, Cullen, and Gersten (1986) report that when police and mental health workers negatively label adolescent offenders, more deviant behaviors follow. Morash (1982) suggests that parents, peers, and adult neighbors often disagree with police impressions and reaction. A negative label placed by friends is more believable and credible than those assigned by police. These findings point to the importance of both formal and informal sources of labeling in contributing to future delinquent behavior.

Research also suggests that relationships with peer-oriented groups (sociability) and schools constitute basic building blocks in explaining adolescent crime and delinquency (Lotz & Lee, 1999). When teenagers experience difficulties in school, receive negative feedback from school officials, and associate with disruptive, troublesome peers, delinquent acts are likely to occur. Sensitivity to demographic and social-economic status is an important consideration. For example, results of Lotz and Lee's (1999) study indicate "that sociability is a strong predictor of delinquent behavior for African American and White teenagers. Negative school experience predicts delinquency only among Whites" (p. 199).

Family processes also play an important function in adolescent delinquency (Vazsonyi & Pickering, 2003). Parental influences include emotional closeness, involvement, support, consistent discipline, and active supervision. Although Perez McCluskey and Tovar (2003) suggest variations by gender and ethnicity, adolescents with weak, negative, and/or detrimental family relationships appear inclined toward delinquency. Research findings, for example, indicate family use of illegal substances is as an appreciable predictor of adolescent delinquent behavior, even while controlling for gender, friend substance use, social support behavior by peers, support orientation, and future beliefs (MacNeil, Stewart, & Kaufman, 2000, p. 373).

For social workers, a major dilemma involves support for or opposition to various **adolescent diversion programs** established to shield and divert teenagers from the negative aspects associated with labeling and stigmatizing in the criminal justice system. While the overall value of juvenile diversion programs is debatable (Binder & Geis, 1984), recent research suggests that diversion programs and projects are more likely "to result in less official delinquency than the 'warn and release' or juvenile justice processing conditions" (Smith et al., 2004, p. 29).

If one accepts the premise that teenagers who misbehave are reachable, diversion programs are useful, especially for young, first-time offenders. Court systems can reprimand and punish unacceptable behaviors by teenagers while making special efforts not to brand juveniles as delinquents. The distinction is between "You did something wrong" versus "You are a bad person."

SELF-CONCEPT

As stated earlier, adolescents wrestle with the development of self. Generally, adolescents view themselves in positive terms and ways. Many factors contribute to the formation of self-concept and self-esteem, including gender, age, parental relationships, school activities, and part-time work (Bacchini & Magliulo, 2003; Steitz & Owen, 1992). There is a particular social-psychological element in the emergence of one's identity via social interaction with significant others—how appraisals from parents, teachers, and peers provide teenagers with important feedback in building self-image.

As social workers, we need to explore with our clients the consequences of being labeled as deviant. Matsueda (1992), testing a multivariate causal model, indicated that both parental appraisals and prior delinquency influence the adolescent self. When deviant behavior occurs and negative social sanctioning is coupled with parental labeling, teenagers are more likely to cognitively view themselves as rule violators (secondary deviance). For many adolescents, labeling may constitute a turning point, where self-perception as a delinquent becomes lodged into the young person's self-concept. The mix of community and parental labeling serves as an important catalyst in the adoption of deviant identities in the adolescent self.

Al-Talib and Griffin (1994) lend support to the premise that both public (community) and private (parental or peer) aspects of the labeling process serve to influence self-concept. Comparing labeled, unlabeled (participating in delinquent acts but uncaught), and nondelinquent British adolescents, Al-Talib and Griffin found "a significant difference exists between the groups in the patterns of their self-concept. Adolescents who had been labeled as delinquents had a lower self-concept than their unlabeled delinquent counterparts" (1994, p. 47). They found both labeled and unlabeled adolescents who committed delinquent acts to have lower self-concepts than those who were not delinquent.

Not all research concludes that deviant social labeling results in a lower self-concept. One study, for example, found little difference in self-esteem between a sample of adolescents labeled as deviant and a sample of normal peers. Instead, only "subjects who believed that the societal view of their group was similar to the self, who had a negative evaluation of the deviant label, had lower self-esteem" (Stager, Chassin, & Young, 1983, p. 3).

Conflict with societal norms is particularly pertinent to adolescents with strong group affiliations, for example, those labeled as "thugs" as a result of their association with the hip-hop movement. If a hip-hop follower believes that society views hip-hop negatively, then self-esteem is in jeopardy. Conversely, when a teenager understands that the societal view of hip-hop is negative but does not internalize this view, then self-esteem is less affected.

As we reflect on these ideas, social opinion about a particular adolescent group becomes relevant. Given your knowledge of the movement, do you believe that hip-hop members are deviant? Do they see themselves as different, cool, and radical, or as troublemakers? Is judgment about the image of hip-hop members based on credible information or anecdotal evidence? What are sources of feedback to group members about their public reputation? To what extent are deviant adolescents isolated from the larger society? To what extent is an association with hip-hop culture only a temporary or intermittent phenomenon? Does membership in a hip-hop peer group contribute to a sense of actual self or represent a facade of the ideal self?

Social workers often serve adolescents experiencing low self-esteem. In assessing the effects of being labeled as deviant, it is important to attempt to understand the impact of any group membership stigmatized by the community. While group identity and individual identity may not be synonymous, group identity is an important social force influencing adolescent self-esteem as well as community response.

DRUG USE

In assessing the relationship between social control and deviant behavior, Becker considered marijuana use. In the early 1960s, when Becker wrote, marijuana use was punishable by severe penalties. It was considered dangerous to physical and mental health, and arrest and imprisonment were the legal penalties. In complex societies, the process of assessment can be quite complicated because breakdowns in social control are often the consequence of becoming a participant in a group whose own culture and social controls operate at cross-purposes to those of the larger society. Important factors in the genesis of deviant behavior, then, may be sought in the processes by which people are emancipated from the controls of society and become responsive to those of a smaller group (Becker, 1963, pp. 59–60).

Becker suggests that the career of a drug user can be divided into three stages: beginner, occasional user, and regular user. Crucial in problem definition is the impression by family, friends, or employer that a person is a regular marijuana user. At this point, others believe the regular user to be "irresponsible and powerless to control his own behavior, perhaps even insane. They may punish him with various kinds of informal but highly effective sanctions, such as ostracism or withdrawal of affection" (Becker, 1963, p. 61). The labeling process can be instrumental in shifting the alliance of drug users from acceptance of negative social controls of the larger society to the welcoming arms of a drug-related subculture.

A common developmental phase of adolescents often involves experimentation, use, and/or abuse of drugs. "In general, the profile of abusers suggests that they are individuals who spend a lot of time involved in drug/alcohol-related activities with friends . . . adolescents who abuse drugs tend to associate more with drug-using peers" (Shilts, 1991, p. 615).

Adolescent drug use, however, is a function not only of peer association; labeling and self-rejection also need to be considered. Kaplan and Fukurai (1992, p. 292), for example, tested a research model emphasizing the mediating influence of peer-group affiliation and the level of self-rejection when examining the impact of social sanctions on drug use. Their results suggest that negative social sanctioning has a direct effect on deviant peers and self-rejection, and both predict drug use.

Recent research has affirmed the importance of family in relationship to adolescence drug use. Butters (2002) suggests family stressors increase the probability of adolescent drug use. Other research suggests that effective monitoring and rule setting by parents can serve to deter teen drug use (Stewart, 2002; Svensson, 2003). Given these findings and the apparent importance of family, it is interesting to speculate about the impact of parents interceding on behalf of their children to avoid stigmatization and labeling as a result of drug use. Articulate, caring, and well-connected parents can effectively say to school and law enforcement officials that their teenager "used bad judgment," "is in need of help," or "was influenced by others." Potentially, any of these tactics could effectively be used to subvert labeling.

To summarize, negative social sanctions can have both direct and indirect (through self-rejection and peer-group affiliations) effects on adolescent drug use/abuse. Findings in this area further support labeling theory's implication that some forms of punishment may actually increase the tendency of teenagers to commit deviant actions, including the abuse of drugs.

As social workers, we are left to question the wisdom of national and state policies emphasizing punishment and incarceration of drug users. What are the ramifications of the current expansion of jail space to detain and punish those who use illegal drugs? What are the real differences between illegal and legal drug use? Are the terms "delinquent" and "criminal" reserved only for certain people and certain drugs, while more influential citizens claim to fall victim to the misfortune of chemical dependency? Is the real issue drug use or social control? How different is the labeling process for teenagers of affluent families caught with illegal substances from that of disadvantaged teens?

ADOLESCENT GANGS

Contrary to popular belief, the study of gang membership and influence in America is not a new phenomenon. Decades ago, Thrasher (1967) pioneered the study of gang life in Chicago. In recent years, worldwide attention has been riveted on street gangs, their existence, and social significance. The defacing of public facilities with graffiti, turf battles, and increasing urban violence has focused public consciousness on gang life in America. The frequent occurrence of drive-by shootings in some areas has forced even the most detached citizen to become more concerned about gangs.

Because gang life has a street existence, the study of gangs is a complicated, dangerous endeavor, even for the most astute researcher. Primary collection of data about gangs requires intense preparation as well as advanced knowledge about group processes, structure, and cohesiveness. Although gangs are an important social problem, assessing gang life can be a hazardous undertaking.

There is little popular consensus and considerable disagreement among researchers as to the definitions of a gang and gang membership (Bjerregaard, 2002). Morash (1983), for example, uses the term "ganglike" with respect to youth groups to achieve objectivity and avoid any reference to delinquency in defining a gang. Bjerregaard (2002) describes the merits of allowing self-identification in relationship to gang membership.

A significant number of scholars refute the notion that gangs are "criminally inclined." Gang life is viewed more as sleeping, eating, and hanging out together. Even commonly accepted athletic and church youth groups would be included in such a definition. On the other hand, delinquent acts of gang members may be a means to participate in a youth culture and a mechanism for "getting by" (Klein, 1995, p. 26).

The heart of the issue is the conceptual link between gang life and criminal behavior. Bjerregaard (2002) states: "Whereas there is little question that the term *gang* carries negative connotations, many of the previously utilized definitions could have also been used to describe nondelinquent organizations and groups . . . it is desirable to develop definitions that do not necessitate the inclusion of criminal activity" (p. 32). Given the premise that criminal activity may constitute a relatively small percentage of a gang's overall activities, it is appropriate to question the legitimacy of defining gangs in terms of their illegal actions. Furthermore, when crime and youth gangs are linked, delinquency seems more the product than the goal of gang members. Irrespective of this conceptual dispute, many people perceive gang members as an antisocial element.

Klein (1995) finds it useful to think of gangs-in-the-making as reaching "tipping points"—junctures in time where citizens begin to think of teenage groups as developing into gangs. Two factors spawn this transition. First, the group adopts a criminal orientation. To Klein, criminal orientation does not constitute "a pattern of serious criminal activity, as many in the enforcement world might require" (Klein, 1995, p. 30). Second, the group takes on an identity by developing special vocabularies, clothing, signs, and colors. At this point, social workers, schoolteachers, and community officials begin to discuss the existence of a troublesome gang. Next, the group acquires gang status in the community, is labeled as such, and eventually begins to interact with others similarly described.

Every youth group that engages in antisocial activities does not become a gang. Some are reluctant to adopt an over-all criminal identity. In other cases, communities may be less inclined to label the group's action as "gang character" and may choose to address deviant behavior on an individual basis. In some instances, a lack of community recognition and response to an emerging gang's identity can downplay their prominence and undercut the growth of group cohesiveness.

Klein openly criticizes traditional gang intervention approaches by suggesting that: "Most social science literature indicates that increasing group cohesiveness also increases group morale and productivity. One of the products of gangs is crime." Upon analysis, most gang intervention programs indicate that they actually contribute to an increase in gang cohesiveness. "The obvious implication is that most gang intervention programs, without meaning to, have the net effect of increasing gang crime. . . . This is a warning to social workers and cops alike and to those public officials who allow, support, and encourage their anti-gang policies and programs. Anti-gang activities may inadvertently promote gang crime and violence" (1995, pp. 7–8).

What characterizes adolescents who join gangs? Who are these teenagers and how do they differ from other adolescents? Are gang members all social outcasts and delinquents?

The answer to these questions may be disturbing. "Gang members are not so much different from other young people as they are caricatures of young people. Their needs and their pleasures are exaggerations of those familiar to us from a more general youth population" (Klein, 1995, p. 76). Gang members comprise a more diverse group of adolescents than often portrayed in the media. Gangs do not always include members labeled as hoods, punks, and defiant personalities, but may be comprised of teenagers who are insecure, aggressive, lonely, or sad. Gangs have leaders, followers, members on the periphery, and members needing to belong somewhere. Thus, a profile of gang members must encompass a broader spectrum of individuals than the stereotypic "hoodlum" image.

As to an association between drugs and gangs, Klein states, "half the connection is pure hype; the other half exists and is worthy of attention along with other equally important gang issues, such as proliferation, crime patterns, ethnic variation, and approaches to control" (1995, p. 40). Media attention to crack-selling gangs has influenced the public to view gangs almost exclusively in terms of a drug-violence subculture.

The development of youth gangs is symptomatic of large-scale underlying social and economic problems in urban areas (Huff, 1989). So, the coexistence of gangs and a viable drug marketplace should not be a surprise.

This does not mean that membership in gangs comes without negative consequences. When examining gang involvement among urban African-American adolescents, Li et al. (2002) found that "current or past membership in a gang demonstrated higher levels of risk behavior involvement, lower levels of resilience, higher exposure to violence, and higher distress symptomatology" (p. 187). Clearly, gang involvement can threaten psychological well-being and place members at risk.

| CASE EXAMPLE | SANTA LOUISA COMMUNITY CENTER |

Samuel Harris is a 55-year-old African American employed as a social worker at the Santa Louisa Community Center, located in a large city in the northeastern United States. This community center coordinates numerous programs for residents in this impoverished section of town. A soup kitchen, free store, meals-on-wheels program, health clinic, day care facility, Head Start program, and the teen outreach program are included in the center's regular programming. The Santa Louisa Community Center is conveniently located between a large housing project and the public middle and high schools.

For the past fifteen years, Samuel, or "S" as he is known on the street, has worked primarily as a community organizer in the neighborhood. His main responsibility is working with teenagers to encourage them to stay in school, seek job training, find employment, and stay out of trouble.

A brief look at the neighborhood indicates a predominance of African-American, Hispanic-Latino American, and Italian-American residents. Over half of the homes are female-headed, with most families receiving Temporary Assistance to Needy Families (TANF), food stamps, or public housing. Street life is a dominant feature in the neighborhood, with the existence of several gangs organized around race and ethnicity. Although crime has long been a problem in the community, recent years have seen a marked increase in all forms of lawlessness.

Six months ago the neighborhood experienced a tragedy when Harold "Pop" Jones, the 80-year-old owner of a convenience store (and Samuel's close friend), was robbed and shot by a member of a newly formed gang. Pop was loved and respected by neighborhood residents, young and old, irrespective of race or ethnicity. Pop's Stop was more than a convenient market; it was a local landmark. Pop was known for his cantankerous ways, but his store was a popular place to buy snacks, catch up on local gossip, and see a familiar face. Pop sat on his stool at the front by the cash register so as not to miss any activity in his store or on the street.

Since Pop's death, Samuel has observed two phenomena. First, disapproval of gang membership has increased among parents and adolescents. Pop's death caused people to observe the neighborhood youth and question them about gang-like activities. Even existing gangs have tried to distance themselves from the murder of this elderly man as well as from other forms of violent crime.

Second, Samuel's colleagues at the local juvenile justice center have observed an increase of nongang-related petty crimes among teenagers. Teenagers began to hang out in or near several local pool halls, resulting in numerous arrests for disorderly conduct and petty theft. An initial assessment suggests that the timing might be ideal for engaging community teenagers in alternative activities. Court officials at Juvenile Hall and representatives from several human service agencies serving adolescents expressed an interest in working with Samuel and cooperating in programs to divert teenagers from both the criminal justice system and gang life.

The shocking death of Harold "Pop" Jones attracted the attention of neighborhood residents, court officials, the city council, business leaders, and local media to the problems of teenagers in the area. At his funeral, family members asked that a foundation be established in Pop's name to benefit local youth. While Pop's Stop will not reopen, Samuel and others are moving quickly to assess the use of Pop Jones Foundation funds for developing community projects for adolescents.

TIME TO THINK!

Samuel has spent most of the last fifteen years trying to improve the quality of life for residents served by the Santa Louisa Community Center. Samuel has a unique opportunity to address the needs of neighborhood adolescents more effectively. Brainstorming with community leaders and colleagues provided Samuel with insight concerning macro-level issues to consider. For example, are macro-level interventions prejudged or discarded because the client population involves inner-city teenagers who have been in trouble with the law? Would the intervention modalities be different if the gangs were from middle-class, white neighborhoods? If so, in what ways? Finally, must a tragedy occur in order to prompt community reaction and analysis focusing on macro-level issues? What part could media take in sensitizing the community to the urgency of this situation? How could Samuel help to bring about such consciousness-raising?

Macro Systems and Troubled Teenagers

As we have said, a major emphasis in this book involves seeing the big picture in social work practice. Although community organizers may be better trained to assess the influence of various macro-level systems, like all social workers, they are not immune to influences of their own practice environment.

Samuel sees a special opportunity to develop programming to entice teenagers away from gang membership and street life. As we scan macro-level systems, a goal is to identify organizational, community, societal, and global factors that Samuel might fail to consider due to his closeness to the neighborhood and the emotional nature of the circumstances.

Organizational Level In his practice at Santa Louisa, Samuel has developed relationships with various community organizations, including the local schools, Juvenile Hall, the police department, juvenile gangs, city government, and local businesses. He is a member of several interagency cluster groups examining adolescent problems and has served on numerous community task forces, including a now defunct antigang coalition formed five years ago.

Samuel's general observation is that organizations with the goal of confronting adolescents and teenage gangs often result only in uniting community teenagers against them. Disappointingly, when a tragedy like the shooting of Pop occurs, some agencies engage in finger-pointing to absolve themselves from responsibility. This was a very conscious strategy employed by a couple of agency officials who hoped

continued

"to move high-risk difficult adolescents out of an agency, and therefore away from liability" (Li et al., 2002, p. 12).

Meanwhile, entrepreneurs establish pool halls and teen nightclubs to profit from adolescents struggling with self-identity crises and an abundance of free time. As adolescents gravitate toward an activity (e.g., shooting pool, doing drugs, or hanging out at the club), they learn to identify with socially nonconforming groups (e.g., hoods, druggies, or clubbers). When their particular group becomes labeled as undesirable or deviant, negative self-esteem is further enhanced.

Two of the more productive community undertakings of Santa Louisa for adolescents are a teenage boxing club and a traveling basketball team called the "Rims." In both cases, former professional athletes from the area have volunteered time and money to provide healthy alternatives to teenagers in the community. Sponsored by several agencies, both of these programs were administered through the Santa Louisa Community Center.

By keeping abreast of current and relevant research, Samuel has become interested in innovative programs that reach out to teenagers in new and energizing ways. Delgado's (2000) work on community capacity development in urban areas is of particular interest. Social programs and services emphasizing the creative and artistic talents and abilities of adolescents to create, enrich, or enhance neighborhood murals, gardens, playgrounds, and sculptures appear to be a valid consideration. In Samuel's neighborhood, he senses encouragement, support, and a willingness from many organizations to examine fresh ways to reach out to teenagers. Innovative projects seeking Pop Jones Foundation monies, however, would need to both embrace the spirit of the foundation and form a consensus among participating organizations as to popular and appropriate activities for gaining teenage participation.

Community Level The Santa Louisa Community Center is located in an area that can best be described as economically depressed. New jobs for adults and teenagers are virtually nonexistent in this section of town. For many residents, the local metro bus system is the only viable link to employment outside the community. Unfortunately, a centralized routing system makes bus transportation around the city both inefficient and time-consuming.

The dire socioeconomic climate of the community creates a feeling of pessimism for many adolescents. Samuel has focused on finding jobs for teenagers in other parts of the city, but employment opportunities are scarce. Potential employers often cite limited transportation as the reason for their reluctance to hire. Samuel believes another reason may be even more important: teenagers from his neighborhood have been labeled negatively by fast-food and service enterprises. Comments from prospective employers have been discouraging: "Your kids are too streetwise!" or "Why would I hire those teenagers when I can hire college-prep students?"

Samuel is deeply concerned about the negative image of the community. Recent media coverage has focused on gang life, crime, and welfare fraud. The several neighborhood churches that offer adolescent support programs have received little recognition and insufficient funding. Moreover, although group discussions, rap sessions, seminars, and gospel music groups organized by the churches appeal to only a segment of the adolescent population, these programs highlight positive attributes of community life and provide opportunities for adolescents to create constructive peer associations while avoiding negative labels.

Samuel is mindful that the community image can influence adolescent self-concept and self-esteem. In assessing program development, one priority is to promote a positive community outlook. Toward achieving this goal, Samuel favors using Pop Jones Foundation funds to encourage activities that appeal to adolescents and promote the strengths of the neighborhood to the surrounding region.

Societal Level Samuel is engaged in social work practice with adolescents who are trying to survive even as they seek growth and self-actualization despite bleak, dismal living conditions. When Samuel explains that he is a social worker involved in community organizing with teenagers in this neighborhood, people frequently ask what it is like working with "thugs and inner-city hoods." Samuel realizes that many are unable to look beyond social labels to see the pain and needs of others.

In the United States, impoverished "ghetto" sections of cities are seen as forms of urban cancer. Using this analogy, inhabitants of less desirable neighborhoods—the minority urban underclass—are seen as malignant cells to be removed by radical surgery. The strategy becomes to identify, isolate, and eliminate. Federal, state, and local officials express negative attitudes in both their attention and appropriations.

In the United States, highway systems are often constructed to avoid contact with this "cancer" or its cells. Suburban drivers speed by the "infected" areas of the city, refraining from even casual interaction with the "disease," hoping that it will not afflict them. If a cell is perceived as irregular or deviant, it may be labeled and isolated or eliminated in the fear that "healthy cells" might be affected.

"The larger society certainly does label some minority persons, a priori, as 'probably deviant' . . . to be young, male, and black or Chicano in white America is to be a suspect person" (Moore, 1985, p. 2). Moore uses **ascribed deviance** to describe the labeling of a particular segment of the population based only on generalized minority stereotypes.

Samuel knows that ascribed deviance exists. Call it "racism," "discrimination," "stereotyping," or "prejudice," teenagers from impoverished areas are viewed and treated differently and as inferior. Samuel must deal with these societal attitudes each day as he sees teenagers doubt their worth and turn toward negative alternatives.

International Level As part of a large metropolitan city in the northeastern United States, the Santa Louisa Community Center has experienced a steady flow of first-generation Hispanic-Latino American immigrants into the community. As a result, Samuel attempts to familiarize himself with the ways of each ethnic group in order to keep abreast of various cultural influences on teenagers.

continued

CASE EXAMPLE | *continued*

Samuel has found interesting distinctions with regard to clothing, music, and value orientations that distinguish African-American, Hispanic-Latino American, and Italian-American adolescents. In some sections of the community, one needs only to look at the graffiti and listen to the beat of the music to ascertain the ethnic origin of the residents.

Samuel has recently discovered that the murder of his friend Pop Jones was by the hand of a member wearing the colors of a newly formed gang, housed in a bordering community. Hoping to "take new turf," this white youth gang has been associated with several brutal acts in the city.

Samuel is familiar with the violent reputation of youth gangs and has learned that many of them link their identity to street gangs and criminal syndicates from years past (Klein, 1995, p. 217). He has made a special effort to learn about the historical and cultural foundations of the ethnic and racial gangs in the neighborhood. Samuel has an added advantage in that he is fluent in several languages used in the community.

Recently, Samuel has received information suggesting that some of the gangs in his neighborhood have nurtured and developed relationships with organized crime in other countries. Based upon country of origin, some gangs are importing ideas and contraband from their homelands. In addition, money and other spoils of gang activity in the United States are being exported to counterparts in other countries. Local criminal justice officials have confirmed these suspicions.

In an effort to better understand gang behavior in his community, Samuel is contemplating the usefulness of contacting social workers in other countries that might be able to provide him with insight. First, he will discuss these ideas with his supervisor and then possibly ask his professional team for input. The police liaison for Samuel's community center might also be a helpful resource.

Of all the reasons cited for participating in gang life, one of the most compelling is the need for belonging, companionship, self-worth, or excitement (Clark, 1992). Were they not alienated at home, school, or from other peers, it is likely that these youth would be less inclined to drift toward gang involvement. For gang members, the gang life becomes family, a potent form of security.

Gangs do perform positive functions for some adolescents. Klein identifies four parts to the "gang-as-positive-mechanism philosophy." This philosophy suggests that gangs might: "facilitate their members' self-actualization," "provide local empowerment," "be co-opted for social goals," and "serve to stabilize disorganized communities" (1995, pp. 82–85). However, to expect gangs to become positive forces in a community is probably both naive and unrealistic. Gang life is complex and multifaceted and continues to be viewed by most Americans as a very negative and undesirable phenomenon.

With respect to community-based initiatives, Okamoto (2001) describes the advantages of interagency collaboration when intervening with youth gangs. When social service agencies and professionals work together in collaborative ways, they are better able to reduce service gaps, offer a wider range of services, address legal mandates, and attain organizational and treatment goals (Okamoto, 2001, p. 6). Frequent and regular communication, cooperation, and the timely sharing of information among youth serving agencies aimed at developing and improving integrated service and intervention delivery systems for teenagers appears to be imperative (Quinn & Cumblad, 1994).

REFLECTION ON DIVERSITY: MULTIRACIAL IDENTIFICATION

Teenagers in the United States live in a multiracial and ethnic society. Traditionally, Americans have thought of race in terms of a large white majority, a small black minority, and a much smaller multiracial group. Lee and Bean (2004) suggest: "Increased racial and ethnic diversity brought about by the new immigration, rising intermarriage, and patterns of multiracial identification may be moving the nation far beyond the traditional and relatively persistent black/white color line" (p. 221).

Much of this change can be attributed to growing Hispanic-Latino and Asian populations in the United States. The National Research Council suggests that by the year 2050, the Hispanic-Latino and Asian populations will triple and comprise nearly 25 percent and 8 percent of the U. S. population, respectively (Smith & Edmonston, 1997). Additionally, "multiracial identification is not uncommon among the members of new immigrant groups such as Asians and Latinos (particularly for those under the age of 18)" (Lee & Bean, 2004, p. 232). The growing number of adolescents with a multiracial identification are found primarily in ten states—California, New York, Texas, Florida, Hawaii, Illinois, New Jersey, Washington, Michigan, and Ohio (Bean & Stevens, 2003).

The implications for America's changing color lines are many, especially when considering adolescence and the variety of topics examined in this chapter: labeling, self-concept, drug use, and gangs. The challenge for teenagers to manage and negotiate exceedingly complex forms of cultural diversity in everyday life is an especially interesting consideration. Based upon the work of Fine, Weis, Powell, and Wong (1997), Hamm and Coleman (2001) assert: "By virtue of belonging to the culturally defining group, White adolescents are often not pressed to develop a repertoire of ways to relate to cross-ethnic peers [of any kind]: This responsibility falls to members of minority groups" (p. 284). Given an opportunity to avoid embracing racial, cultural, and multiracial diversity, it might be reasonable to assume that many teenagers as well as adults will take a somewhat passive, wait-and-see approach. For many of us, it is easiest to opt to do little or nothing until confronted with a challenging situation or circumstance, rather than to anticipate the problem and promote positive interventions.

As others sense the world changing around them, more curious and forward-looking adolescents seek to expand their knowledge and skills. In public and private school systems across our nation, a growing number of adolescents are seeking service opportunities and volunteer experiences to become knowledgeable about people from an expanding set of cultures, races, and social-economic backgrounds. The popularity of educational and service trips to impoverished areas in the United States as well as in other countries is further testimony to the eagerness of many teenagers to embrace multiple forms of diversity.

It is exciting to recognize how readily teenagers will adapt to new cultures abroad as well as to cultural diversity in the United States. Hamm and Coleman (2001) speculate that regular cross-ethnic interaction will contribute to social-cognitive abilities "permitting more integrative and flexible thinking about ethnic groups and ethnic relations" (p. 297). Research by Onyekwuluje (2000) "focuses on the special obligations of adult role models to assist adolescents in expanding their diversity skills" (p. 76). Optimally, cross-ethnic interaction by adolescents accompanied by thoughtful dialog with parental figures can prove to be mutually beneficial for both teens and adults.

APPLYING A SOCIAL WORK FRAMEWORK: LABELING THEORY

In this chapter, labeling theory was introduced as an appropriate theoretical orientation for assessing developmental issues during adolescence. Our intent is to encourage readers to focus on social reactions to teenagers rather than to concentrate on adolescent behaviors and actions. Social workers must consider the consequences when teenagers are labeled in such terms as deviants, punks, druggies, thugs, and gangsters.

This chapter demonstrates a layering effect with regard to social labels. Teenagers can be stigmatized, at one or more levels, as individuals, group members, members of subcultures or minority groups, residents of a community, or any combination of these. The significance of labeling at each tier lies in its potential for generating negative or antisocial lifestyles (secondary deviance) for teenagers because labeling evokes images of aberrant behavior (Moore, 1985, p. 1).

In this chapter's case example, Samuel assesses mechanisms for breaking down existing social labels and for creating positive teenage alternatives. Teenagers need to connect with affirming, healthful activities and groups. Samuel has seen too many adolescents from his neighborhood enter the criminal justice system. Those in power too often quickly judge, incarcerate, and forget the life that needs rebuilding. Pop Jones's death created an opportunity to rally residents and community leaders into action to change this cycle.

As labeling theory dictates, Samuel Harris endeavors at every turn to identify and accentuate the strengths of neighborhood adolescents. Choosing to minimize legal confrontations, Samuel and other social workers in the neighborhood hope to use Pop Jones Foundation funds to offer original and responsive programs.

Suggested Activities

1. Visit the city or county juvenile court. What are your impressions of the building, people, and atmosphere? Is it possible to differentiate between first-time and repeat offenders? How do these individuals differ? Are there people who seem very familiar with the court whereas others appear to be newcomers? How are juveniles labeled? Identify special terms or slang used to distinguish certain teenagers.
2. Interview a social worker at a community center serving adolescents. Inquire about the clientele, community needs, and programs currently offered. Ask the social worker to identify primary public misconceptions about teenagers in the area. Discuss the strengths of adolescents in the community and programs designed to draw attention to their talents and abilities.
3. Talk to an adolescent relative about different student groupings at her or his school; mention hip-hop. Let the adolescent describe and articulate the characteristics of as many groups as possible. Ask also about the presence of any gangs at school. Let the adolescent be the expert and you the listener.

References

Abrams, L. (2003). Sociocultural variations in adolescent girls' expressions of distress: What we know and need to know. *Child and Adolescent Social Work Journal, 20*, 135–150.

Adams, M., Robertson, C., Gray-Ray, P., & Ray, M. (2003). Labeling and delinquency. *Adolescence, 38*, 171–186.

Al-Talib, N., & Griffin, C. (1994). Labeling effect on adolescents' self-concept. *International Journal of Offender Therapy and Comparative Criminology, 38*, 47–57.

Aronson, E. (1972). *The social animal.* San Francisco: W. H. Freeman.

Bacchini, D., & Magliulo, F. (2003). Self-image and perceived self-efficacy during adolescence. *Journal of Youth and Adolescence, 32*, 337–350.

Balesent, K. (2005). *Africa News Service,* June 2, NA.

Bean, F., & Stevens, G. (2003). *America's newcomers and the dynamics of diversity.* New York: Sage.

Becker, H. (1963). *Outsiders: Studies in the sociology of deviance.* New York: Free Press.

Becker, H. (1964). *The other side: Perspectives on deviance.* New York: Free Press.

Binder, A., & Geis, G. (1984). Ad populum argumentation in criminology: Juvenile diversion as rhetoric. *Crime and Delinquency, 30*, 624–647.

Bjerregaard, B. (2002). Self-definitions of gang membership and involvement in delinquent activities. *Youth and Society, 34*, 31–54.

Butters, J. (2002). Family stressors and adolescent cannabis use: A pathway to problem use. *Journal of Adolescence, 25*, 645–654.

Carnegie Council on Adolescent Development. (1996). *Great transitions: Preparing adolescents for a new century.* New York: Carnegie Corporation of New York.

Chappell, K. (2005). Celebrated, controversial, and influential: 30 years of hip-hop music. *Ebony, 60*, 52–56.

Clark, C. (1992). Deviant adolescent subcultures: Assessment strategies and clinical interventions. *Adolescence, 27*, 283–293.

Delgado, M. (2000). *Community social work practice in an urban context: The potential of a capacity-enhancement perspective.* New York: Oxford University Press.

Devaney, P. (2004). Hip-hop's "bling" culture is wooing corporate America: Despite the violent associations with "gangstar" rappers, hip-hop music and their bling-bling culture are a sure-fire moneyspinner. *Marketing Week, 27,* 38–39.

Fashimpar, G. (1991). From probation to mini-bikes: A comparison of traditional and innovative programs for community treatment of delinquent adolescents. *Social Work with Groups, 14,* 105–118.

Fine, M., Weis, L., Powell, M., & Wong, F. (1997). *Off-white: Readings on race, power, and society.* New York: Routledge.

Hamm, J., & Coleman, H. (2001). African-American and white adolescents' strategies for managing cultural diversity in predominantly white high schools. *Journal of Youth and Adolescence, 30,* 281–303.

Horwitz, A., & Wasserman, M. (1979). The effect of social control on delinquent behavior: A longitudinal test. *Sociological Focus, 12,* 53–70.

Huff, R. (1989). Youth gangs and public policy. *Crime and Delinquency, 35,* 524–537.

Invik, J., Mills, S., & McCreary, T. (2005). The third sex: Supporting the struggles of transgendered people. *Briarpatch, 34,* 14–16.

Javors, I. (2004). Hip-hop culture: Images of gender and gender roles. *Annals of the American Psychotherapy Association, 7,* 42.

Kaplan, H., & Fukurai, J. (1992). Negative social sanctions, self-rejection, and drug use. *Youth and Society, 23,* 275–298.

Kazdin, A. (1995). *Conduct disorders in childhood and adolescence.* Thousand Oaks, CA: Sage.

Klein, M. (1995). *The American street gang.* New York: Oxford University Press.

Lee, J., & Bean, F. (2004). America's changing color lines: Immigration, race/ethnicity, and multiracial identification. *Annual Review of Sociology, 30,* 221–242.

Lemert, E. (1951). *Social pathology.* New York: McGraw-Hill.

Li, X., Stanton, B., Pack, R., Harris, C., Cottrell, L., & Burns, J. (2002). Risk and protective factors associated with gang involvement among urban African-American adolescents. *Youth and Society, 34,* 172–194.

Lotz, R., & Lee, L. (1999). Sociability, school experience, and delinquency. *Youth and Society, 31,* 199–223.

MacNeil, G., Stewart, J., & Kaufman, A. (2000). Social support as a potential moderator of adolescent delinquent behaviors. *Child and Adolescent Social Work Journal, 17,* 361–379.

Matsueda, R. (1993). Reflected appraisals, parental labeling, and delinquency: Specifying a symbolic interactionist theory. *American Journal of Sociology, 97,* 1577–1611.

Moore, J. (1985). Isolation and stigmatization in the development of an underclass: The case of Chicano gangs in east Los Angeles. *Social Problems, 33,* 1–12.

Morash, M. (1982). Juvenile reaction to labels: An experiment and an exploratory study. *Sociology and Social Research, 67,* 76–88.

Morash, M. (1983). Groups, gangs, and delinquency. *British Journal of Criminology, 4,* 316.

New York Times. (1995). Rock star's forum grows too raucous for on-line service, April 12, A19.

Okamoto, S. (2001). Interagency collaboration with high-risk gang youth. *Child and Adolescent Social Work Journal, 18,* 5–19.

Onyekwuluje, A. (2000). Adult role models: Needed voices for adolescents, multiculturalism, diversity, and race relations. *Urban Review, 32*, 67–85.

Palamara, F., Cullen, F., & Gersten, J. (1986). The effect of police and mental health intervention on juvenile deviance: Specifying contingencies in the impact of formal reaction. *Journal of Health and Social Behavior, 27*, 90–105.

Perez McCluskey, C., & Tovar, S. (2003). Family processes and delinquency: The consistency of relationships by ethnicity and gender. *Journal of Ethnicity in Criminal Justice, 1*, 37–61.

Pipher, M. (1994). *Reviving Ophelia: Saving the selves of adolescent girls.* New York: Ballantine.

PR Newswire. (2003). Hip-hop teen superstar Bow Wow supports computers for youth and its computer distribution to inner-city children; HBO to sponsor free concert in Bryant Park. July 21.

Quinn, K., & Cumblad, C. (1994). Service providers' perceptions of interagency collaboration in their communities. *Journal of Emotional and Behavioral Disorders, 2*, 109–116.

Rosenbaum, J. & Prinsky, L. (1991). The presumption of influence: Recent responses to popular music subcultures. *Crime and Delinquency, 37*, 528–535.

Ruffolo, M., Sarri, R., & Goodkind, S. (2004). Study of delinquent, diverted, and high-risk adolescent girls: Implication for mental health intervention. *Social Work Research, 28*, 237–245.

Sherman, L., & Berk, R. (1984). The specific deterrent effects of arrest for domestic assault. *American Sociological Review, 49*, 261–272.

Shilts, L. (1991). The relationship of early adolescent substance use to extracurricular activities, peer influence, and personal attitudes. *Adolescence, 26*, 613–616.

Smith, E., Wolf, A., Cantillon, D., Thomas, O., & Davidson, W. (2004). The adolescent diversion project: 25 years of research on an ecological model of intervention. *Journal of Prevention and Intervention in the Community, 27*, 29–47.

Smith, J., & Edmonston, B. (1997). *The new Americans.* Washington, DC: National Academic Press.

Stager, S., Chassin, L., & Young, R. (1983). Determinants of self-esteem among labeled adolescents. *Social Psychology Quarterly, 46*, 3–10.

Steitz, J., & Owen, T. (1992). School activities and work: Effects on adolescent self-esteem. *Adolescence, 27*, 37–50.

Stewart, C. (2002). Family factors of low-income African-American youth associated with substance use: An exploratory analysis, *Journal of Ethnicity in Substance Abuse, 1*, 97–111.

Svensson, R. (2003). Gender differences in adolescent drug use: The impact of parental monitoring and peer deviance. *Youth and Society, 34*, 300–329.

Thomas, C., & Bishop, D. (1984). The effect of formal and informal sanctions on delinquency: A longitudinal comparison of labeling and deterrence theories. *Journal of Criminal Law and Criminology, 75*, 1222–1245.

Thrasher, F. (1967). *The gang: A study of 1,313 gangs in Chicago.* Chicago: University of Chicago Press.

Traub, S., & Little, C. (1975). Labeling and deviance. In S. Traub and C. Little (Eds.), *Theories of deviance.* Itasca, IL: Peacock.

Vazsonyi, A., & Pickering, L. (2003). The importance of family and school domains in adolescent deviance: African-American and Caucasian youth. *Journal of Youth and Adolescence, 32*, 115–128.

6 CHAPTER | YOUNG ADULTHOOD

"Cathy," a syndicated cartoon found in the comic section of many newspapers, depicts a young, single adult in a fictional world. She reflects a segment of working women who struggle with identity and coping issues. This daily comic strip is dedicated to the humorous trials and tribulations of Cathy's work, her dating, her ever-ticking biological clock, and her ambivalent relationship with her parents.

Cathy, like many young adults, is continually anxious about her body image. She spends hours deliberating about life's difficult choices: how to achieve the "right" appearance, create the most attractive body image, and choose clothes to enhance that image. She struggles with the problem of relationships with coworkers, men, and her parents. An emerging adult, Cathy is rarely satisfied with herself and seeks reassurance from others at nearly every turn. In her quest for independence, she vacillates between seeking her parents' approval and wanting to define her own person. Indeed, Cathy is in a perpetual, modern-day frenzy.

Cathy appeals to a wide audience in the United States as young women identify with her relentless introspection and difficulty with everyday decision making. Yet, does Cathy portray reality? Does she reflect a perception of common issues facing young adults in our society? Does Cathy typify the conflicts of young adults in our era?

In the exaggerated manner of television and movies, the comic strip often portrays life as a carefree journey without economic or social limitations. Like many middle- and upper-class individuals, Cathy has the resources to make choices concerning work, clothes, personal relationships, and residence. Many of Cathy's readers probably view these choices as the normal way of life for most young adult Americans. But this is a comic strip, not reality. Many less fortunate Americans do not have money for a daily newspaper and would deny that Cathy's turmoil in any way reflects the dilemmas of the working class or the poor.

Cathy is a white, privileged young adult, oblivious to the plight of African Americans, Hispanic-Latino Americans, and other people of color in America. She does not frequent neighborhoods characterized by high crime and drug trafficking. The economic and social decline experienced by northern industrial cities has little impact on Cathy's perception of life or sense of social well being.

Cathy has not yet confronted important issues such as job discrimination, tax reform, home ownership, civil unions, or the AIDS epidemic. Yet, to equate a comic strip with reality is certainly to make an improper comparison. Cathy is a fictional creation intended to entertain and amuse the reader, and to provide escape from reality. Nevertheless, these daily strips provide commentary on significant social issues.

THEORY: VALUE CONFLICT

In this chapter, we have chosen a value-conflict orientation for viewing young adulthood. Although other theories could be of equal importance or merit with regard to this developmental period, this perspective will stimulate thinking and enliven discussion.

Value-conflict theory focuses explicitly on environmental conditions rather than on individual behaviors (Hardert, Gordon, Laner, & Reader, 1984, p. 14). This theory asserts that there are certain groups of people in our society who espouse specific value-centered positions. Groups that organize around a special interest often find themselves directly in competition with other groups attempting to define social realities and policies. DiNitto (1995) contends that it is the exception when social values are agreed upon in a societal context. Instead, it is typical that groups will have conflicting values. She suggests:

1. Defining social problems is difficult. People do not agree on what constitutes a social problem, since what may be a social problem for one group may be a benefit for another.
2. Groups differ in their power and ability to advance a special interest.
3. Policy makers are motivated less by social values and more by the potential to maximize rewards given by special interest organizations. (DiNitto, 1995, pp. 8–9)

Affirmative action initiatives are an example of value conflicts. Civil rights activists argue that without concrete plans for mandating the employment of underrepresented groups of people in the U.S. labor force, advancement for minorities in the workplace will be either nonexistent or staggeringly slow. Business groups, however, hold that affirmative action policies restrict individual choices and undermine a free economic system, creating a burden for employers.

From a value-conflict orientation, various special interest or value-centered groups compete, politically and socially, for their own points of view and rights. Each group hopes to define reality from its vested-interest position. The goal for each group, if it is influential enough, is to define the other group and its stance as undesirable, unacceptable, or deviant. Ultimately, "outcomes of value conflicts are often influenced by power; the group with the most power may use its position to influence the outcome of value conflicts" (Mooney, Knox, & Schacht, 2002, p. 13).

For each of us, membership in or affiliation with value-oriented groups is influential in shaping our perception of reality. Each social grouping (e.g., political, religious, or work-based) offers a set of values and principles for adoption and adherence. Eventually, after a period of socialization and indoctrination, people internalize these orientations and outlooks. People then act and come to perceive their expectations of their social world and society in terms of group values and beliefs (Gil, 2002, p. 48).

As a result of the proliferation of special interest groups, laws regulating lobbying groups have been enacted in the United States. Such legislation requires special interests to identify themselves when acting as political lobbying entities, and it defines what constitutes acceptable lobbying activity. While there is considerable debate concerning the willingness of lobbyists and politicians to adhere to these rules and the net impact of this kind of regulation, the need to monitor and provide oversight with regard to the behavior of special interest groups and government officials is evident (Lowery & Gray, 1994).

DEVELOPMENTAL ISSUES

Theodore Lidz's (1976) classic work *The Person* depicts young adulthood as a life-cycle phase, usually between the ages of 18 and 35, filled with important choices. These choices include marriage, occupation, and parenting. Lidz (1976, p. 81) clearly recognized the influence of family and peers with respect to life expectations and tasks, but are parenting, marriage, and occupation to be considered only as individual choices? Or do environmental factors play a major role in choice?

Each day people make choices that affect their lives in significant ways. Individuals, to varying degrees, are able to consider life circumstances, to actively set goals, and to plot the pathways they wish to pursue. However, to more fully enter the world of the client, the social worker needs an in-depth appreciation of social influences, restraints, and parameters that facilitate or curtail personal choices.

Social class distinctions affect employment, marital status, and parenting. Is the Cinderella story reality? Is it typical for poor Americans to be courted by the rich elite in business or marriage? Do you attend parties and other functions with those from privileged segments of our society? Have you entered a career in which you will rub elbows with the movers and shakers of our society? Or, will you now identify with working-class Americans, the poor and homeless, the hungry, the mentally and physically challenged, and the impoverished of our world? That is the privilege and responsibility of the social worker.

Clearly, we live in a segregated society where social inequality and injustice continue to be implicit—if not explicit—elements in the daily lives of people in the United States. This is especially evident in the ability to secure decent housing because "the goal of home ownership is an elusive one for many American families" (Whiting, 2004, p. 851). It would be naive to believe that young adults choose a community in which to live, select a career, commit to a spouse, or decide upon the number of children they will bear solely on the basis of cognitive functioning and desire (Rosenbaum, 1994).

As a social worker, you will meet clients who have several children, but who do not understand how children are conceived. Other clients may be knowledgeable about human reproduction but lack specific information concerning birth control. To assume that all young adults in the United States make cognitive, informed choices about parenting is erroneous. Instead, many children in our society are conceived out of ignorance, misinformation, or thoughtless emotion.

A major challenge for novice social workers is setting aside one's personal experiences and avoiding case generalizations about clients of a similar age. Each young adult has been uniquely influenced by sets of person-specific social influences and systems and by individual circumstances. Unfortunately, research suggests that some social workers overemphasize personal choice as an explanation for human behavior (McDonell, 1993). Therefore, the social worker must assess the impact of particular groups, organizations, the neighborhood, the community, and societal norms while remaining alert to a tendency to "blame the victim" and to demand a higher degree of personal responsibility than the client is capable of assuming.

As an example, not every student has been prepared to enter college. And not all young adults can afford the high costs of higher education. The school that one attends during primary and secondary education has an enormous impact on the individual's educational aspirations, future academic opportunities, and view of life (Palmer & Little, 1993, p. 316). Children do not choose to be born into a particular family, neighborhood, or social status. As a result of socioeconomic circumstances, parents are often unable to choose the school they want their children to attend or to consider higher education for their offspring (Stolzenberg, 1994). Many factors are beyond individual control during young adulthood.

INTERRELATIONSHIPS OF DEVELOPMENTAL ISSUES

The remainder of this chapter focuses mainly on dilemmas young adults routinely face with regard to marriage, parenting, and occupation or career attainment. Although each developmental issue is examined separately, these topics are related. As before, our emphasis is on the macro-level social systems and their pervasive influence on life stages.

The manner in which society focuses on the virtue of marriage as a prerequisite to parenting provides a helpful illustration. Expectations concerning the timing, occurrence, and sequence of marriage and childbearing are an important component of American culture (Trent, 1994). For example, premarital childbearing is often viewed as an inappropriate transition during young adulthood and one that contributes to the persistence of poverty in America. The more traditional and acceptable sequence of events is to marry and then to coordinate childrearing with educational and occupational aspirations.

Marriage, parenting, and employment are interconnected and present complex developmental issues during young adulthood. "Due to the demand for both men and women to manage the multiple roles of parenthood, marriage, and career, it is important to consider the balance preferences of young adults, as well as the timing of role entry that young adults anticipate" (Kerpelman & Schvaneveldt, 1999, p. 191). As you read this chapter, you are challenged to construct examples and scenarios that emphasize the interdependent nature and balance of these roles as well as to consider differences on the basis of gender and race.

MARRIAGE

Typically, books examining young adulthood and marriage focus on issues of self-identity, parental influences, attraction, dating, and marital happiness. While these are certainly important topics, let's examine some additional macro-level considerations for social workers with respect to marriage during young adulthood.

SEXUAL ORIENTATION   The issues of same sex partners, civil unions, and marriage for gays and lesbians have captured the attention of many Americans in recent years. During the 2004 presidential campaign, the right of each state to determine the legitimacy of marriage for gays and lesbians was a major topic of debate and discussion. People representing fundamentalist religious groups and politically conservative organizations argue that the institution of marriage should be reserved for the union between a man and woman. Understandably, gays and lesbians continue to lobby for the legal right to marry.

Marriage constitutes more than a formal and publicly recognized commitment between two people. It entails legal rights (e.g., insurance), responsibilities (e.g., mutual support), and obligations (e.g., fidelity). Steeped in religious and political values and tradition, various groups in America have been zealous in their efforts to define marriage.

May any two adults of legal age choose to marry? Yes, but only if they are opposite in gender. Each of the fifty states allows two consenting adults of opposite sex to marry. Massachusetts was the first state in the United States to sanction marriage between consenting adults of the same sex.

The debate regarding homosexual marriages has been an extended one. Since 2004, a number of states have advanced legislation restricting marriage to the union of a man and a woman. Businesses reflect a similar perspective, a fact most observable in company policies regarding health and retirement benefits. Religious groups continue the ethical debate regarding gay and lesbian couples and their full participation in the life of the church as pastors and professional leaders.

Even for some social workers, the idea of a homosexual couple or family presents a dilemma, a conceptual leap. Some social workers may not feel comfortable working with lesbians and gays (Green, 2000). Swann and Anastas (2003) point out: "As knowledge about gay, lesbian, bisexual, and transgender people continues to mature, social work research must address the complexity of key issues, including sexual identity" (p. 109). Each social worker needs to consider the psychosocial impact of discrimination against homosexuals and bisexuals during young adulthood. Love, irrespective of sexual orientation, involves emotion and passion. People in a loving relationship have a desire to express their feelings for each other. Should gays be expected to suppress their emotions in order to conform to society's norms?

The institution of traditional marriage in the United States has been defended by heterosexual, religious, or politically conservative people and special interest groups, who find it difficult to accept the ideas of domestic same-sex partnerships and especially of gay marriage. For homosexuals and lesbians who wish to publicly proclaim their committed relationships, society has until recently continued to hold the closet door tightly closed. The "coming out" movement initiated by gay and lesbian organizations during the last decade demonstrates an organized effort that lobbies for the rights of people to openly and freely express their love for a person of the same sex and share the legal and religious formality of marriage.

The desire for long-term relationships is common to a majority of homosexual couples (Longres, 1995). The expression of love within a legal, socially approved setting is the hope of many gay and lesbian couples, who continue to push social boundaries as they demand recognition and legitimizing of their sexual orientation.

In addition to traditional lifelong marriage, there are other arrangements:

1. Staying single—never marrying
2. Living together—cohabitation
3. Civil unions
4. Marrying, then divorcing
5. Divorcing, marrying someone else

Bullough (2002) states, "singleness is growing, although men and women have different trajectories. While women are catching up with men in engaging in sexual intercourse with partners they do not intend to marry, women are much more likely than men to spend long periods of time in the single status" (p. 22). Bullough (2002) suggests that Americans need to be open to change, broaden perspectives, and "develop programs to help serve the needs of these newly emerging groups" (p. 23).

As an example, the research of Lee (2000) indicates: "Lesbian, gay, bisexual, and transgendered patients are at increased risk of suicide, eating disorders, substance misuse, and breast and anal cancer" (p. 403). She suggests that: "As many as two thirds of physicians never ask patients about their sexual orientation" (p. 403). Health care professionals and those in related fields can improve service delivery systems and enhance the efficacy of intervention strategies by creating open and more embracing practice environments.

People in our society who are involved in nontraditional relationships often compete for equal opportunities and legitimacy in a variety of spheres. Employers, for example, may offer jobs or promotions to individuals because they view them as "family types" having family members to support. Imagine the added difficulties in becoming a leader in community youth groups, running for local political office, adopting children, or securing a loan for a home if one is engaged in a same-sex relationship.

Single or divorced people, as well as gays and lesbians, often sense a public perception of themselves as less desirable or social outcasts. Seeking understanding and support, they frequently meet in churches and temples, in public meeting areas, or wherever space is available to explore mutual needs, and advocate for their common rights and benefits. A necessary skill for social workers is the ability to adopt a nonjudgmental attitude toward diverse lifestyles while maintaining the integrity of one's own values.

DIVERSITY IN MARRIAGE   Those who fall in love with people different from themselves in race, nationality, age, and religion face unique social pressures and constraints in life. While many will argue that people who enter heterogeneous types of marriages should realize the potential for social discord, love knows few bounds. People have intense emotions, fall in love, and often hope their relationship will be immune to the prejudices and beliefs of others.

In social work practice, your clients will reflect a wide range of social associations and arrangements in their intimate bonds. The challenge is to be sensitive and nonjudgmental in response to each type of relationship. One also must become familiar with community and national organizations that are available to address special needs.

WIVES AND DEPENDENCY   We would be remiss, however, in exploring alternatives to the institution of marriage in the United States if we failed to acknowledge the continued plight of many women in heterosexual marriages. Women often enter marriage with the hope of having it all —career, marriage, and motherhood (Hoffnung, 2004). Despite the fact that adult gender roles are changing and women may have come a long way, women and men often enter marriage with different expectations of love and romance, the division of labor in the home, (Sabattini & Leaper, 2004; Sprecher & Toro-Morn, 2002) and of the demands of equality (Phipps, Burton, & Osberg, 2001). Many women in heterosexual relationships find themselves economically and socially less powerful and overly dependent on men. An aggressive woman in our society may be labeled a "bitch," whereas an aggressive man is seen as a "go-getter" or over-achiever. Often, automobile salespeople talk to the husband about the car and offer refreshments to the wife and children. In many marriages, women have not reached full partnership with men.

Through organizations such as the National Organization for Women (NOW), women have come together to confront the many "super women" expectations placed upon females in our society as well as to demand equal pay and recognition in the workforce. Women's organizations have been histori-cally important in raising issues, demanding change, and in counseling women. During the mid-1880s in urban areas of the United States, women organized for the right to vote. Later, women banded together to achieve full legal, social, economic, and educational equality. Their efforts continue in their struggle for liberation from sexual harassment and gender stereotyping. The establishment of professional networks (legal, medical, and economic) has enabled women to define their special needs in gender-specific ways.

When women see their family physicians or therapists because they feel depressed, controlled, and/or discontented in their marriages, they frequently encounter a variety of responses. Traditionally, male doctors have interpreted these complaints as signs of depression. The treatment suggested often involves the use of antidepressant drugs (Cowley, 1994). Although the use of psy-chotropic medications can be highly effective in the treatment of affective dis-orders, physical complaints and distress can be symptoms signaling a need to gain social power in relationships and/or to seek involvement in the broader cause of improving conditions not only for themselves but for all women.

For women, as for any other special interest group, power is necessary to apply the political and social muscle required for social change. Improved domestic conditions for women occur as a result of social movements by people who are organized to give support and bring about change. Although antide-pressant therapies have clinical importance for treatment with certain diag-noses, they are not prescriptions for social change.

A traditionally cited prerequisite for such change is the involvement of an influential group of people, or a large number of less powerful individuals, confronting a specific social problem or cause (Zastrow, 2000). Therefore, it is important for women to support women's causes actively, to gain strength col-lectively, and to identify new directions for creating change.

Regardless of social class, women may experience loss of self-esteem, may feel controlled, and in some cases experience physical abuse in marriage. Dur-ing the 1990s, the publicity surrounding the death of Nicole Brown Simpson and the alleged domestic violence in her relationship with O. J. Simpson brought this issue to national attention. The suffering and pain of one well-known woman served to awaken a nation to an important social issue affecting many women.

A pivotal dilemma for the social worker to explore with each client in-volves personal problem versus social problem. Does your client seek mental health, membership in a social cause, physical protection, or all of the above?

Have you as a social worker assessed both the macro and micro elements of a particular case and considered social change as well as personal change?

PARENTING

Parenting issues for young adults include the reasons people have children, when to have children, how to parent, and choosing not to have children (Papalia & Olds, 1989). Each of these topics focuses on intrapsychic aspects of the phenomenon. Here, we consider the social conditions that surround and influence having children.

PARENTHOOD AND PLANNING   Should parenthood be planned or unplanned? Contraception, artificial insemination, adoption, and surrogate parenting all involve rational approaches. In these instances, people wish to be parents and utilize time-consuming and expensive processes to achieve that goal. Similarly, if a young adult practices abstinence, the decision not to have children is implicit.

Although modern technology has provided us with an array of birth control measures for planning parenthood, birth control is problematic and involves important qualifiers. Birth control pills, diaphragms, and condoms, for example, are readily available. However, effective use of birth control devices assumes not only availability but also knowledge and education concerning the standard procedures for using each method. The person who is able to follow instructions for using a birth control device greatly enhances his or her opportunity for successfully planning parenthood.

Accurate and straight talk concerning birth control, sterilization, and sexually transmitted diseases varies from family to family, school to school, and community to community. Now with the impact of AIDS, individuals may be more willing to speak openly and freely about sex and birth control. However, books and manuals on sex education still have restricted access in those libraries that fear violating community or societal norms. As Federico (1990) suggests, sex education must go well beyond the biological aspects of sex. As social workers, you will often need to explore with clients the relationship between human sexuality and individual aspirations, economic stability, and lifestyle issues, knowing that this dialogue might not occur elsewhere.

Sex education and planned parenting are emotionally laden subjects for many Americans. At one end of the continuum, certain religious and political groups lobby in favor of sex education being taught exclusively in the family rather than in the classroom. These groups may also view abortion as murder and advocate that it be outlawed. They organize protests and picket at family planning and abortion clinics to champion their position.

Conversely, planned-parenthood organizations and pro-choice organizations seek to openly disseminate information concerning procreation, birth control, and abortion for women of childbearing age. Groups like NOW sponsor marches, rallies, and forums to promote women's rights to make their own reproductive choices.

Moreover, parenting is a social-class issue. If individuals possess the necessary knowledge and resources to effectively implement birth control, then parenting is likely to involve a rational, planned choice. But if sexually active individuals lack the information or do not have the resources to secure birth control devices, then parenting becomes a random event.

SOCIAL POLICY AND PARENTING   Over the past several decades, states and the federal government have examined the implementation of policies that would reduce or curtail benefits to parents with dependent children. In 1996, President Clinton signed into legislation the Personal Responsibility and Work Opportunity Reconciliation Act (PRWORA). This historic piece of legislation was created to save the federal government tens of millions of dollars by shifting the responsibility to assist economically disadvantaged parents and their children from the federal level to state and local jurisdictions.

Aid to Families with Dependent Children (AFDC), a long-standing public assistance program for poor families, was replaced by a new federal block grant program titled Temporary Assistance for Needy Families (TANF). Under TANF, states and local governments were granted considerable discretion in determining eligibility requirements and income assistance levels for parents with dependent children. In addition, greater emphasis was placed upon time restrictions and transitioning parents off public assistance to employment.

Long (2000) suggests that the formation and implementation of the PRWORA was grounded in dominant ideological beliefs of the period. Conservative political groups were calling for a renewed sense of fiscal responsibility, a greater emphasis on self-sufficiency, more reliance on the traditional family and work ethic, and state and local control in public assistance programs (pp. 65–66). However, it is important to note that it was not just conservatives who pushed for the acceptance of the PRWORA. President Clinton and many Democrats supported the passage of this legislation.

The ability of single-parent mothers to comply with the complex work rules and sanctions of the PRWORA is difficult. Although it is relatively easy to document that time limits and other restrictions effectively pushed families off of public assistance rolls, "the human consequences—both positive and negative—of forcing people in need off welfare remain largely unknown" (Long, Tice, & Morrison, 2006, p. 14). For single parents, employment in the labor force often presents challenges involving day care, transportation, and medical coverage. Parents experiencing difficulty in locating or maintaining employment may need to move in with extended family members or friends. This is commonly referred to as **doubling up**. Research by Lindhorst, Mancoske, and Kemp (2000) indicates that only 10 percent of former recipients in their sample believed they were better off as a result of the PRWORA.

PROMOTING EFFECTIVE PARENTING   Parenting is a complicated task, requiring information, insight, skills, and emotional stability. Fortunately, a variety of organizations can help provide young adults with basic information, social support, and advocacy services to promote healthy parenting. Most child and family service agencies sponsor parenting seminars and classes in local communities. School-based programs, church-supported workshops, YWCA classes, single-parent clubs, child support enforcement agencies, Parents of Murdered Children, Sudden Infant Death Syndrome chapters, Mothers Against Drunk Drivers, the National Alliance for the Mentally Ill, and many others instruct, support, and counsel parents who face special needs or concerns related to parenting. In assessing the social environment of a young adult, social workers should be aware of the function that special interest groups for parents can play in the life of the client. Parents of children with special needs often join social action organizations whose main purpose is to protect the child and link parents in similar situations with one another. These organizations, via meetings and newsletters, provide parents with recent research findings, social support, and an organized setting for exploring advocacy issues to benefit their children and families.

For example, advocacy groups have recently become a significant force for change in laws affecting children and are active lobbyists for child mental health issues. Imagine the stresses facing a family or parent of a child who is mentally ill. Loneliness and bitterness are common emotions experienced by these people. Organizations like the National Alliance on Mental Illness (NAMI) help parents to realize that they are not alone. People in need benefit from knowing that they share common concerns.

NAMI keeps parents aware of legislation, existing or pending, that may affect their children. NAMI members are regular participants and sponsors at mental health meetings and functions. They serve as strong voices on mental health issues, advancing the views of consumers with regard to future directions for mental health policies and programs.

In a similar fashion, family preservation movements across the country have initiated programs to provide timely and effective services for parents, enabling them to keep at-risk children in home environments (Berry, 1992). Early assessment and intervention in these programs bring valuable problem-solving techniques and adaptation skills to parents. School law has also changed to include the right to education for every child, regardless of limitations, expanding local programs to provide mental health treatment as well as care for children with physical disabilities.

HOME OWNERSHIP   The hope of many American couples and families is to purchase and eventually own a home. The dream of living in a house with a spacious front- and backyard surrounded by a picket fence is rooted in American folklore. A sense of achievement and security comes with living in a dwelling that you can claim as your own.

From a more practical aspect, home ownership for the typical American constitutes an important investment and tax break. The goal of many people is to secure a home loan at a reasonable interest rate and acquire a house or condominium that will appreciate over time. As the home loan matures, the buyer builds equity. Home equity can eventually be leveraged to provide an equity line of credit or to purchase a larger or more expensive residence.

Beyond the investment value, home ownership can contribute to a sense of stability and well-being. Owners identify with their home. They spend time and money to decorate and remodel their homes to reflect their personalities, values, and lifestyles. Home ownership can contribute to quality of life. An adequate and safe home is viewed by many professionals as fundamental to one's health and well-being (Whiting, 2004).

Unfortunately, not everyone in our society can afford to purchase a home. While "home ownership seems to be more accessible to demographic groups previously excluded from the housing market . . . the gap in home ownership between white and nonwhite households remains" (Wiens-Tuers, 2004, p. 882). Wiens-Tuers also found that it is particularly difficult for temporary workers employed by temporary, consulting, or contracting agencies in non-standard jobs to own a home.

Home ownership also appears to enhance the quality of the social and learning environment for children. Research conducted by Boyle (2002) suggests that for low-income families home ownership can contribute to enhanced emotional and behavioral functioning and well-being. Haurin, Parcel, and Haurin (2002) found that "owning a home compared with renting leads to a 13 to 23% higher quality home environment, greater cognitive ability and fewer child behavior problems" (p. 635). Their results indicate higher math and reading achievement scores for children living in owned homes. Similarly, Zhan and Sherraden (2003) found that home ownership is a positive asset for single mothers and is associated with higher educational achievement for children.

WORK

A fundamental value orientation for people in the United States involves the American work ethic. Where this value is strongly held, children at an early age are socialized to believe that work is healthful, wholesome, and a major source of personal identity. At the next party or social gathering you attend, be an active listener and direct your attention to the conversation of people around you. Your friends and acquaintances may be discussing their academic major, job, or career aspirations. Irrespective of socioeconomic class, race, or gender, most young adults view work not just as a functional necessity but as a source of identity. While Americans learn to value work, we are also socialized to view certain types of occupations as more gender appropriate than others. If you doubt this premise, consider this anecdote from the recent past:

> A man and his son, traveling down a narrow road at night, become involved in a car accident. The son is seriously injured and taken to the closest hospital for immediate medical care. As the father and son enter the hospital, they are separated and the boy is taken to the emergency room. The attending emergency room doctor looks at the boy and quickly proclaims, "I can't treat this boy; he is my son!" How can this be?

Some people have guessed that the physician is the boy's stepfather and are surprised to find that the emergency room doctor is the boy's mother. Childhood stories, television, and other media reinforce gender stereotypes.

This exercise illustrates social boundaries and parameters that affect attainment of certain occupations by people in the United States. Typically, literature describing human development during young adulthood focuses on occupational choice as a major developmental task. Yet, occupational choice assumes that people are actually free and able to pursue a particular career, profession, or vocation of their liking. Unfortunately, research indicates that gender, race, socioeconomic class, sexual orientation, disability, nationality, and other social statuses serve as social barriers that inhibit entry into a chosen field (Jacobsen, 1994), create differential access to workplace power (Elliot & Smith, 2004), and contribute to salary inequities (Kilbourne, England, & Beron, 1994).

For women, equitable compensation in the labor force is restricted by two key elements: "the differential distribution of women and men across jobs and occupations that vary with respect to pay, and within-job pay differences" (Cohen & Huffman, 2003, p. 882). Women are employed in occupations and professions that typically receive less pay, and women receive less compensation than men even when in the same jobs. As if this were not enough, the segregated nature of female employment in certain occupations and professions often leads to a devaluation of women's work roles (Cohen & Huffman, 2003).

In our society, it is often only the economically advantaged who can afford to attend the prestigious undergraduate universities and accumulate the years of graduate school education necessary to hold many professional positions. In the United States, licensing and certification requirements serve a gatekeeping function that allows certain members of our society to enter and turns others away.

Standards required for admission into many helping professions routinely lead to rejection of many applicants. As a result of marketplace demands and self-imposed professional control, applications for a job opening is often restricted to individuals holding a special license or degree. The field of psychology presents a useful example. In most states, the practice of clinical psychology requires a PhD or PsyD. And while there are an appreciable number of doctoral degree programs in psychology in the United States, entry is restricted and very competitive. It is difficult to gain admission into a doctoral program in clinical psychology because applicants far outnumber the limited number of openings available for students.

As an undergraduate or graduate student in social work, could you choose to enter a doctoral program in psychology? If you experience some misgivings or hesitancy at this question, imagine the sense of hopelessness that many of your clients feel with respect to meaningful employment and upward job mobility. If your client is mentally disabled or has special needs, you will need to understand the pain, frustration, and social barriers that come with seeking employment beyond beginning-level or service-oriented positions.

KNOWLEDGE OF SPECIAL INTERESTS   As a social worker, you will be able to join forces with colleagues to advance the special interests of both clients and social workers. The National Association of Social Workers (NASW) and its political action committee (PACE) represent two of these possibilities. In addition, the Council on Social Work Education (CSWE) and social work clinical associations constitute professional organizations that provide information about and advocate for the role of social work in the labor force.

Labor unions and professional associations in the United States have historically played vital roles in protecting the rights of workers and in formulating and shaping important social policies (Marmor, 1973). Many young adults are unfamiliar with labor reforms (e.g., policies promoting healthy and safe working conditions or fair wage and medical benefits for workers) that were initiated and supported by organizations like the AFL-CIO, the Teamsters, and the United Auto Workers (Western, 1994).

Because young adults are still relatively new to the world of work and have not yet attained seniority in the labor force, they are especially vulnerable to manipulation and exploitation in their employment. Ironically, the hiring of youths sometimes affords significant advantages as companies downsize or restructure their labor force. Preference is often given to younger workers who can be hired at lower salaries while laying off more costly older workers. Other young adults fall victim to the "last hired/first fired" pattern. When young adults do not comply with the expectations of the employer, they face swift termination. The availability of applicants waiting to fill a position places the burden on the new worker to meet the demands of management or face loss of his or her job.

Thus, for the social worker, knowledge concerning organizations and programs dedicated to promoting and protecting the rights of young adults in the labor force is paramount. Community-based employment education and training programs help young adults prepare for and seek meaningful work. Equal opportunity commissions, the National Urban League, women-in-work conferences, labor unions, and professional associations constitute a few examples of potentially powerful allies available to clients.

Companies implement policies concerning health insurance coverage, day care provisions, flexible time, and fair rights hearings when forced to see the need and the benefits to the company. It takes organization for individuals and groups to demand these employment practices. Where is the young consumer of your services with respect to participation in work-related groups and forums that focus attention on specific employment issues or needs? As an example, Callahan and Cooper (2004) suggest that lack of health insurance is a particular concern for young working adults, especially "men, Hispanics, and those in low- and middle-income households" (p. 291). Women, single or married, also have an urgent need to have medical insurance in place for themselves and their children. As a social worker, you will need to be informed about and involved in activities that emphasize empowering clients who enter the labor force.

| CASE EXAMPLE | A JAMAICAN STUDENT CONFRONTS CULTURAL ISSUES |

David Hewan is a 27-year-old, third-year engineering student at Florida State University (FSU). David's current grade point average is 3.5 out of a possible 4.0. During the last several months, however, David's grades have dropped. David appears sad; the student counseling center at FSU made a preliminary diagnosis of depression.

A social history reveals that David grew up in Jamaica in the small town of Sandy Bay, several miles west of the active tourist port of Montego Bay. David's father has been a tour bus driver for many years; his mother is a secretary in Immigration Services at the airport. David has one younger sister, Denise, aged 14. David is the only member of his immediate family who has left Jamaica.

As a child growing up on this Caribbean island, David was very fortunate to have attended private primary and secondary schools in Montego Bay. Following secondary school, David completed high school, fulfilling the first part of a lifelong dream of his parents.

Since he was 6, David's parents saved money to enable him to attend college. Funds were deposited regularly in the bank for David's education. This involved many sacrifices and hardships for his parents, who lived a meager life in a simple and sparsely furnished home.

The plan for years had been for David to come to the United States, where he could live with his maternal uncle, Cameron, and attend FSU. Because attaining a visa for study abroad is very difficult in Jamaica, it took David's parents over two years of political maneuvering to secure an educational visa for him. They agreed he would live with Cameron while in the United States and return to Jamaica following graduation.

Although he has experienced academic success at FSU, David's social experiences have been confusing and a source of personal turmoil. Though David appreciates living in the United States with his uncle and enjoys the many modern conveniences of his new home, he is aware of changes within himself. He is becoming more ambivalent about his eventual return to Jamaica. He often feels pleased about being a successful student who is quickly learning American customs. At the same time, he experiences a sense of guilt at losing his Jamaican ways and roots. A promising career and an enduring relationship with his girlfriend, Juanita, are dependent upon living in the United States. Yet, David is continually troubled by his promise to return to Jamaica.

David yearns to stay in the United States, but he feels the pull of his parents' expectations. Would he be disloyal not to return to his beloved Jamaica where his engineering knowledge and skills could be a significant asset to his country in its need for advanced technology? Would failure to return to his homeland be interpreted as breaking his word? Keeping one's promises and honoring fiscal responsibilities are values highly regarded by his parents.

In addition, David feels that if he stays in the United States, he stands to lose his identity as a Jamaican. He resents being referred to as a person of color or an African-American. He is a Jamaican! For this young man to be called anything else negates his sense of being and the heritage of his proud people.

At an early age, David learned the symbolism of the colors of the Jamaican flag. The green is for Jamaica's abundant vegetation, the yellow represents the sun that shines over Jamaica's land and sea, and the black symbolizes the hardships and struggles that the Jamaican people have endured. How can David forget his family, country, and people? Once life seemed to be "no problem"; now life seems just too difficult.

Time to Think!

David presents a fairly common dilemma for people who come to the United States from other countries. He appears distraught by intrapsychic conflict, but what macro-level issues are germane to his case? How is your thinking influenced by the fact that David comes from Jamaica? Are there national or international considerations that might be appropriate to consider in your assessment? Though many of David's concerns are related to cross-cultural issues, which life-stage issues are similar to those of any other young adult?

Macro Systems and David

Our goal is to encourage social workers to incorporate macro-level issues and factors into their daily routine when working with clients. With David as your client, you are challenged to explore organizational, community, societal, and global considerations.

Organizational Level As a student at FSU, David is strongly influenced by the policies and programs of this institution of higher education. Thus, it would be beneficial to know about the presence of student organizations and/or university programs designed specifically to assist international students. Many universities have developed student organizations, clubs, and support programs designed to address the unique needs of such students.

We know that David has family in Florida and the FSU area. We do not know about contacts with organizations that David's family has made in the community. Does Cameron belong to any clubs or civic organizations that might take an interest in David or provide assistance?

The social worker should find out about Jamaican or Caribbean organizations in the community that provide opportunities for socializing, mutual support, and acquiring information. The local Traveler's Aid Society may be of assistance. Additionally, listings of agencies in the Yellow Pages or directories of community agencies often provide such information. Churches serving the neighborhood may also offer programs and insight concerning available resources.

What do we know about David's interests and priorities in life? Does he have a religious affiliation, participate in athletics (e.g., cricket and soccer are popular sports

continued

CASE EXAMPLE | *continued*

in Jamaica), or enjoy a musical interest? Does David attend a church, play on an athletic team, or belong to a musical group? These are areas to explore as the worker takes a social history. What are David's interests in the political process; is he interested in political advocacy or in joining a political action group?

As a social worker, view David's case as an opportunity to become familiar with Jamaican culture, mores, and organizations. In the United States, there are travel agencies specializing in visits to Jamaica. Travel centers, libraries, and government bureaus dealing with immigration could be important sources of information. A resourceful worker will gain increased insight from organizations that can contribute to a better understanding of the social/cultural framework.

Community Level While David attends FSU, he lives with Uncle Cameron in the city of Conway, located just west of Tallahassee. It is important to examine the match between David and the community in which he lives. Florida, specifically the Tallahassee vicinity, is accustomed to sharing daily life with people from other countries and with diverse cultural backgrounds. David feels comfortable living with his uncle. People of the city have made him feel welcome.

David's girlfriend, Juanita, is employed as a leasing representative in a nearby apartment community. Because Juanita is a Latino-American from Puerto Rico, most local acquaintances initially believed that David also belonged to this ethnic group. When David first moved to live with Cameron, he was quick to correct people and to identify himself as Jamaican. Usually this did not present difficulties for David, as most people only inquired about life in his native land. But, the longer David has lived in the United States, the more reluctant he has become to identify himself as Jamaican. Cameron identifies himself as American when he chooses. David struggles daily with the temptation to enter fully into American life, thus weakening his ties to his Jamaican heritage. Would identifying himself as American bring more acceptance and if so, from whom?

Rather than discovering prejudice, David has found life at FSU and in Conway almost too accommodating. Because Conway is open to people of different ethnic origins, David is not seen as unusual and is viewed by the citizens as just another international college student. On the other hand, this positive view is not necessarily helpful to David, as he struggles with maintaining his Jamaican heritage.

As a social worker, you will practice in communities that appear to place a strong emphasis on particular ethnic or racial customs and traditions, that is, **cultural pluralism**. In these communities, the festivals, parades, and gatherings help people to remain connected to their racial and ethnic roots.

Other communities may dictate uniformity in behaviors and customs based on the prevailing (often white) norms and values of the community. This is known as **Anglo-conformity.** In these communities, people from other countries have few opportunities to celebrate their heritage and country of origin other than within their immediate families.

Still other communities attempt to combine the cultural and ethnic uniqueness of the people who reside in a location into one distinctly new entity—a **melting pot**. In this environment, ethnic and racial backgrounds are deemphasized in favor of unity and community wholeness.

At first glance, David appears to be experiencing the community as a melting pot. While this initially appears to be a positive community attribute, David's living circumstances relate directly to reevaluating his self-concept.

Sentiments toward people from foreign nations vary according to nation of origin (Herring, 1993). Because David is from Jamaica, would you anticipate any unique community-based difficulties or advantages in the future? As a social worker, you will need to be sensitive to the community's response to an immigrant group.

Finally, what opportunities exist in Conway to allow David to connect with his Jamaican upbringing? Are there international organizations at FSU or other resources in neighboring communities that would provide avenues for David to maintain his Jamaican heritage?

Societal Level What is the general perception that American people have of Jamaicans? How much accurate information do U.S. citizens possess about them? In our society, exposure to Jamaica for many people has been limited to depictions in popular media (e.g., films and television shows), of Red Stripe beer, Jamaican rum, news accounts of Jamaican drug rings, or vacation tales from Caribbean tourists. David has been fortunate during his stay in the States to avoid stereotypes associated with Jamaican males, but this might not always be the case.

What were David's expectations on coming to America? Did he believe all Americans were rich and self-centered or altruistic and privileged? Was David's perception of people from the United States distorted by limited contacts with American tourists and by media?

Perhaps some Americans, upon learning that David is from Jamaica, wonder if he is working with a proper green card or if he is involved in illegal drugs. Other Americans might hold prejudicial views, questioning the work ethic of a Caribbean islander. In order to refrain from stereotypes, it is important to attempt to gain an understanding of how David may be viewed and how he perceives people in his new environment.

The social worker should also be familiar with special policies, laws, or rules governing a Jamaican student's stay in the United States. Toward this end, the U.S. Immigration Service or U.S. congressional offices might be able to assist in identifying any special provisions or requirements that regulate academic study by Jamaicans in the United States.

Finally, the social worker should explore the existence of any national organizations that focus on Jamaica or the needs of Jamaicans in the United States. While national Jamaican associations may not have a local chapter in the FSU area, such organizations could broker information to Jamaicans across the United States or serve to network Jamaicans regionally via newsletters, websites, electronic chat rooms, or referral services.

continued

CASE EXAMPLE | *continued*

International Level David's situation is well suited for a discussion of international issues in social work practice. First, David reminds us of the many people living in the United States who have emigrated here from other countries. Indeed, America is a nation of people from other countries. Mindful that our clients often originate from diverse backgrounds in a global sense, social workers need to become "world wise" in their approaches to the client-worker situation. Each client who has grown up in a different culture represents a new journey and adventure in assessment for the social worker.

Jamaica is a country whose economic health relies heavily on bauxite and sugar exports as well as on tourism. During the early 1980s, the Reagan administration attempted to strengthen a weakened Jamaican economy by making it a model of a free market society. The strategy was to increase Jamaica's foreign aid from the United States to over $495 million a year, double the amount given in previous years (Braun, 1991, p. 70). This monetary infusion, however, had little impact on the wage scale of Jamaicans (with minimum wage below $9 per week) and resulted in few new jobs while creating a windfall profit for investors and entrepreneurs. This is an example of how the wealthy prosper and common citizens benefit marginally from foreign aid.

David comes from a strong working-class family that failed to experience any positive impact from the economic policies initiated in the 1980s by the United States in Jamaica. Indeed, David's presence in the United States is a testimony to a combination of his family's determination, the political contacts nurtured by his mother, and the willingness of his uncle, Cameron, to provide support for David while he is living in the United States. From the perspective of David's family and Jamaican government, he is clearly obligated to return to his homeland following completion of his degree.

As social workers, what do we know about immigration laws and research describing trends in transnational migration that may impact David (Massey, Goldring, & Durand, 1994)? Juanita, David's girlfriend, is a U.S. citizen. David's rights concerning citizenship and his visa are topics for assessment. If they were to marry, would Juanita be allowed to return with David to Jamaica or could David apply for U.S. citizenship? Ultimately, for David to make an informed decision as to where to live, he needs to understand his choices and their consequences. The answers to some of David's questions involve both immigration law and differing customs between the two nations.

REFLECTION ON DIVERSITY: REFUGEES

In a number of cities and states across America as well as in Britain and Germany, social workers are actively engaged in practice with various refugee and asylum seekers from Africa, Central America, Southern Asia, Asia Minor, the Far and Middle East, Afghanistan, the Balkans, and Eastern and Central Europe. The United States is one of the larger receptor nations in the industrialized world. Over the last thirty years (since 1975), the United States has helped over 2.4 million refugees resettle, with 77 percent being people from either Indochina or the former Soviet Union (Administration for Children and Families, 2005). Social workers help refugees to identify and obtain needed resources (e.g., food, shelter, health care, money) and navigate the complex and often burdensome myriad of policies, laws, and offices governing their presence in a new land.

According to Okitikpi and Aymer (2003): "An **asylum seeker** is someone who has crossed an internationally recognized border and is looking for sanctuary, because they face persecution and they believe they are in danger" (p. 214). By contrast, a **refugee** is "someone fleeing persecution, torture or war, and who applies for refugee status" (Okitikpi & Aymer, 2003, p. 214). A refugee typically is unable or unwilling to return to his former country. Traditionally, Article 1 of the United Nations Convention (1951) and the New York Protocol (1967) have provided the definitive resources for defining what constitutes a refugee.

People seeking refugee status frequently meet with resistance and feel "unwelcome by the indigenous population because they are seen as competitors for what is perceived as limited resources. Their presence is seen, by some, as a threat to the continuing economic prosperity of individuals and an unwelcome burden on the social welfare system of the countries concerned" (Aymer & Okitikpi, 2000, p. 52). As a result, the process of declaring refugee status is often a lengthy and sometimes demeaning process that involves cumbersome paperwork and stringent guidelines and rules.

Especially since the attack on the World Trade Center and Pentagon of September 11 (2001), there has been a growing sentiment among various groups that heightened border control and the tightening of various forms of immigration are imperatives in the United States. Although organizations such as Catholic Social Services and Lutheran Immigration & Refugee Services (LIRS) have for many years sponsored and provided refugee programs and services in the United States, public compassion toward and support for people fleeing persecution can be impacted by social–historical events. It is certainly true that human services in America have suffered as politicians and government officials have directed national resources to support wars in Afghanistan and Iraq, combat international terrorism, and promote homeland security.

Research by Okitikpi and Ayner (2003) is particularly helpful for identifying and highlighting the various problems and difficulties confronting young adults and their children as refugees in foreign lands. Difficulties cited include psychological problems, emotional issues, health problems, cultural adaptation, lack of housing, educational problems, loss of contact with families, financial woes, and language barriers (p. 218). It is clear that refugees need a range of services, but social workers interviewed in the study "reported that providing practical support meant little thought and time was available to look at the emotional and psychological aspects" (p. 219).

As social workers seek ways to enhance practice with and services to young adults and families from other countries seeking a place of safety, sensitivity needs to be given to public sentiment. Long, Tice, and Morrison (2006) suggest that phenomena such as war, catastrophe, economic crisis, unemployment, fluctuations in the stock market, population shifts, technological advancement, and international threats affect public and professional opinion concerning the use of community and societal assets for social services. Refugees enter countries with both urgent and long-term needs and are many times greeted by government officials and citizens with less than open arms. Social workers need to consider ways to heighten public consciousness and awareness of the complex troubles experienced by refugees. Brawley and Martinez-Brawley (1999) suggest the use of mass media in promoting issues related to social justice and human dignity.

According to the Administration for Children and Families (2005), two factors have contributed in meaningful ways to the effectiveness of refugee services in the United States. First, the use of case managers to track the progress of each case has been helpful. Second, regulations requiring services to be provided by bilingual, bicultural workers have eased communication barriers.

For social workers whose clients are migrating from other countries, it is important to note that many people and professionals view an asylum seeker as a pre-refugee who has not yet received refugee status. Yet, sensitivity needs to be given to time limits or "clocks" for receiving assistance. For example, the typical eight-month clock for receiving financial or medical assistance usually begins the date she or he entered the United States or the date the grant of asylum was made.

APPLYING A SOCIAL WORK FRAMEWORK: VALUE-CONFLICT THEORY

Earlier in this chapter, basic tenets of a value-conflict perspective were examined. Social policies and programs were viewed as products of special interest groups competing with each other for limited resources. From this perspective, what is deemed legitimate or illegitimate is a result of particular groups successfully exerting dominance and influence over the interests of other groups.

For David, the values and positions set forward by special interest groups and systems are also important elements. For example, David's family and country have firm expectations that David will return to Jamaica. However, David's girlfriend, his uncle, the community in which David now lives, and the university he attends support his staying in America.

Various constituencies in the United States continually compete to define the rights and opportunities of immigrants. Legislation in California aimed at prohibiting aid to illegal immigrants and their children is a product of this kind of effort. Some political groups oppose state and federal aid to immigrants because of the financial obligations and consequences of such support. Other religious or social welfare groups favor aid to immigrants for humane and altruistic reasons.

In part, David's future is shaped by groups who organize to promote their vested interests. It is important for David and his social worker to ascertain which groups have the greatest potential impact on this young man's situation and what level of advocacy is appropriate to assist him in attaining his goals.

Suggested Activities

1. Most universities sponsor an international student coalition. Seek information concerning this organization and plan to attend some of their cultural events and programs. Become familiar with the special needs of international students at your school. Ask a student from another country about his/her experience in obtaining a student visa.

2. Plan to visit or vacation in a foreign country. If this is not feasible, attend a travel show or exposition focusing on a country you hope to visit. Strive to gain an appreciation of the culture, values, norms, and ways of people in this country. Explore university-sponsored service learning or an immersion experience in a semester abroad, and determine if this type of opportunity is possible for you. What facts would you want to know before you opted for such a program?

3. Attend a political or special interest group meeting or rally. Ask for brochures, pamphlets, and literature describing the group's positions on important social issues. Inquire about politicians or media personalities who champion the group's cause. What types of policy or legislative initiatives are of major concern for the group?

References

Administration for Children and Families. (2005). *U.S. Resettlement program: An overview.* Available online at: www.acf.dhhs.gov/program/orr/programs/overviewrp.htm.

Berry, M. (1992). An evaluation of family preservation services. *Social Work, 37,* 314–321.

Boyle, M. (2002). Home ownership and the emotional and behavioral problems of children and youth. *Child Development, 73,* 883–892.

Braun, D. (1991). *The rich get richer.* Chicago: Nelson-Hall.

Brawley, E., & Martinez-Brawley, E. (1999). Promoting social justice in partnership with the mass media. *Journal of Sociology and Social Welfare, 16,* 63–86.

Bullough, V. (2002). Changing lifestyles and perspectives. *Free Inquiry, 23,* 22–23.

Callahan, S., & Cooper, W. (2004). Gender and uninsurance among young adults in the United States. *Pediatrics, 113,* 291–297.

Cohen, P., & Huffman, M. (2003). Occupational segregation and the devaluation of women's work across U.S. labor markets. *Social Forces, 81,* 881–908.

Cowley, G. (1994). The culture of Prozac. *Newsweek,* February 7, 41–42.

DiNitto, D. (1995). *Social welfare: Politics and public policy.* Boston: Allyn & Bacon.

Elliot, J., & Smith, R. (2004). Race, gender, and workplace power. *American Sociological Review, 69,* 365–386.

Federico, R. (1990). *Social welfare in today's world.* New York: McGraw-Hill.

Gil, D. (2002). Challenging injustice and oppression. In M. O'Melia and K. Miley (Eds.), *Pathways to power: Readings in contextual social work practice.* Boston: Allyn & Bacon.

Green, R. (2000). Introduction to special section: Lesbian, gay, and bisexual issues in family therapy. *Journal of Marital and Family Therapy, 26,* 407–408.

Hardert, R., Gordon, L., Laner, M., & Reader, M. (1984). *Confronting social problems.* St. Paul: West.

Haurin, D., Parcel, T., & Haurin, R. (2002). Does homeownership affect child outcomes? *Real Estate Economics, 30,* 635–666.

Herring, C. (1993). Ethnic notions about alien nations: American ethnic groups' changing sentiments toward foreign nations. *Sociological Focus, 26,* 315–332.

Hoffnung, M. (2004). Wanting it all: Career, marriage, and motherhood during college-educated women's 20s. *Sex Roles, 50,* 711–723.

Jacobsen, J. (1994). Trends in work force sex segregation. *Social Science Quarterly, 75,* 204–211.

Kerpelman, J., & Schvaneveldt, P. (1999). Young adults' anticipated identity importance of career, marital, and parental roles: Comparisons of men and women with different role balance orientations. *Sex Roles, 41,* 189–217.

Kilbourne, B., England, P., & Beron, K. (1994). Effects of individual, occupational, and industrial characteristics on earnings: Intersections of race and gender. *Social Forces, 72,* 1149–1176.

Lee, R. (2000). Health care problems of lesbian, gay, bisexual, and transgender patients. *The Western Journal of Medicine, 172,* 403–408.

Lidz, T. (1976). *The person.* New York: Basic Books.

Lindhorst, T., Mancoske, R., & Kemp, A. (2000). Is welfare reform working? A study of effects of sanctions on families receiving temporary assistance to needy families. *Journal of Sociology and Social Welfare, 27,* 185–201.

Long, D. (2000). Welfare reform: A social work perspective for assessing success. *Journal of Sociology and Social Welfare, 27,* 61–78.

Long, D., Tice, C., & Morrison, J. (2006). *Macro social work practice: A strengths perspective.* Belmont, CA: Thomson Brooks/Cole.

Longres, J. (1995). *Human behavior and the social environment.* Itasca, IL: Peacock.

Lowery, D., & Gray, V. (1994). Do lobbying regulations influence lobbying registrations? *Social Science Quarterly, 75,* 382–384.

Marmor, T. (1973). *The politics of Medicare.* Chicago: Aldine.

Massey, D., Goldring, L., & Durand, J. (1994). Continuities in transnational migration: An analysis of nineteen Mexican communities. *American Journal of Sociology, 99,* 1492–1533.

McDonell, J. (1993). Judgments of personal responsibility for HIV infection: An attributional analysis. *Social Work, 38,* 403–410.

Mooney, L., Knox, D., & Schacht, C. (2002). *Understanding social problems.* Belmont, CA: Wadsworth Thomson Learning.

Okitikpi, T., & Aymer, C. (2000). The price of safety: Refugee children and the challenge for social work. *Social Work in Europe, 7,* 51–58.

Okitikpi, T., & Aymer, C. (2003). Social work with African refugee children and their families. *Child and Family Social Work, 8,* 213–222.

Palmer, E., & Little, G. (1993). The plight of Blacks in America today. *Social Behavior and Personality, 21,* 313–325.

Papalia, D., & Olds, S. (1989). *Human development.* New York: McGraw-Hill.

Phipps, S., Burton, P., & Osberg, L. (2001). Time as a source of inequality within marriage: Are husbands more satisfied with time for themselves than wives? *Feminist Economics, 7,* 1–21.

Rosenbaum, E. (1994). The constraints on minority housing choices, New York City 1978–1987. *Social Forces, 72,* 725–747.

Sabattini, L., & Leaper, C. (2004). The relation between mothers' and fathers' parenting styles and their division of labor in the home: Young adults' retrospective reports. *Sex Roles, 50,* 217–225.

Sprecher, S., & Toro-Morn, M. (2002). A study of men and women from different sides of Earth to determine if men are from Mars and women are from Venus in their beliefs about love and romantic relationships. *Sex Roles, 46,* 131–147.

Stolzenberg, R. (1994). Educational continuation by college graduates. *American Journal of Sociology, 99,* 1042–1077.

Swann, S., & Anastas, J. (2003). Dimensions of lesbian identity during adolescence and young adulthood. *Journal of Gay and Lesbian Social Services, 15,* 109–125.

Trent, K. (1994). Family context and adolescents' expectations about marriage, fertility, and nonmarital childbearing. *Social Science Quarterly, 75,* 319–339.

Western, B. (1994). Unionization and labor market institutions in advanced capitalism, 1950–1985. *American Journal of Sociology, 99,* 1314–1341.

Whiting, C. (2004). Income inequality, the income cost of housing, and the myth of market efficiency. *American Journal of Economics and Sociology, 63,* 851–879.

Wiens-Tuers, B. (2004). There's no place like home: The relationship of nonstandard employment and home ownership over the 1990s. *American Journal of Economics and Sociology, 63,* 881–896.

Zastrow, C. (2000). *Social problems: Issues and solutions.* Belmont, CA: Wadsworth Thomson Learning.

Zhan, M., & Sherraden, M. (2003). Assets, expectations, and children's educational achievement in female-headed households. *Social Service Review, 77,* 191–327.

7 CHAPTER | MIDDLE ADULTHOOD

In this chapter, we examine the macro issues of middle adulthood and focus on the role of the social worker as facilitator during this turbulent passage. The midlife aspirations of many men and women center on personal achievement. There is something exciting about entrepreneurs, inventors, and entertainers who have "made it big." The success of a Bill Gates, a Colin Powell, a Ted Turner, or an Oprah Winfrey confirms the American dream. We see them as people who began with few resources but through hard work and determination and fortunate circumstances became rich and famous.

Professional athletes often seem to emerge quickly from relative obscurity to stardom. Who has not heard of Roger Clemens, Tiger Woods, or Venus Williams? Their names are symbols of success to many American children and adults. Yet, their celebrity status is often gained at great cost.

Athletes, entertainers, powerful politicians, and business tycoons, like others striving to achieve success, struggle to balance various roles and responsibilities as spouse, parent, daughter, or son while pursuing life ambitions. To become a celebrated person in our society requires an extensive commitment of time and energy.

George Lopez is arguably the most recognized Hispanic-Latino television star since the late Freddie Prinze. Best known for his hit sitcom *George Lopez*, he is recognized by many Americans for his award-winning smile and quick and clever humor. He is an accomplished actor, comedian, author, writer, and producer.

However, life for George Lopez has not always been glamorous or easy. In San Fernando, California, George's father abandoned the family when George was only two months old. At the age of 20, George's mother entrusted his upbringing to her parents (Horsburgh & Wang, 2002). "His no-nonsense grandparents reared him. And he was funny as a kid, often teasing his classmates until their parents complained" (Lee, 2004, p. NA). His maternal grandparents "had little money—or affection—to shower on their grandson [according to George]. 'They were tough on each other and on me, emotionally'" (Horsburgh & Wang, 2002). Reared by strict, working-class grandparents, George's upbringing was far from ideal.

Success in the field of entertainment did not come overnight. After working a variety of odd jobs and spending nearly two decades on the comedy-club circuit, George's first major showbiz break came in the form of a radio show in Los Angeles. At the same time his acting career in movies had begun to take off via roles in *Bread and Roses* and *Real Women Have Curves* (Horsburgh & Wang, 2002).

George's life-changing break occurred when he met Ann Serrano, currently a successful producer. Ann had been scouting for a Hispanic-Latino actor and watched his comedy act. Shortly after this encounter they began dating. Ann became George's partner and confidant; their marriage soon followed. "Lopez says meeting his Cuban wife, Ann, changed him forever" (Lee, 2004, p. NA).

George and Ann Lopez led busy and successful lives. They are parents of one daughter, Mayan. In addition to their careers, they are both known for their philanthropic efforts and willingness to share with others. For example, George has lent his support to a national advocacy campaign to promote enrollment and use of libraries. The initiative for use of library cards is called "The Smartest Card" (*PR Newswire*, 2004).

In 2005, the Lopez family revealed to the public that George had been suffering from a serious kidney ailment for over a decade. The condition necessitated a transplant. As his kidneys were failing, George received a transplant from the person closest to him, his wife, Ann (*People Weekly*, 2005). According to George, "Whatever happens to me professionally and wherever my golf swing goes, nothing is more important than the fact that my wife gave me a chance to live. I can't pay her back, but what I can do is make her as happy as she thought I would be when we first got married" (*People Weekly*, 2005, p. 83).

As a busy middle-aged entertainer, husband, and father, George Lopez appears firmly committed to his wife and daughter. As one of the few Hispanic-Latino giants in the entertainment field, demands from acting, public appearances, media events, and charity work are enormous. George, like other people with demanding and challenging work schedules, is presented with the daily dilemma of looking for ways to better accommodate family obligations and to gain greater satisfaction in relationships with family members and close friends.

Similarly, knowing how to balance personal and professional roles and time becomes a necessary skill for the social worker. Some employers expect an excessive number of hours of work each day although compensation is based on a forty-hour workweek. Other administrators want their employees to volunteer time and energies at community events and functions in the spirit of advancing the mission of the agency.

Flexible and creative time arrangements and strategies that restructure employment to address both agency needs and personal responsibilities have been implemented in recent years. For example, many people (including social workers and nurses) have gone to four-day workweeks. Other employers have provided workers with latitude regarding daily starting or ending times. Some employers have defined their full-time work and benefits in terms of a thirty-two-hour workweek. While labor laws can work to constrain the ability to bank time for later use, it is not unusual for employers to provide employees each year with a designated number of personal and sick days. These variations on the traditional work schedule often meet the needs of both agency and worker.

THEORY: ROLE

Role theory is a helpful perspective as we view macro issues of the middle years. Role theorists frequently quote this well-known passage from Shakespeare's *As You Like It* (act 2, scene 7):

> All the world's a stage,
>
> And all the men and women merely players:
>
> They have their exits and their entrances;
>
> And one man in his time plays many parts, . . .

The analogy of actors on a stage and role-players in society can be very useful. This **dramaturgical approach** provides a means to assess individual behaviors in relationship to social structure. Role theory has become so prominent that it "has become part of the very web of social work thinking and literature" (Strean, 1967, p. 77).

Just as actors learn and perform clearly defined parts from written scripts, people in real life acquire various statuses and roles that dictate behavioral conformity and adherence to social norms. In much the same way as actors perform parts as villains and heroes, people act out roles as student, worker, friend, spouse, and parent. Each role involves social expectations that define how to behave, think, and feel. As role-players, we must adapt our lives to bosses, teachers, and other people who occupy positions of power over us. Rather than playing to audiences, people in real life respond to the situation and to those around them.

A **role theory perspective** requires that:

> Individuals in society occupy positions, and their role performance in these positions is determined by social norms, demands, and rules; by the role performances of others in their respective positions; by those who observe and react to the performance; and by the individual's particular capabilities and personality. The social "script" may be as constraining as that of a play, but it frequently allows more options. (Biddle & Thomas, 1966, p. 4)

For role theorists, the social script is defined predominantly by the expectations and behaviors of others. From the standpoint that the social script is powerful and demands conformity, role theory reflects social determinism. While individuals occupying positions and playing roles may be viewed as having different role-playing skills and capabilities, heavy emphasis is placed on social conformity and the power of those with whom one interacts.

One notable contrast to role theory's social-deterministic ways involves Goffman's (1959) emphasis on individual control in his book *The Presentation of Self in Everyday Life*. Although clearly using a structural approach, he gives added attention to how "the individual may deeply involve his ego in his identification with a particular part, establishment, and group." Through analysis of concepts like "impression management," Goffman explores individual interpretation and control over "the presentation of self" in social roles (1959, p. 243).

The concept of role is the point of articulation between society and the individual. While recognizing that much debate exists over a clear and concise definition of social role, Turner offers three basic conceptualizations:

Prescribed Roles. When conceptual emphasis is placed upon the expectations of individuals in statuses, then the social world is assumed to be composed of relatively clear-cut prescriptions. The individual's self and role-playing skills are then seen as operating to meet such prescriptions, with the result that analytical emphasis is drawn to the degree of conformity to the demands of a particular status.

Subjective Roles. Since all expectations are mediated through the prism of self, they are subject to interpretations by individuals in statuses. When conceptual emphasis falls upon the perceptions and interpretations of expectations, then the social world is conceived to be structured in terms of individuals' subjective assessments of the interaction situation. Thus, conceptual emphasis is placed upon the interpersonal style of individuals who interpret and then adjust to expectations.

Enacted Roles. Ultimately, expectations and the subjective assessment by individuals of these expectations are revealed in behavior. When conceptual priority is given to overt behavior, then the social world is viewed as a network of interrelated behaviors. The more the conceptual emphasis is placed upon overt role enactment, the less analytical attention to the analysis of either expectations or individual interpretations. . . . (Turner, 1974, pp. 165–166)

Two helpful concepts when considering the impact of roles on everyday life are role strain and role conflict. **Role strain** refers to the difficulties associated with the enactment of a single role. Because a role has numerous and oftentimes competing expectations attached to it, people often find it difficult or stressful to meet such demands. Having the role of student likely requires class attendance, participation in out-of-class projects, reading, and the completion of papers.

Role conflict recognizes the fact that people occupy more than one role at a time and that it is often difficult to enact the expectations of one role without violating expectations of another role. This can be seen when students also work as paid employees. As a student, regular class attendance and participation in course-related activities is expected and often required. In the role of worker, the student-employee is expected to be at work and dedicated to their corporate mission. When the expectations of two separate roles collide, role conflict occurs.

It should be noted that while considerable attention is given to how individuals actualize roles in a given script, less attention is given to how various social scripts can develop and change. People can alter expectations and rules governing their behavior.

DEVELOPMENTAL ISSUES

Social scientists refer to middle age as a time of reflection and self-evaluation. Prompted by physical changes and the realization that one's life is half completed, people at middle age begin to review. What have I already accomplished? What have I left undone? What are priorities in my life? Using Neugarten's (1970) notion of "social clock," people shift in their thinking about their lives "from time since birth to time until death" (Bee & Bjorklund, 2004, p. 382). Although a time of major transition and role changes for women and men, this is a developmental period often "neglected or de-emphasized in the intervention context" (Dziegielewski, Heymann, Green, & Gichia, 2002, p. 65).

The term "midlife crisis" characterizes the struggle of people from their late thirties to sixties as they react to a perceived "time squeeze" (Friedan, 1993). How do I achieve all that remains important to me in the time left? Sometimes feeling as if they have lived their lives for others, middle-age people often remark that "it is time to start doing what I want to do" as they chart new directions. Others see this as a time to turn away from egocentric pursuits and to begin to focus their efforts more on contributions to the welfare of the community.

Using a role-theory perspective, we find that middle age is a prime time for evaluating social roles (worker, father/mother, husband/wife, daughter/son, grandparent), role salience or importance, and one's commitment to roles as well as to the norms and rules that oversee each. Our focus in this chapter is twofold: emphasizing role shifts or adjustments experienced during middle age and the impact of changing social scripts for role enactment during middle age.

Multiple role involvement, characteristic of our society, is often labeled as a negative—time-consuming and mentally draining. Yet, Gilbert (1988) and others suggest that the opposite may be true. When an individual embraces multiple roles, her or his identity transcends any single role. In other words, if a person forfeits or vacates any single role through job loss, divorce, childlessness, retirement, or even illness, other roles are available to contribute to self-definition.

Conversely, when people invest heavily in a single role (e.g., worker or parent) but later relinquish this role, either voluntarily or involuntarily, loss of identity may occur. Understandably, this void may be psychologically and emotionally devastating. John Updike's 1960 novel *Rabbit, Run* is about a middle-aged man who lives in the tarnished glory of his high school basketball days. Although he was a husband, father, son, and employee, Rabbit's energy and role identification had terminated his psychological growth at an adolescent marker. In the interest of growth and psychic health during middle age, it is wise not to invest all one's energy in a single role.

GENDER DIFFERENCES

Life experiences differ for males and females during middle adulthood. Although there are increasing opportunities and choices available to women during middle age, equitable roles between women and men in the worlds of both work and family still do not fully exist (Gilbert, 1993, p. 106).

We know, for example, that women and men enter different kinds of occupations and that women continue to be employed in lower-paying occupations, hold lower ranking positions within their occupations, and earn appreciably less income than men in the labor force (Coleman & Kerbo, 2003, pp. 264–265). The needs of husbands and children continue as major concerns for women who are employed (Moen, 1991). Although husbands and fathers are assuming a more equal share of home chores and child care, a careful look reveals that employed women still take primary responsibility for work in the home. Furthermore, results from research by Keith and Malone (2005) indicate that "hours spent on housework adversely affect married women's wages and have an indeterminate effect on married men's wages" (p. 239). Other research indicates that middle-aged women are disproportionately called upon to provide care to older parents (Brody & Schoonover, 1986). Indeed, women are not only called upon to attend to the needs of their own parents, but they are often asked to care for their male partner's parents as well.

These examples reflect larger societal views defining the scripts and roles played by women and men during middle adulthood. Women of middle years, like other women in the United States, live in a male-dominated society. Although societal norms concerning a "woman's place" are slowly changing, the way in which middle-aged women perceive, weigh, and enact various social roles is still influenced by their social position and their community.

Is it reasonable to expect a middle-aged man to change jobs and move to a new area to accommodate a spouse's career move? Men often point out the impracticalities of relinquishing their jobs or taking a pay reduction to support a wife's occupational pursuits: "We will lose income! How would we live? Why would you want to do that? Can't you be satisfied just raising a family?"

However, women are often expected to make such adjustments. Changing employment for males may be seen as best for the family, a step up the ladder regardless of any other considerations. Traditionally, women have been asked to give husbands' jobs priority regardless of the investment they have in their own positions. It is assumed that the wife can seek another job. The implication is that the husband's career is more important. As we begin to explore the performance of various roles during the middle years, consider the impact of gender as well as other sources of power on social scripts and role expectations.

Why do standards and rules differ for various individuals in the United States? Do some groups of people exert greater control over social roles and scripts than others? Is it easier in middle adulthood to define and determine one's own life direction? If predominantly white, male professionals can modify their job conditions, why is it not reasonable to assume others can?

WOMEN AT MIDDLE AGE

Literature has created an overemphasis on the negative aspects of middle age for women. Middle age for women is often described as the worst of years—as a time of family crises, suicides, the departure of husbands, empty nests, fading charms, melancholia, responsibilities for aging parents, and pressures to prepare for financial security in their final years. In addition, there are all sorts of physical reminders that one is not as young as one used to be, such as wrinkles, weight gain, menopause, and screenings for breast and uterine cancers. (Hunter & Sundel, 1994, p.114).

This negative account of midlife women is one-dimensional. A more balanced perspective describing both limitations and opportunities for women in middle age is needed. While recognizing the existence of emotional ups and downs for women during midlife, let's see the glass as half full rather than half empty. "Without alternative images these demoralizing cultural stereotypes can become a self-fulfilling prophecy" (McQuaide, 1998, p. 21).

Middle age is not by definition a time of crisis, turbulent change, or disaster. Research by Spitze and Logan (1990), for example, suggests that actual time spent performing duties—juggling of full-time work, interactive marriage, active parenting, and helping parents—may not be unduly burdensome. For example, in instances where women care for both parents and children in the home, older children have been found to serve important supportive functions for women (Raphael & Schlesinger, 1994). It can be a rewarding experience when family members pull together to help each other during times of need.

Approaching this time for women from a positive perspective, midlife can be a time of self-actualization, characterized by new and exciting opportunities and challenges. Peterson and Klohnen (1995) observe that women in midlife are likely to become politically active. Their findings suggest that "expressions of generativity are not limited to family or work life but are manifested as well in concerns for the wider national and international spheres" (Peterson & Klohnen, 1995, pp. 27–28). Results from research conducted by McQuaide (1998) suggest that most women in her study "were satisfied with themselves and their lives" (p. 29). McQuaide found that "menopausal symptoms and the empty nest are irrelevant to well-being in midlife for certain women." Other findings of McQuaide indicate that women most satisfied with their lives had an annual family income above $30,000, were healthy, and were not involuntarily out of work (p. 29). Many middle-aged women lead positive, fulfilling lives and may use the time frame to seek opportunities for the acquisition of new roles and activities.

ROLE OF PARTNER OR WIFE   Divorce for people of middle age in the United States is a very real phenomenon. Consider for a moment that research by Kreider and Fields (2002) reveals that an estimated 90 percent of adults 45 years of age or younger will get married at least once and up to 50 percent of these marriages will result in divorce (Walker, Logan, Jordan, & Campbell, 2004, p. 144). "Furthermore, about 75% of those divorced from their first marriage will remarry (Kreider & Fields, 2002), and a significant proportion of those marriages are estimated to end in divorce as well (estimates of 60%) (Bumpass, Sweet, & Castro Martin, 1990; Cherlin, 1992)" (Walker, Logan, Jordan, & Campbell, 2004, p. 144).

Years ago, those who divorced were stigmatized and were viewed as irresponsible or immoral. In recent years, however, divorce has become more acceptable. Ultimately, the availability of divorce provides women with additional choices and increased freedom. Still, the strong emphasis on family values and monogamous marriages, and the desire of courts as well as religious and community groups to see children reared in two-parent families, tends to undergird traditional role assignments.

In our society, it is clear that men and women take on different roles and assume different responsibilities in marital relationships. It probably is of little surprise to many middle-aged women that wives often "have a better sense of the marital relationship and that they are often depended on to be responsible for the maintenance of their marriages" (Heaton & Blake, 1999, p. 42). This is not meant to absolve men from assuming more responsibility for success in marriage. Instead, findings by Heaton and Blake (1999) suggest the need for a more balanced approach between partners for emotional maintenance during marriage.

Bogolub (1991) describes the typical dilemma faced by women who become divorced in middle age as "loss of a long-held position, the possibility of over-dependence on young adult children, a shrinking remarriage pool, socially denigrated body changes, and unfair labor market conditions" (p. 428). Although Bogolub recognizes the need for women to view divorce as a challenge to growth, she does not clearly express a sense of the abilities of women experiencing divorce to create and sustain close links with other adults.

In minimizing the harmful effects of divorce, Hunter and Sundel (1994) propose that midlife can constitute an opportunity for women to redevelop intimate relationships with partners. Liberated from worry over pregnancy, they can acknowledge sexual interest and enjoyment. With children out of the home, women also feel a new sense of freedom and control over their lives. In a positive sense, marital relationships and their role expectations can facilitate expansion, renegotiation, and redefinition in middle age.

On the other hand, the decreased income that frequently accompanies divorce cancels out advantages anticipated by those who see promising possibilities in the single life. The cost of child care, support of family, and adequate housing are economic realities. Both income and status often go down for women, while men—especially those who do not meet child support payments—fare somewhat better (Amato, 2000; Holden & Smock, 1991; McKeever & Wolfinger, 2001; Shapiro, 1996).

Women do not march to the beat of a single drum. A variety of relational paths are available to them in middle age. Some restructure relationships with husbands; others decide to stay single but to be sexually active. Still others gravitate toward other women as support and sexual partners (Gilbert, 1993). The traditional assumption that all middle-aged women eventually either become passive, depressed wives or assume "divorcee" roles is both outdated and sexist. Social workers can empower women to make both micro- and macro-level choices that result in satisfying relationships.

Research by Lesser et al. (2004) suggests that women supporting women through the use of mutual aid groups can be particularly helpful during midlife. This type of intervention "can have a powerful influence on women who are self-sacrificing to the point of ignoring their own needs. Women can recognize this dynamic in themselves and in each other and thereby gently encourage changes" (p. 77). Women are often adept at listening to each other in compassionate ways, particularly in relationship to their husbands, work, children, and caretaking of parents (p. 86).

PARENTING   The focus of much attention regarding women and middle age relates to the "empty nest" syndrome. Following menopause and the departure of children from the home, some women experience depression and despair. Yet, many eagerly await the day their children leave the home. As offspring become more independent and move away, they require less parental time, energy, and resources. Now mothers can gain further control over their lives and seek new interests and activities as they rechannel energy into work, education, the arts, and volunteerism.

The stereotype of a middle-aged housewife sitting at home depressed and bewildered by the emotional void and idle time produced by the "empty nest" is overstated, if not misleading. Many women welcome the opportunity to develop alternatives or engage in new roles at the completion of child rearing. Freed of parenting responsibilities, women in middle adulthood can more easily concentrate on defining and developing themselves.

Blaker (2000) shares her thoughts on celebrating fifty in the following ways. "I've reached an awareness in my own life of the possibilities surrounding this threshold. . . . With less of my time devoted to doing things for others, more time would be available for me. I could feel the focus shifting; the spotlight was on my life for the first time in more than twenty-five years" (pp. 173–174).

In *The Fountain of Age* (1993), Betty Friedan recounts her Outward Bound wilderness survival expedition at the age of 60. Finding resources deep within herself, her identity unknown by the group, she emerged from the experience with heightened awareness of new spiritual, mental, and physical strengths, realizing she could play the old games or could experience new adventures in work and love.

OCCUPATIONAL ROLE   Current and future financial status is a major concern for women in middle age. The threat of poverty for older women is both profound and severe (Hunter & Sundel, 1994). In large part, fear of poverty can be attributed to reliance on husbands for financial security. Women who face divorce or widowhood but lack employment experience are at greatest risk. Early work experience may provide a basis for exploring new career or work opportunities in middle age.

Expectations relative to middle-aged women and employment are changing. Now many women welcome the chance to work outside the home and view their careers as an important source of their identity (Barnett, Biener, & Baruch, 1987). The benefits of middle age may include an increased opportunity to develop "professionally and to have established a sense of self separate from a man and children, economic independence, and perhaps greater intellectual companionship and contentment" (Gilbert, 1993, pp. 111–112).

However, for this group to attain self-actualization through participation in the labor force, discrimination in employment based on age and sex must be eliminated. These women often rely upon temporary, dead end, or sex-segregated jobs—such as unskilled secretarial and retail sales positions—for employment (Weitzman, 1988).

It is noteworthy that social work as a profession is not immune from gender pay differentials. Although social work is a female-dominated profession, research demonstrates that the income of female social workers continues to be lower than the income of male counterparts (Gibelman & Schervish, 1997). Gibelman (2003) provides a comprehensive analysis of the status of women's pay and the realities of gender inequalities in our profession. As one consideration, it is not uncommon for males to disproportionately assume administrative roles in female-dominated professions. Gibelman notes: "It is the men who are 'tracked' into the higher paying jobs" (2003, p. 29).

Women in the mid-years bring valuable knowledge and skills to the workforce, even when they have limited prior employment experience. But, much like actors who become typecast in particular roles, many find themselves trapped in jobs that limit their progress and fail to provide challenges. Upgrading and acquiring strategic skills to obtain better paying occupations becomes a necessity. However, attaining these skills requires advocacy for policies and legislation that challenge corporate America to rewrite the social script and assure middle-aged women fair access to higher-status positions.

THE PARENTAL CARETAKER ROLE   Who cares for older parents in need? The resounding answer is women. "This patriarchal society officially recognizes the social need to *care about* children and the elderly by assigning women to *care for* them" (Sancier & Mapp, 1992, p. 63). It is frequently expected that women should be able to undertake a combination of homemaking, a job, and care of an aged parent—a challenging, if not unrealistic, association of roles.

When middle-aged daughters are asked to take primary responsibility for their elderly parents, they do so with difficulty and sacrifice. Typically, daughters help with such tasks as shopping, cleaning, transportation, and emotional support. They are also likely to become involved with cooking and personal care for their parents (Brody & Schoonover, 1986). A daughter may also be expected to adjust her job to meet parental needs.

Middle-aged women in these circumstances struggle for balance. How can they manage home, work, and caregiving? Overburdened by conflicting demands of work and family, such a woman is like an actor asked to play too many roles in an overly demanding, emotionally draining drama.

The long-term resolution to this dilemma, however, does not lie in encouraging or enabling middle-aged women to do more. The broad issue of dependent care by daughters is a gender issue that demands solutions. "Women should become leaders in finding solutions that are woman friendly" (Sancier & Mapp, 1992, pp. 62–76).

But does this place another demand upon those who already are overburdened? Perhaps corporate America, with its preponderance of men in leadership roles, should assume this onerous responsibility. Redefining the care of older parents as societal, family, and workplace responsibilities is required.

Men also need to serve as caretakers. Currently when men address the needs of others, it is viewed as an expression of compassion; for women it constitutes an expected duty (Sancier & Mapp, 1992). By what unwritten law were women assigned to—and men excused from—serving as parental caretakers?

Governments and employers should consider family-friendly policies that enable both men and women to effectively address the needs of elderly parents. The Family and Medical Leave Act of 1993 constitutes a noteworthy step in the right direction. Public and private employers with fifty or more employees are required to offer family or medical leave when an employee or family member experiences serious illness or for maternity-related reasons (Marx, 2004, p. 152). However, although employers are mandated to continue health care benefits, workers using family leave are not required to be paid. When considering the higher earning power of men in our country, one can readily understand why many couples opt to have the woman take a leave of absence.

MIDDLE-AGED MEN

Because of the uneven balance of socioeconomic power between men and women, men are able to be more selective with regard to participation in basic roles: marriage, work, and the care of dependents. As seen daily in the workplace, men exert greater influence than women in defining social scripts and in the enactment of roles.

We do not suggest that middle adulthood is uneventful for men. In this life stage, they may experience divorce, career changes, and the redefining of relationships with children and parents. New relationships are traumatic and life-changing for men as well as for women. A major difference, however, is that men often have more resources to effect role changes.

Predominantly white, middle-aged men are the investors, writers, producers, and directors in the drama of life in America. Scripts and roles are developed to serve the purposes and desires of those in power, and when this does not occur, the scripts are rewritten or recast.

Many employers in the United States have established affirmative action policies for hiring. Frequently, affirmative action officers implement and monitor these practices. It is interesting, however, to view the employment process when executive-level positions such as chief executive officers, vice presidents, and general managers are selected.

Often, company presidents and boards of trustees create special rules for executive-level hires. The rules are often cloaked in a spirit of urgency and secrecy requiring immediate action. Because there is an assumption that few people are qualified for such major positions, decisions are made "confidentially."

In these "special cases," the affirmative action officer may be informed by the board or president of the intent to circumvent normal hiring practices. In fact, such exceptions are often explicitly authorized in an affirmative action policy manual. The result is that the president hires "his man" and the good old boy system remains intact. Women as well as other minorities identify in this system a well-polished and maintained glass ceiling. Notable exceptions in recent years include newly elected female presidents of Michigan State University and University of Michigan. Condoleeza Rice as Secretary of State is also a reminder that exceptions exist, particularly in high profile positions.

Those who have followed affirmative action employment guidelines over the years understand the closed door discourse in these situations. The justification for such decisions may include: "We have known and respected Jeffrey for years, and we know he is a good man." "I hear he is ready for a change, especially since his recent divorce." "This promotion would provide John with new opportunities in a different city, and he's someone we can count on!"

Like those who can influence the casting of prime parts in productions, men have traditionally helped each other by making a few phone calls to important people involved in hiring processes. They are also known to provide buddies with opportune introductions to assist in their job hunting. Men who have developed various connections over the years are in a position to call in favors to assist in their midlife transitions and those of their associates. Conversely, women who divorce in middle age often have fewer influential contacts and must approach the process as if they are starting over (Hayes, Anderson, & Blau, 1993, p. 104).

While men can claim certain advantages from role changes in middle adulthood, following divorce they do not fare as well in their relationships with adult children. Findings by Cooney and Uhlenberg indicate:

> Divorce has a pronounced negative effect on the frequency of men's contacts with their adult offspring, significantly reduces the likelihood that men have an adult child in their household, and sharply reduces the probability that fathers consider their adult children as potential sources of support in times of need. (1990, p. 677)

So although middle-aged men may find change relatively easy, the consequences in relationships with their children may be profound. Though middle-aged men in our society appear capable of generating appreciable influence over the definition and enactment of various social roles, after divorce they may find it hard to maintain satisfactory contact with their children, especially after remarriage.

| ## ECONOMICS, EMPLOYMENT, AND WOMEN

Mrs. Pamela Stern is employed as a social worker at the Western Hills Office of Mental Health Services, Inc. (MHSI). Located in the western suburbs of a large metropolitan city, the Western Hills office offers a wide range of community mental health and family services.

Several years ago, two utility companies, a clothing retail group, and a large department store chain began a contractual arrangement with MHSI to address problems faced by employees: family issues, day care, worker alienation, mental health concerns, substance abuse, and retirement planning. Following the program's success, fifteen other companies and businesses have established agreements with MHSI for employee assistance services.

Pamela's caseload is evenly divided between referrals from the community and contracted businesses. Her major responsibility involves intervention with individuals and families.

Mrs. Jean Royer, a 53-year-old employee of the department store chain that is in the contract group, approached Pamela for help. Jean has had over 15 years of experience with the company, first as a secretary and later as a clerical supervisor. Recently, as the result of a restructuring of personnel in the company, Jean was promoted to support staff manager at their regional corporate headquarters.

Given a small monetary increase and a new title, Jean originally was pleased with her promotion. The leap from an hourly job to a more prestigious position—with a salary increase at this stage of life—was exciting. Soon, however, Jean became discouraged with her work situation and how it had altered her life.

Jean recently discovered that the company is engaged in a 12-month plan aimed at "right sizing" the labor force. One element of the plan is a 15 percent reduction in the secretarial staff. This change is to be accomplished by arranging secretaries into centralized secretarial pools, one of which Jean administers.

Now a part of management, Jean feels overwhelmed with company secretarial demands. The workload created by laying off 15 percent of the secretaries has become excessive. Jean averages 50- to 55-hour workweeks as she continues to do her part in the secretarial pool. Because she is now a salaried employee, her male superiors expect her to shoulder responsibility for job completion in secretarial services. When approached about the situation, Jean's boss stated, "Welcome to management. You will have to learn how to handle long days and nights."

Jean's relationship with her husband, Fred, began to suffer as a direct result of her promotion. The couple is contributing toward their son's college tuition and board. Although her small pay increase is useful, Jean is more interested in having time with Fred and in seeking new hobbies, interests, and relationships. Jean finds that her excessive hours affect quantity and quality of time spent with Fred. Originally supportive of Jean's promotion, Fred has expressed increasing frustration over the new position.

TIME TO THINK!

As a social worker at MHSI, Pamela performs several professional roles. She is an individual and family therapist as well as a consultant and advocate for planned change in organizations.

For funding, MHSI depends heavily upon service contract arrangements with local businesses in the community. Given the agency's financial reliance and the presenting situation, what ethical considerations emerge for Pamela in assessing macro-level systems? Can Pamela be objective in her assessment of Jean's presenting situation, knowing that Jean's employer contributes to an important MHSI contract? Is being a female social worker an advantage or disadvantage for Pamela?

Macro Systems, Middle Adulthood, and Gender

As you have likely surmised, a major premise in this chapter is that midlife experiences for women and men are significantly different. Considering organizational, community, societal, and global factors, examine the relevance of gender in this case example. Would males find themselves in this kind of dilemma? Why or why not?

Organizational Level Because of her tenure with the company, Jean has expressed an interest in exploring change from within the system rather than resigning her position. Pamela has collected information describing the organization's structure, job descriptions, employment policies, and procedures, as well as employee rights as described in the department store's newly revised personnel manual. As the department store is nonunion, a labor relations specialist is available through MHSI to assist in assessing procedural and legal aspects involved in realigning the department store's labor force.

Over the years, Jean has been troubled by the demeaning manner in which women are viewed and treated in the company. Expectations of long work hours are often accompanied by low pay and minimal recognition of individual skills or needs. Many company officials see women in supportive positions as secretaries, clerks, cleaning people, and food-service workers, but rarely in leadership roles. Jean's promotion confirmed her perceptions when it became apparent that support staff managers possessed little power and were not invited to attend management meetings or functions.

It seems that these attitudes can be traced to the founder of the company. His son will assume the leadership upon his father's retirement. It is believed that his view of women in the company is even less progressive than that of his father. This is cause for concern because nearly all of the current executives are men.

Community Level The client in this example lives in the western suburbs of a Great Lakes city. Once a thriving, heavy-industry and automobile manufacturing center, the city's economy has suffered greatly as a result of decreased production in the manufacturing sector.

continued

CASE EXAMPLE | *continued*

The downtown area of this city has been decimated by business failures. Plagued by high unemployment and crime, many major businesses and stores have moved to the suburbs for survival. However, even there, opportunities for people seeking long-term employment are very limited. In many instances, employers can select employees from a large and stable labor pool. Those who have steady employment are made to feel fortunate.

Jean and other employees have heard rumors that the department store might relocate its regional corporate headquarters to another city, but the recent office reorganization suggests that these reports, for the time being, are inaccurate.

Employment opportunities for women around the city are primarily service and clerical or staff support positions. Additionally, the marketplace for these openings is highly competitive. If Jean were to leave the department store and pursue another job in the community, she would likely lose credit for her years of experience and find it necessary to accept a lower-paying, less prestigious position.

A recent survey funded by Working Women, a local advocacy group, confirms a high degree of worker alienation among women in the area. The department store chain appears to treat female employees as second-class workers as do other employers in the city.

Societal Level When changes occur in employment and earnings because of recessions and the loss of manufacturing jobs, such as those experienced in the now famous Rust Belt of the United States, women often seek and assume stronger economic roles (Zippay, 1994). As they take on a greater share of the financial support of their families, many women feel trapped into taking and maintaining jobs that are unfulfilling and represent underemployment (Briar, 1988). Particularly in times of economic downturn, women feel pressured to take positions with little power and limited opportunity for advancement.

Nationally, businesses are driven by the dual goals of increasing earnings and survival. Fierce competition exists among department store chains in the United States. Corporate managers in this field are granted promotions and bonuses for devising

---

Gay Men and Lesbian Women: Middle Age and Parenthood

Gays and lesbians face many forms of institutional and social discrimination both with family members and at work. However, in middle age many people feel compelled to make a last attempt at parenthood. This can be a special concern for gays and lesbians as from an "institutional perspective, same-sex couples and individual homosexuals do not have the same civil and legal rights as do heterosexuals" (DePoy & Noble, 1992, p. 49). Parenthood is a role our society has been unwilling to accord to gays and lesbians in a just manner. Holleran gives some insight to this complex issue:

> In middle age, everything you see appears in a different light. Fathers and sons included. In middle age, not only do you hear Time's winged chariot hurrying near,

less costly ways of producing greater revenue. A focus on increased profits with minimal concern for human rights and fairness has become a norm. In order to cut costs, department stores have learned to rely heavily on a disposable labor force of low-paid employees. Except at the very top of the corporate ladder, long-term commitment and loyalty to a company have given way to cost containment strategies.

Middle-aged women are particularly vulnerable to employment exploitation. Like many other women in America, Jean senses that she is unappreciated and feels manipulated by her bosses. Quitting would only allow the company to hire a younger, less experienced, and lower-paid person as her replacement. It would be a difficult challenge after age 50 to find employment with equal benefits.

International Level Several important international themes appear in this case example. International trade and industry have affected the client system in several distinct ways. The loss of jobs and commerce in automobile-related industries—a result of the success of foreign imports—has clearly contributed to the economic downturn in this Great Lakes city. Employers know jobs are scarce and take full advantage of the deluge of applicants in their hiring and employment practices.

Competition among department store chains has also been fueled by foreign rivalry. The introduction of hypermarkets by international investors has created a revolution in the industry. By hiring low-cost workers, the hypermarket stores have forced American competitors to rethink employee relations and methods for delivering service. On more than one occasion, Jean has been told that, given the competitive nature of the marketplace, restructuring the regional office is necessary for economic survival.

"Gender bias in occupational distribution and pay is also a worldwide phenomenon" (Nichols-Casebolt, Krysik, & Hermann-Currie, 1994). The labor of women is exploited throughout the globe. In order to undercut prices, companies in less-developed nations often pay women and children shockingly low wages to produce products for American markets. If women in industrialized regions have not been adequately involved in business decisions, women in developing countries have few, if any, rights with regard to shaping their roles in employment.

you also catch the shrill ring of that biological alarm clock mentioned in articles about women wondering if they should have children before it's too late. It rings, I suspect, with decreasing volume, for the rest of one's life. But it never quite stops. If, as Carlyle wrote, the answer to life is either Yes or No, then the answer to "Will I have children?" is equally stark. There are no in-betweens: nieces, nephews, friends' children can be pleasures, but no answer. . . . So you wanna have a baby? I know gay men who have had children and are very proud of them; gay men who are ashamed of theirs (because they left their children, after the divorce which followed their coming out); gay men thrilled to be not associated with kids; and gay men patiently walking their dogs through Washington Square who think deep down that the one thing that would have made them happiest in life is—children. (Holleran, 1989, p. 3)

One of the more depressing aspects of stage life for any actor involves lead roles never played. Knowing that one could have played the part, but was never cast for it, is disheartening.

Most of us in the field of social work acknowledge that discrimination, whether a result of sexual orientation, gender, race, socioeconomic status, or any combination of elements, is a powerful force in American culture. For middle-aged people, it may be a harsh realization that discrimination was the basis for never acquiring one or more of the desirable lead roles in life.

REFLECTION ON DIVERSITY: RELIGION AND SPIRITUALITY

Frequently, social workers conceptualize diversity in practice in terms of gender, race, ethnicity, sexual orientation, social-economic status, age, disability, geographical region, subculture, and religion. While it is useful to organize and categorize diversity using these distinctions, human diversity in social work intervention is a complex and encompassing concept that merits consideration beyond the use of classification systems.

For example, a thorough analysis of diversity in the context of practice often reveals several diverse forms existing concurrently. The ability of social workers to work with clients and sort out the relevant social conditions and factors that contribute to the social situation is crucial. Seeing the big picture as it relates to presenting circumstances typically necessitates a clear vision of the influence of various shapes of diversity on the lives of consumers of social services.

As suggested earlier in this chapter, the marriage relationship and marital roles are commonly reevaluated during middle age. When engaged in marriage and family counseling, Wolf and Stevens (2001) offer religion and spirituality as valid considerations. **Religion** implies shared values and beliefs concerning a supreme being (e.g., God) that includes a religious community. **Spirituality** may be more expansive and yet more personal and can include notions involving a life-giving or essential force without specific reference to a supreme being. Important for social work practice, both religion and spirituality emphasize values and beliefs as well as a sense of meaning in life. When working with couples, "the therapist should simply be open to the values and beliefs of the family" (p. 72). In assessing the social environment, the social worker should not only entertain religion as a salient factor, but should ask clients to "share, explore, and perhaps draw on their beliefs" when considering change strategies (p. 74).

Sabloff (2002) suggests that many professionals recognize and favor the use of spirituality and religion in helping processes but often neglect to do so. She theorizes that helping professionals may lack the appropriate background and training needed "to understand how or to what extent religion strengthens families" (p. 46).

We live in an era where various world religions—Christianity, Judaism, Islam, Hinduism, and Buddhism, to name a few—have an increasingly powerful impact on American culture. The war in Iraq and turbulence in the Middle East have brought religious differences and tensions to the forefront of media and American thought. Imagine for a moment the complexities associated with attempting to understand any one religion with its associated denominations or factions. Consider how the beliefs from any one religion influence role expectations for women, men, racial or ethnic groups.

Research conducted by Carolan and Allen (1999) suggests that when working with African-American couples during midlife, religion and commitment to faith "provide a foundation for familial and intimate relationships and mediate the constraints of aging and racism" (p. 3). In their sample, results indicated that: "Religiosity permeated every aspect of the participants' lives, their commitment to one another, their attitudes about men and women, and their regard for family and community" (p. 9). Ardent religious commitments were deemed to be very valuable in empowering African-American couples to address the various demands associated with midlife and in confronting barriers presented as a result of race (p. 8).

The work of Carolan and Allen (1999) provides an excellent illustration of how a comprehensive understanding of diversity often involves several factors (e.g., age, race, and religion). Developmental issues associated with any life cycle phase or stage are susceptible to a variety of social influences. When considering human diversity and the effect of macro systems on human behavior, it is important to develop and refine skills for scanning and exploring the strengths and limitations of various forms of diversity. This can be an arduous task for helping professionals. Hurdle (2002) suggests that recognition of the strengths of people and communities (e.g., on the basis of race or religion) may necessitate "interpreters or cultural mediators to ensure that communication is fully understandable" (p. 190).

APPLYING A SOCIAL WORK FRAMEWORK: ROLE THEORY

We introduced this chapter with a brief examination of the life of George Lopez. As busy professionals in the field of entertainment, George and Ann Lopez are presented with the dilemma of how to juggle their roles and responsibilities as workers, spouses, and parents. Using role theory, an analogy was drawn between life and the stage. The Lopezes were viewed as actors in a play, each performing parts written in social scripts.

In the case example, role theory was the underlying theme used to identify factors influencing the creation of a workplace script and the enactment of occupational and family roles. Unlike successful entertainers, Pamela's client, Jean Royer, has far less power and control in defining her work environment.

As an actor on a stage, Jean finds herself cast in a role created and interpreted by male directors. Several unique factors have given store executives freedom and options to write, cast, and direct this department store drama. A male-oriented business, a city experiencing economic decline, and employment needs in a highly competitive industry present a challenging plot to be resolved. Feeling powerless, Jean seeks ways to alter the organizational pattern that defines her role and those of her coworkers.

In this situation, Pamela plays a vital part. As an agent of change in a contract-for-service agency, she must approach problems with an awareness of a multitude of systems, including the individual, family, organization, community, and society. Attending to immediate needs, Pamela has initiated both individual and family intervention for Jean. However, because Pamela has established a close and trusting relationship with Jean and also has the respect of business leaders who contract for MHSI services, she is well-positioned to suggest ways that will reshape Jean's role in the company. Each of these strategies is an important consideration, but as we focus on macro changes, let us look at what Pamela may be able to do.

Several macro issues are apparent to Pamela as she repeatedly hears female employees complain of oppressive working conditions. Women are routinely subjected to subservient work roles and scripts written and produced by men. Lack of flexibility in the work arena produces severe psychological stress and family dysfunction and requires attention through policy formation/development and social legislation.

At a macro level, Pamela will explore the feasibility of a flexible time program and will introduce a team decision-making model at Jean's workplace. Pamela is also on the planning committee for a local Women and Work Conference. She has asked Jean to organize a workshop to examine dilemmas experienced by women in entry-level management positions.

Garvin and Tropman stress that "coalition building, establishing networks, developing data bases, and engaging in various kinds of public relations and societal information activities set the stage for societal change and become an important component of it" (1992, p. 205). Pamela is committed to individual and family intervention as well as to seeking ways to resolve differences between her client and business leaders at the department store chain. She is committed to working with her clients in groups and individually to explore ways to eliminate sexism, ageism, worker alienation, and other forms of oppression against middle-aged women in the marketplace.

SUGGESTED ACTIVITIES

1. Many professors and university administrators are middle-aged. As a class, examine the leadership positions at your school in relationship to gender. What percentage of full professors are women? Check your college catalog. Identify factors contributing to the ratio of women to men in higher rank and leadership positions. Ask a female professor for her opinion as to how advancement through the rank-tenure process differs for women and men.

2. Develop a class debate. Argue the merits of the "bring-your-daughter-to-work day" as a means of sensitizing girls to work roles. Is this practice outdated or useful? When should children learn about discrimination and power in the labor force? Could "bring-your-daughter-to-work day" be used as a forum by parents to examine themes of diversity in the workplace?

3. Ask a friend or a group of friends about the merits and benefits of middle age. Structure questions around positive changes that middle-aged people have experienced, both individually and as a group. Ask your group to share their thoughts concerning the impact of religion or spirituality on their lives.

References

Amato, P. (2000). The consequences of divorce for adults and children. *Journal of Marriage and the Family, 62,* 1269–1287.

Barnett, R., Biener, L., & Baruch, G. (1987). *Gender and stress.* New York: Free Press.

Bee, H., & Bjorklund, B. (2004). *The journey of adulthood.* Upper Saddle River, NJ: Pearson Prentice Hall.

Biddle, B., & Thomas, E. (1966). *Role theory: Concepts and research.* New York: John Wiley.

Blaker, K. (2000). Celebrating fifty. In D. Sattler, G. Kramer, V. Shabatay, & D. Bernstein (Eds.), *Lifespan development in context: Voices and perspectives.* Boston: Houghton Mifflin.

Bogolub, E. (1991). Women and midlife divorce: Some practice issues. *Social Work, 36,* 428–433.

Briar, K. (1988). *Social work and the unemployed.* Silver Spring, MD: National Association of Social Workers.

Brody, E., & Schoonover, C. (1986). Patterns of parental care when adult daughters work and when they do not. *Gerontologist, 26,* 372–381.

Bumpass, L., Sweet, J., & Castro Martin, T. (1990). Changing patterns of remarriage. *Journal of Marriage and the Family, 52,* 747–756.

Carolan, M., & Allen, K. (1999). Commitments and constraints to intimacy for African-American couples at midlife. *Journal of Family Issues, 20,* 3–24.

Cherlin, A. (1992). *Marriage, divorce, remarriage.* Cambridge, MA: Harvard University Press.

Coleman, J., & Kerbo, H. (2003). *Social problems: A brief introduction.* Upper Saddle River, NJ: Pearson Prentice Hall.

Cooney, T., & Uhlenberg, P. (1990). The role of divorce in men's relations with their adult children after midlife. *Journal of Marriage and the Family, 52,* 677–688.

DePoy, E., & Noble, S. (1992). The structure of lesbian relationships in response to oppression. *Affllia, 7,* 49–64.

Dziegielewski, S., Heymann, C., Green, C., & Gichia, J. (2002). Midlife changes: Utilizing a social work perspective. *Journal of Human Behavior in the Social Environment, 6,* 65–86.

Friedan, B. (1993). *The fountain of age.* New York: Simon & Schuster.

Garvin, C., & Tropman, J. (1992). *Social work in contemporary society.* Englewood Cliffs, NJ: Prentice-Hall.

Gibelman, M. (2003). So how far have we come? Pestilent and persistent gender gap in pay. *Social Work, 48,* 22–32.

Gibelman, M., & Schervish, P. (1997). *Who we are: A second look.* Washington, DC: National Association of Social Workers.

Gilbert, L. (1988). *Sharing it all: The rewards and struggles of two-career families.* New York: Plenum.

Gilbert, L. (1993). Women in midlife: Current theoretical perspectives and research. In N. Davis, E. Cole, & E. Rothblum (Eds.), *Faces of women and aging.* New York: Hawthorne Press.

Goffman, E. (1959). *The presentation of self in everyday life.* Garden City, NY: Doubleday Anchor.

Hayes, C., Anderson, D., & Blau, M. (1993). A startling report on women and divorce. *Ladies' Home Journal, 110,* 98–106.

Heaton, G., & Blake, A. (1999). Gender differences in determinant of marital disruption. *Journal of Family Issues, 20,* 25–45.

Holden, K., & Smock, P. (1991). The economic costs of marriage disruption: Why do women bear a disproportionate cost? *Annual Review of Sociology, 17,* 51–78.

Holleran, A. (1989). Time's scythe. *Christopher Street, 5,* 3–5.

Horsburgh, S., & Wang, C. (2002). Pool sharp: Factory-worker-turned-comic George Lopez dives into his own life to create his hit ABC sitcom. *People Weekly, 58,* 129.

Hunter, S., & Sundel, M. (1994). Midlife for women: A new perspective. *Affilia, 9,* 113–128.

Hurdle, D. (2002). Native Hawaiian traditional healing: Culturally based interventions for social work practice. *Social Work, 47,* 183–192.

Keith, K., & Malone, P. (2005). Housework and the wages of young, middle-aged, and older workers. *Contemporary Economic Policy, 23,* 224–241.

Kreider, R., & Fields, J. (2002). *Number, timing, and duration of marriages and divorces: 1996* (Current Population Reports, P70–80). Washington, DC: U.S. Census Bureau.

Lee, L. (2004). Sitcom star George Lopez reflects on humble beginnings. *Knight Ridder/Tribune,* May 3.

Lesser, J., O'Neill, M., Burke, K., Scanlon, P., Hollis, K., & Miller, R. (2004). Women supporting women: A mutual aid group fosters new connections among women in midlife, *Social Work with Groups, 27,* 75–89.

Marx, J. (2004). *Social welfare: The American partnership.* Boston: Pearson Allyn & Bacon.

McKeever, M., & Wolfinger, N. (2001). Reexamining the economic costs of marital disruption for women. *Social Science Quarterly, 82,* 202–217.

McQuaide, S. (1998). Women at midlife. *Social Work, 43,* 21–31.

Moen, P. (1991). Transitions in midlife: Women's work and family roles in the 1970s. *Journal of Marriage and the Family, 53,* 135–150.

Neugarten, B. (1970). Dynamics of transition of middle age to old age. *Journal of Geriatric Psychiatry, 4,* 71–87.

Nichols-Casebolt, A., Krysik, J., & Hermann-Currie, R. (1994). The povertization of women: A global phenomenon. *Affilia, 9,* 9–29.

People Weekly. (2005). The greatest gift: With his kidneys failing, sitcom star George Lopez got a transplant from the person closest to him—his wife, *63,* 83.

Peterson, B., & Klohnen, E. (1995). Realization of generativity in two samples of women at midlife. *Psychology and Aging, 10,* 20–29.

PR Newswire. (2004). Actor-comedian George Lopez joins "smartest card" library campaign, October 4.

Raphael, D., & Schlesinger, B. (1994). Women in the sandwich generation: Do adult children living at home help? *Journal of Women and Aging, 6,* 21–45.

Sabloff, J. (2002). The role of religion and spirituality in marriage and family therapy. *Journal of Pastoral Counseling, 37,* 45–49.

Sancier, B., & Mapp, P. (1992). Who helps working women care for the young and the old? *Affilia, 7,* 61–76.

Shapiro, A. (1996). Explaining psychological distress in a sample of remarried and divorced persons. *Journal of Family Issues, 17,* 186–203.

Spitze, G., & Logan, J. (1990). More evidence on women (and men) in the middle. *Research on Aging, 12,* 182–198.

Strean, H. (1967). Role theory, role models, and casework: Review of literature and practice applications. *Social Work, 12,* 77–87.

Turner, J. (1974). *The structure of sociological theory.* Homewood IL: The Dorsey Press.

Updike, J. (1960). *Rabbit, run.* New York: Knopf.

Walker, R., Logan, T., Jordan, C., & Campbell, J. (2004). An integrative review of separation in the context of victimization: Consequences and implications for women. *Trauma, Violence, and Abuse, 5,* 143–193.

Weitzman, L. (1988). Women and children last: The social and economic consequences of divorce law reforms. In S. Dornbush & M. Strober (Eds.), *Feminism, children, and the new families.* New York: Guilford Press.

Wolf, C., & Stevens, P. (2001). Integrating religion and spirituality in marriage and family counseling. *Counseling and Values, 46,* 66–75.

Zippay, A. (1994). The role of working-class women in a changing economy. *Affilia, 9,* 30–44.

8 CHAPTER | LATER ADULTHOOD

Tools in hand, roof tiles tucked under his arm, the retired chief executive of the nation startled America as he clambered over roof peaks. As a volunteer builder of homes for the poor, this man has modeled the use of resources and skills of the older adult.

Former President Jimmy Carter epitomizes the potential and integrity of America's seniors. The media continues to picture President Carter and his wife, Rosalynn, as hands-on builders for Habitat for Humanity and as ambassadors negotiating peace in troubled areas of the globe.

In dedicating his book of poems, *Always a Reckoning* (1995), Jimmy Carter reveals the roots of his post-White House activities:

> To my mother, Lillian, who never let racial segregation, loss of loved ones, ravages of age, or any other principalities or powers stop her sharing what she had or was with the least of those she knew. . . . (vii)

We begin this chapter with our observations of the present Jimmy Carter rather than the President Jimmy Carter. In the image of his mother, James Earl Carter has refused to be defined as inept and "over the hill." To the disappointment of Carter detractors, he refuses to be relegated to the shadows in his later years. Although no longer the leader of our nation, Jimmy Carter rejects the premise that a retired person loses value in his or her later years.

Now, as a former president and senior citizen, Jimmy Carter is known for his peacemaking activities in such troubled sites as Central America, North

Korea, Haiti, and Bosnia. He has become a college professor and author and is deeply involved in policy analysis at the Carter Center. He is respected internationally for his peacemaking and humanitarian efforts. Some suggest that Jimmy Carter should be recognized as the United States' most outstanding president.

In many respects, Jimmy and Rosalynn Carter feel fortunate. In *Everything to Gain: Making the Most of the Rest of Your Life,* their coauthored book, they say:

> What we had come to realize as "retired" people is that we have a lot more leeway than ever before to choose our own path, to establish our own priorities. We had a lifetime of training and experiences on which to base these decisions, and our financial resources would be adequate to meet our needs. We had nothing to lose in whatever we did and everything to gain. (1987, p. 33)

These words come from a one-term First Family that was devastated upon losing its reelection bid to Ronald Reagan. Rosalynn Carter recalled, "There was no way I could understand our defeat. It didn't seem fair that everything we had hoped for, all our plans and dreams for the country could have been gone when the votes were counted on Election Day" (1987, p. 9).

After losing the election, they could have left the White House and returned to Plains, Georgia, to live in isolation and bitterness. Instead, the Carters refocused their energies. They became involved by helping others both domestically and internationally.

As exemplified by the presidential couple, older age can be a time for growth, new adventures, and the opportunity to make a difference in the lives of others. When wisdom and experience are used in voluntary service, older people often gain a newfound sense of enrichment and self-worth. Schools, libraries, hospitals, social service agencies, businesses, and other community organizations benefit from the helping hand of senior citizens in America.

Older adults often struggle with their place in society. They are led to believe that their usefulness and competency have passed. However, the potentials of older adults are underdeveloped in the United States. Active community and societal participation by senior citizens not only contributes to our nation, but enables seniors to maintain personal competencies and acquire social power.

How the story of a peanut farmer from Georgia ends and how historians note him is yet to be determined. However, how Jimmy Carter wishes to be remembered is clear.

In "A Committee of Scholars Describe the Future Without Me," Jimmy Carter wrote,

> Some shy professors, forced to write
> about a time that's bound to come
> when my earthly life is done

described my ultimate demise
in lovely euphemistic words
invoking pleasant visions of
burial rites, with undertakers,
friends, kinfolks, and pious pastors
gathered round my flowery casket
eyes uplifted
breaking new semantic ground
by not just saying
I have passed on
joined my maker
or gone to the Promised Land
but stating the lamented fact
in the best and gentlest terms
that I, now dead, have recently
    reduced my level of participation. (1995, p. 25)

Source: From *Always a Reckoning and Other Poems*, by Jimmy Carter., copyright © 1995 by Jimmy Carter. Illustrations copyright © 1995 by Sarah Elizabeth Chuldenko. Used by permission of Time Books, a division of Random House, Inc.

THEORY: SOCIAL RECONSTRUCTION

So far we have selected and applied general sociological theories to each developmental time period. However, in this chapter we describe **social reconstruction theory,** an orientation specific to older age.

The basic tenets of social reconstruction theory are found in Kuypers and Bengtson's (1973) analysis of social breakdown and competence in older age (p. 182). They suggest that, as a result of social reorganization that occurs in later life, older people are devalued and develop negative self-images.

Older adults typically experience the loss of occupational roles and established social networks. As this loss occurs, they receive feedback from others that they are less needed and less valued. In this way, older people are stripped of their dignity and opportunities to productively use knowledge and abilities they have spent a lifetime developing.

Rice (1995) defines social reconstruction theory as "a theory of aging describing how society reduces the self-concept of the aged, and proposing ways to reverse this negative cycle" (p. 635). He identifies the following four steps:

1. *Our society brings about role loss,* offers only sparse normative information and guidance, and deprives the elderly of reference groups, so that they lose the sense of who they are and what their roles are.
2. *Society then labels them negatively* as incompetent and deficient.
3. *Society deprives them of opportunities* to use their skills, which atrophy in the process.

4. *The aged accept the external labeling,* identify themselves as inadequate, and begin to act as they are expected to act, setting the stage for another spiral. (p. 635)

Most sociological theories provide only an analytical framework for gaining insight about social phenomena, but social reconstruction theory proposes three considerations to help end social breakdown during older age. Kuypers and Bengtson (1973) suggest that on a macro level society members should reflect upon:

1. **Defining personal competence as successful role performance.** A person's worth in our society is disproportionately weighted in relationship to one's performance in economically productive roles—work. When an older person retires, self worth suffers. What alternatives exist for defining personal worth? While recognizing that a shift in values is no simple task, greater emphasis on wisdom, experience, creativity, and volunteerism as a personal basis for assigning worth would benefit older adults.
2. **Defining competency in terms of capacity to adapt to change.** Various helping professions have a rich tradition of providing clinical services to assist older people in adapting to environmental change. However, the competency of older adults should not be judged solely on their ability to adapt and to provide for themselves. When society helps assure adequate health care, housing, and financial security, senior citizens are freed to pursue personal meaning and expression in later life, as in the case of Jimmy and Rosalynn Carter.
3. **The ability of older adults to exert control.** People in older age are susceptible to losing control over their lives. Senior citizens must be empowered to be decision makers regarding the social policies and programs that affect them and their positions in life. Self-worth in older age can be directly equated to the ability to maintain power and engage in self-determination. (pp. 194–198)

To summarize, social reconstruction theory provides social workers with a perspective for assessing planned change at the societal level that will benefit older adults. These general themes include focusing on ways to reduce the importance of work and encourage alternative activities as sources of self-worth; promote societal responsibility for health care, housing, financial status, public transportation, and other social services for older adults; and empower senior citizens to establish self-rule.

Recent research conducted by Warr, Butcher, Robertson, and Callinan (2004) in Britain underscores the importance of the ability of older adults to exercise role preference, especially in relationship to employment and retirement. People tend to be happier when they experience a degree of control over their lives. This can be particularly true in older age. Participants reported enhanced feelings of well-being when they felt comfortable and fulfilled in their current role. The ability to exercise power and control over one's role in life appears critical.

DEVELOPMENTAL ISSUES

Old age is viewed negatively and stigmatized by many in our society. Loss of independence, physical health, sexual appetite, activity level, employment, and financial security are reported in the literature as common problems for senior citizens.

Ageism, that is, prejudice and discrimination against older adults, continues to be experienced by a high proportion of those over 65. It may take the form of discrimination or bias in employment situations, forced retirement, substandard care in nursing homes, or restrictive attitudes toward sexuality. When society limits older adults to subsistence and maintenance goals, it contributes to a negative view of this age group.

Beryl Williamson, a 75-year-old ice skating instructor at Michigan State University, believed her age was a factor that kept her contract from being renewed. Though there is no required retirement age for contracted employees, she was replaced after 43 years of teaching. Her income dropped $12,000 without the contract renewal (Pena, 1996).

Sensitivity and interest concerning issues confronting people in older age have risen over the years as the number of senior citizens in our society continues to grow. As the post-World War II baby boomers age, it is estimated that by 2030 the number of people between the ages of 66 and 84 will have risen in the United States to 61 million (Knickman & Snell, 2002, p. 850). This is an important demographic projection. It suggests that in such an aging society more people are living longer and potentially healthier lives than ever before. Indeed, many Americans no longer view 65 as a benchmark for physical or mental decline.

Business leaders and government officials have learned to appreciate the over-65 group as vital constituents. When senior citizens organizations like the AARP (formerly the American Association of Retired Persons) speak, business leaders and politicians listen. AARP maintains a comprehensive website at www.aarp.org and provides publications covering a variety of topics such as consumer information, finances, health, and personal planning that inform members about important issues. AARP fosters and supports strong participation of seniors in relevant laws and policy making. Senior citizens constitute a powerful force in our society, united like no other age group.

Since 1950, there has been a White House Conference on Aging approximately every ten years. These have been used to inform government leaders of the needs of seniors. During the Reagan and Bush administrations, there was limited if any expansion of social service policies and no 1990 White House Conference on Aging (Cox, 1993, p. 315). To date, the most recent White House Conference on Aging was held in June, 2005. Using modern technology, many communities and social service organizations now participate in the White House Conference on Aging as well as other conferences dedicated to issues of aging from remote locations via teleconferencing capabilities.

As noted earlier, our review of macro-level developmental issues for later life is guided by social reconstruction theory. Consequently, the literature presented focuses on mechanisms for enhancing the image and integrity of older adults, as opposed to a description of the various physical and mental problems encountered during older age (Hancock, 1990).

SENIOR CITIZENS AS VOLUNTEERS

AARP's long-standing motto has been "to serve, not to be served." AARP's commitment to volunteering is offered as a means for helping others and as a model for keeping older adults connected and involved in communities across the nation.

As with Jimmy and Rosalynn Carter, senior citizens in general represent an inestimable resource for community and national service in the United States. Research by Gallagher (1994) indicates that when compared to younger adults, seniors do their fair share in volunteering time, particularly to the needy. Gallagher suggests that older adults help others in informal ways, providing emotional support during crises, supplying goods, or helping them cope with their daily problems. Assisting relatives as well as more public volunteering was found to be an important element in the lives of many older adults, especially older women.

Gallagher's findings refute the common belief that older adults disengage from social relationships and caring for others. "When it comes to hours of volunteering, specifically volunteering to help the needy, older men and women actually spend more time than do their younger counterparts, even when controlling for employment status" (Gallagher, 1994, p. 576). As health and energy permit, senior citizens are a rich source of volunteer assistance in many communities. While **disengagement theory** asserts that older age can be a time when people interact with fewer others and assume fewer roles in life (Cumming & Henry, 1961), clearly it is possible to choose and commit one's self to an active and engaged lifestyle that includes volunteerism during older age.

An older person's interest, aptitude, or willingness to serve as a volunteer or enact a particular role should be placed into a life span context. **Continuity theory** suggests that as people age, they learn and develop patterns of interaction with others in the social world (Atchley, 1989). "People maintain continuity in roles, personality, relationships, and activities, which helps them to adjust (or not) to aging" (Rogers, 2006, p. 322). Volunteerism and service to others are likely to endure into older age when such values have been nurtured early in life.

Several negative factors have to be considered, however, when using senior volunteers: racism, ageism, and sexism are subtle and often concealed in routine procedures within companies and agencies. Morrow-Howell, Lott, and Ozawa, for example, caution social workers that for senior citizens, while "race itself does not affect volunteer helping behavior . . . higher levels of contact and client satisfaction are reported when the volunteer and the client are of the same race" (1990, p. 395). They suggest that problems associated with using older adults as volunteers, including the impact of race, can be effectively addressed by professional instruction and support.

When social workers do more than troubleshoot by also giving professional training and supervision to elderly volunteers, they help provide structure, purpose, support, recognition, and meaning to volunteer activities. Seniors better serve others, and probably experience greater satisfaction, when social workers make a concerted effort to match volunteer with client and services rendered. A major role for social workers in these instances is to produce "successes." Successes are defined as effective delivery of volunteer services, enhancing the self-worth and integrity of the volunteer.

Just as President Clinton used Jimmy Carter's expertise to help establish peace in Haiti, social workers maximize the potential for success by utilizing volunteers' strengths. Perkins and Tice (1995) remind us that older adults and clients share an important common thread: they are survivors. Both long for control and independence in daily living. Social workers must become stockholders in volunteerism, continually assessing ways to build upon strengths and to enhance the value of clients, volunteers, and the helping enterprise.

The potential rewards associated with being a volunteer can be many. Greenfield and Marks (2004) suggest that when older adults become formal volunteers they report a higher degree of positive affect and can experience renewed feelings of purpose in life. Other research suggests that the issue of time is an important motivator for older volunteers as volunteering constitutes a means to remain active and keep busy (Kovacs & Black, 1999). Because social workers frequently encounter older adults with valuable life experiences, it is important for social workers to be knowledgeable and skillful in recruiting volunteers and retaining their expertise and service for use in social service organizations (Kovacs & Black, 1999).

To optimize successes and retain elderly volunteers, Fischer and Schaffer provide five important suggestions.

1. Selective recruitment, or matching volunteers with appropriate assignments and screening out people who are likely to be uncommitted volunteers.
2. Careful monitoring of new volunteers can help avert the post-honeymoon blues effect during the first few months of volunteering.
3. To maintain the commitment of volunteers, it is important to offer intrinsic rewards—that is, jobs that are challenging, interesting, and important.
4. A critical factor in sustaining the commitment of volunteers is to provide for successful experiences.
5. Friendship is an important factor in volunteer commitment. (1993, p. 205)

While older adults should be thought of as potential volunteers in various ways, a body of research demonstrates their usefulness with regard to peer education and counseling. Shannon and colleagues (1983), for example, found success in recruiting and training older adults as peer educators in a nutrition-awareness program. Similarly, Hoffman (1983) described her program for peer counseling with the elderly. Goodman (1984) reported the merits of the "helper bank" in which older people enter reciprocal arrangements to assist each other.

Given the involvement of the elderly in volunteering, one wonders why senior citizens are not more adequately acknowledged and rewarded for their activities. The successful Retired and Senior Volunteer Program (RSVP), active in most large communities, provides a model for appreciating seniors while society benefits from well-structured services. Better recognition of their efforts could be instrumental in reshaping the image of senior citizens from dependent recipients of care to healthy and involved citizens.

Unfortunately, older adult volunteers are rarely viewed as having an integral position in society. Is this because volunteer work, compared to paid employment, is not highly valued? Are seniors expected to become volunteers simply because they have extra time?

Three perspectives identified in the literature suggest why seniors should volunteer. Using these views, it is important to pay special attention to how older people are depicted. Is there an emphasis, explicit or implied, on work-role loss? How are older people characterized or stigmatized with regard to their skills and capabilities? Are older volunteers viewed with dignity or as has-beens?

> The **inoculation perspective suggests that** keeping active (and doing good) is "good" for the elderly; that is, older people who are active are happier and healthier than older people who are withdrawn or "disengaged." Thus volunteer work can inoculate, or protect, the older person from the hazards of retirement, physical decline, and inactivity.
>
> The **debit perspective** reflects a contemporary economic concern—that older people are a drain on society, that the elderly have received special privileges and benefits from policies and programs based on age rather than need, and that there are too many of them. . . . Thus, when older persons serve . . . they potentially are reducing the drain on public funds from other elderly in need.
>
> The third perspective, the **leisure perspective**, is different from the other two. This perspective defines volunteerism as a form of leisure activity. Retired persons, under this rubric, are consumers. Volunteer work is their choice; if it is enjoyable and meaningful to them, then maybe they will choose to participate in volunteer activities. (Fischer & Schaffer, 1993, pp. 3–11)

These orientations are disturbing and problematic as they depict public opinion of older adults and volunteerism. From the inoculation perspective, emphasis is not placed on the contributions of elderly volunteers, but volunteerism is cast as an activity primarily benefiting seniors. From the debit perspective, "the idea that older persons have a special debt to society to compensate for the burdens they are imposing is ethically troublesome" (Fischer & Schaffer, 1993, p. 10). Finally, the leisure perspective gives no credence to "the special nature of volunteer service and suggests that volunteerism is no more (or not much more) important than playing bridge or tennis, in terms of its social impact" (Fischer & Schaffer, 1993, p. 11).

Older adults who volunteer deserve respect and credit for their humanitarian efforts. Over two decades ago, AARP constructed a Bill of Rights as a means to promote volunteerism as a recognized, valued, and dignified enterprise for older adults. Many of these tenets and rights continue to be valid and useful considerations.

BILL OF RIGHTS

The Right to be treated as a co-worker—not just free help.

The Right to suitable assignment—with consideration for personal preference, temperament, life experience, education and employment background.

The Right to know as much about the organization as possible—its policies, people, and programs.

The Right to training for the job and continuing education on the job—including training for greater responsibility.

The Right to sound guidance and direction.

The Right to a place to work—an orderly, designated place that is conducive to work and worthy of the job to be done.

The Right to promotion and a variety of experiences through advancement or transfer, or through special assignments.

The Right to be heard—to feel free to make suggestions, to have a part in planning.

The Right to recognition—in the form of promotion and awards, through day-by-day expressions of appreciation, and by being treated as a bona fide co-worker. (American Association of Retired Persons, 1985, p. 15)

Finally, Chambre (1984) poses an extremely salient but multidimensional question. Is it reasonable to conceptualize volunteering as a relief for role loss in older age? Chambre suggests that people who have maintained an active level of participation in the labor force up to retirement do not seek volunteer activities to regain the prestige of a paid job. Instead, the writer proposes that "elderly volunteers may be volunteers who became elderly; that is, their involvement is a continuation of behavior patterns established earlier in life" (1984, p. 297).

Although their prominence in volunteerism accentuates the integrity of senior citizens as a group, America is a country dedicated to paid work, not just work. Volunteerism is commendable but not revered. Therefore, seniors also need to consider ways to promote other aspects of their worth, including, but not limited to, humanitarianism.

SENIOR CITIZENS AND WORK

The advertisement reads: "Highly experienced worker seeks part-time employment. Open to learning on the job, flexible concerning hours, willing to work for reasonable compensation." This notice could appear in any daily newspaper. Senior citizens represent a superabundance of knowledge and experience for the labor force, accompanied by a willingness to be productive. Are there positions for these older, often retired people, in the marketplace? If so, how can golden agers find employment that matches their interests and backgrounds?

At a macro level, Morris and Bass suggest a role for higher education.

1. Urban and metropolitan elderly populations, although characterized predominantly by limited income and education, have the interest and capacity to perform socially useful and significant tasks in their retirement.
2. A university can provide a concentrated period of competency building which will equip interested elders to perform complex and significant tasks and to fill new and significant service or decision-making roles in their communities.
3. The university can develop a liaison and active coalition with nonprofit civic groups and public authorities to ensure that a mechanism exists for moving from competency acquisition into significant community roles. (1986, p. 16)

Collaboration between senior citizens and universities has many merits. Elderhostel, an educational adventure for older adults, is a shining example of such mutuality. A nonprofit educational organization, it offers inexpensive, short-term academic programs hosted by educational institutions around the world. Thousands enroll annually in these programs offered in the United States and throughout the world (Dade, 1994).

The eager return of many older adults to the classroom indicates a readiness for educational growth. At the same time, these seniors share their life experiences and maturity with students and faculty. Participants often return to their neighborhoods eager to volunteer with their newly acquired skills. Such older adults may be placed in prominent positions that contribute to their higher esteem in peer groups.

Social workers need to explore projects and programs that successfully link older adults to the labor force—beyond volunteerism and rudimentary service-oriented employment. Many senior citizens are willing to work part-time or to trade wages for a modest reimbursement for expenses, for the sake of maintaining a desirable status and making occasional use of their experience and background.

In our aging society, older adults face widely different socioeconomic circumstances. Some will struggle to remain in the primary marketplace through full-time employment as long as possible. Others, associated with progressive companies and corporations, will benefit from part-time work, consulting, or postretirement roles. Still others will emphasize their leisure interests in retirement.

It is important to note that the economic well-being of older women is of particular concern. Bear in mind that: "In 2002, the U.S. Census Bureau reported that there were almost 14 million adults in the United States who had lost a spouse by death, most commonly they were in middle or late adulthood. Of these, over 11 million were women and over 2 million were men (Kreider & Fields, 2002)" (Bee & Bjorklund, 2006, p. 354). When considering the longevity of women, "a picture emerges of an increasing number of women facing poverty either in old age or in extreme old age" (Gough, 2001, p. 311).

As suggested by Morris and Bass (1986), one macro-oriented strategy worthy of consideration is the expansion of the marketplace. Stimulation of the economy that creates new businesses and jobs produces opportunities for all Americans. These efforts would assist interested seniors in finding satisfying and valued work roles.

Locally and nationally, social workers have also contributed to the development of a secondary economy, where special needs and social objectives not met in the primary economy are addressed by senior citizens. Through participation in programs such as the Peace Corps, Foster Grandparents, RSVP, Meals-on-Wheels, and Second Harvest, capabilities of seniors outside their career skills may be utilized, with little or modest remuneration or compensation compared to that found in the traditional workforce.

For older adults wishing to resume active employment in the labor force, predictions are that there will be heavy retirement rates over the next couple of decades in the United States (Institute of Management and Administration, 2003). This will lead to the targeting of older workers for employment. Professionals in human resource departments will develop strategies to encourage many older workers to maintain employment beyond retirement age, despite concerns that older adults may lack technological expertise, will increase health care costs, and lack flexibility in the labor force (Institute of Management and Administration, 2003, p. 12).

Retiring from active employment raises many concerns beyond those of finances. Physical and mental health issues, as well as staying connected to one's family, community, and society, are also important considerations (Goldberg, 2002). Research indicates that "social engagement and productive activities have a positive impact on health and longevity" (Cohen, 2002, p. 37). Unfortunately, Szinovacz and Davey suggest that nearly one third of older workers perceive their retirement as being forced rather than voluntary (2005, p. 36).

Few would argue with the statement: "The lifeblood of living in older years is involvement" (Goldberg, 2002, p. 873). Physical and social activities are important ingredients in promoting healthy aging. Marshall and Altpeter (2005) state "anything social workers can do to help older adults maintain or enhance physical activity levels will preserve quality of life and save healthcare dollars" (p. 140).

Choosing to continue work in older age as a personal option to augment quality of life is one issue. Maintaining employment in older age out of economic need is another matter. Many social workers would agree with the assertion that: "It is a failure of national policy when more and more of the elderly have to work out of sheer economic necessity" (Ghilarducci, 2002, p. 38). As one of the mightiest and most powerful industrialized nations in the world, the United States needs to develop policies and initiate legislation that will secure private pension plans for older adults and preserve social security as the stable anchor of the federal retirement system. Particularly for older adults, financial security is an important and necessary prerequisite for the pursuit of personal meaning and expression.

POLITICAL ACTIVISM IN OLD AGE

Traditionally, the elderly have been thought of as a strong political force in America. In addition to the AARP, senior citizen organizations including the National Council of Senior Citizens, the Gray Panthers, and Save Our Security have been influential fact-finding and lobbying entities (Quadagno, 1991). As publisher of *Modern Maturity,* which has one of the highest circulations in the nation, the AARP has repeatedly demonstrated its political clout. The "gray lobby" has given older adults sociopolitical stature and guided age-related public policy formation and development in the United States.

However, Day (1993) suggests that assessing the impact of elderly constituents and interest groups on the aging policy process is difficult and complex. She identifies three divergent views of older people with regard to political activism.

1. Grey peril—where senior citizens are seen as a formidable political group of "greedy geezers" out to bargain for more than their due of community and societal resources.
2. Fading grey—where senior organizations are seen as losing power and influence and becoming increasingly ineffective with regard to protecting existing benefits and raising new issues and policies.
3. A progressive view—where older adults promote broad-minded change aimed at intergenerational unity and promoting a comprehensive and compassionate social welfare system. (Day, 1993, p. 426)

Some will argue that a growing population of older Americans characterized by a propensity for voting and demanding favors from politicians supports a gray peril view of older adults in the political arena. Seniors have the numbers and know they have clout, and government officials are frightened of their power (*Economist*, 1989).

Others will contend that senior citizens are prone to support a liberal government agenda. They emphasize that older adults view government intervention as an important mechanism for addressing societal ills. Indeed, *Modern*

Maturity (1995) reports that 35 percent of senior citizens believe the best way to halt declining values in America comes through strengthening both governmental and individual responsibility.

McKenzie (1993), however, provides an interesting argument supporting the fading gray perspective. He predicts that federal expenditures for programs for the elderly will be curtailed and gradually decline. His contention is based on a perceived reduction in the political power of senior citizens.

McKenzie gives eight reasons "that the sheer growth in elderly numbers and population share will undercut, albeit marginally, the political influence that elderly interest groups and lobbies have on Congress":

1. There is a "free rider" problem, where many older Americans are seen as sitting back and assuming that others will do the lion's share of work to maintain political influence.
2. The cost of mobilizing large numbers of elderly will outdistance the number of elderly, depressing their desire to engage in political activism.
3. Senior citizens are growing more diverse with regard to their political objectives.
4. Younger people are increasing their political effectiveness.
5. Nonelderly political groups are raising objections to the growth in a perceived "Elderly Welfare State."
6. Older adults are continuing to work beyond the typical retirement years with working seniors separating themselves from political efforts of their retired counterparts.
7. Wealthier senior citizens are being taxed more, thus producing another division in the senior citizen voting bloc.
8. New small groups representing well-defined public and special interests (e.g., AIDS, education, or anti-crime) will better compete with the elderly for political influence. (McKenzie, 1993, pp. 75–76)

In assessing the big picture with respect to the position of older adults in the American scene, social workers must carefully consider McKenzie's premises. Political activism and clout are important to senior citizens for maintaining and improving economic, social, and health services. Stated another way, a vital key to self-rule and integrity of the elderly in our society is their ability to influence the politicians who formulate and execute the policies and programs that affect them.

A formidable body of research (e.g., Blackburn & Chilman,1987; Gist, 1992; Meyer & Bartolomei-Hill, 1994; Storey, 1986) has emerged describing the nature of current and proposed legislative and budgetary changes that attack the quality of life for senior citizens. The common theme warns of an erosion of benefits for aged individuals, whether through policy changes, program reductions, or tax reform. Although the impact of these cuts would be felt by all senior citizens, the most severely affected are older adults at or near poverty-level incomes, single women, and the frail elderly.

McKenzie identifies specific areas where Congress has begun to reduce benefits that should create concerns for the elderly now and in the future.

- Raising age requirements for full retirement from age 65 to 67.
- Modifying calculating schemes that reduce the real purchasing power of social security benefits.
- Increasing the taxability of social security benefits.
- Decreasing real Medicare costs covered by federal insurance, accompanied by increases in Medicare premiums.
- Changing the measure of cost of living by the Bureau of Labor Statistics. (1993, p. 80)

PRESIDENT GEORGE W. BUSH AND SOCIAL SECURITY REFORM

At his February 2, 2005, State of the Union address, President George W. Bush formally advocated overhauling the social security system. Earlier, during his bid for a second term in the White House, President Bush had proposed allowing younger beneficiaries to divert a portion of their social security taxes to individual investment accounts. This effort toward privatization of social security would presumably allow taxpayers to assume ownership in their social security benefits by placing a percentage of their dollars in self-directed financial investments.

Many Americans would agree that the social security system as we know it today is in need of change. As a society with an increasing number of older adults and a large number of baby boomers on the verge of retirement, the solvency of the social security trust fund over the next several decades is highly questionable. Indeed, many middle age workers wonder if the current level of social security benefits will be available to them at retirement. A constructive solution needs to found.

Yet, many people believe that the formation of private, manageable accounts under the auspices of social security is a bad idea. Nunberg states: "President Bush's notion of 'ownership' in Social Security really means asking workers to accept risk, volatility, and uncertainty" (2005, p. A16). What happens if the stock market plummets, people invest unwisely, or, as in the case of Enron, companies are able to successfully deceive investors? Under these hypothetical conditions, what would happen to the retirement plans of senior citizens?

Schulz and Gorin (2005) caution that neither politicians nor Americans should gamble with social security. They state: "Although everyone agrees that, in the long run, social security will need to raise more money or reduce some of its benefits, no one really knows exactly how much money we will need. . . . [P]rivate accounts are hardly a solution to financing problems . . . these accounts would require at least $1–2 trillion extra funds (over 10 years)" (2005, p. 75).

The Christian Century (2005) depicts social security in the following manner: "Social Security has been a means by which a mobile, fragmented modern society has honored its elders. . . . Social security payments provide most of their income; for 20 percent of recipients, it is their only source of income. The program has decisively cut poverty rates among the elderly" (p. 5).

Scott (2005) states: "I can't help but wonder how many people, particularly America's senior citizens, who voted in the 2004 election for George W. Bush realized they were voting to privatize Social Security" (p. 30). When considering the Bush Administration's efforts toward privatization of social security, it is understandable that observers are asking if Medicare can be far behind. Many concerned citizens believe that "the cost of transitioning Social Security and Medicare might even throw the country into an economic crisis" (Baker, 2005, p. A8).

Polls suggest that President Bush has lost support for privatization of social security. According to a *USA Today*/CNN/Gallup poll taken near the end of June, 2005: "Bush's numbers on Social Security were worse than any other issue in the poll, including Iraq, the economy and health care. . . . [With respect to social security reform,] 64 percent disapprove, the first time disapproval has risen above 60 percent" (Wolf, 2005, p. A4).

MEDICARE PRESCRIPTION DRUG COVERAGE

In 2003, the Medicare Modernization Act (MMA) was passed by the U.S. Congress and signed into law by President George W. Bush. This was a wide-sweeping piece of federal legislation affecting Medicare benefits. Most notably, as of 2004, beneficiaries received a discount drug card. This constituted a temporary program to provide immediate assistance to Medicare recipients until the Medicare Prescription Drug Coverage Program (Part D) came into effect in 2006.

Under the provisional drug discount card system, recipients selected a Medicare-approved pharmaceutical company and its card. Each pharmaceutical provider offered a predetermined discount on medications. In addition, some low-income seniors qualified for and were granted a $600 annual credit for prescription medications.

The temporary discount card program was not a comprehensive benefit for older adults. Problems associated with the system included: older adults received a relatively small percentage discount per drug, pharmaceutical companies were permitted to remove drugs from their approved lists, recipients struggled to identify the best drug card given their medical needs, and a general sense of confusion occurred concerning the number of cards available and the benefits associated with each card.

As of 2006, under the auspices of the Medicare Prescription Drug Coverage Program (Part D), insurance companies began to work with Medicare to offer specific drug plans and negotiate discounts on the price of medications for Medicare recipients (Ohio KePro, 2005, p. 5). Although drug plans vary according to drugs covered, co-payments, and pharmacy usage, Medicare established guidelines prescribing standard and minimum levels of coverage.

It should be recognized that the temporary drug discount cards and the MMA has provided older adults with a degree of relief from the spiraling costs of prescription drugs. However, the MMA is a good example of a "piecemeal approach" to a major social problem confronting mature adults.

As American pharmaceutical companies continue to prosper, many senior citizens have had to cut daily living expenses and seek innovative solutions to address the costs of their prescription medications. Splitting medications into half dosages and reducing food or fluid intake to save money are dangerous and dehumanizing practices. In a highly industrialized and technologically advanced society like the United States, older adults should be provided with a universal form of health care coverage that addresses their needs in a straightforward, understandable, and comprehensive manner. A universal health care system would relieve a major, life-threatening burden for many older adults and allow senior citizens to more freely direct their energies to issues of personal relevance (e.g., creativity and volunteerism).

Promoting Public Transportation

If you have traveled abroad, you may be familiar with public transportation systems, mainly rail and bus, in such places as Europe and the British Isles. New York City, Boston, Washington, D.C., Chicago, and San Francisco offer well-known forms of mass transit to commuters and travelers. In addition to being environmentally friendly, public transportation offers an alternative to automobiles that is economically viable for people at the lower end of the socioeconomic spectrum as well as people experiencing difficulties with driving (e.g., older adults and people with special needs).

Unfortunately, the American experience with public transportation is not as positive as that found in other countries. For example, Rittner and Kirk's (1995) examination of use of public transportation by older adults in Florida indicated that bus travel was characterized by "missing or late buses, problems with lack of shelters, buses that were difficult to get on and off, dirty windows, and occasional confrontations with other passengers" (p. 370). Such conditions pose barriers, instead of opportunities, for usage among older adults.

Throughout this chapter, we have made the argument that older adults need to be able to remain physically and socially active, adapt to change, exert control over their lives, and maintain as much independence as possible. Social reconstruction theory indicates that society often deprives older adults of opportunities to use their talents and skills. This theory places a heavy emphasis on advancing the value of human capital in policy development and service delivery. With respect to public transportation, the development of a comprehensive, effective system is needed in order to assist older adults in staying "connected—by all possible means—to the communities that enrich them" (Madachy, 2003, p. 24).

For older adults, there is a critical need for specialized public transportation. "Social service agencies, transportation service providers, and governmental entities are searching for ways to develop or improve transportation services to meet local travel needs of older people" (Sterns, Antenucci, Nelson, & Glasgow, 2003, p. 14). Older adults frequently need a continuum of transportation services in order to remain independent and socially integrated. For people unable to drive, the ability to see family and friends, participate in community functions, go to health care appointments, participate in therapy, and attend events is dependent upon the goodwill of others, the availability of public transportation, or the ability to pay out of pocket for private transportation services and/or taxicabs. Straight (2003) suggests that the "[c]urrent level of public investment in specialized transportation does not appear to meet current needs, let alone future ones" (p. 45).

Public transportation for older adults in rural areas in the United States is particularly troublesome. Stunkel (1997) suggests that "cycles of federal regulation and deregulation and chronic underfunding of rural transit" have led to highly ineffective, fragmented transit systems across America (p. 67). For older adults in rural areas, taking advantage of innovations in medicine and behavioral health care management is a formidable challenge. Transportation intended to keep older adults active and integrated into the fabric of community life is many times idealistic at best.

EMPOWERING PEOPLE IN OLDER AGE

Social workers concerned about macro-level issues during older age must assess various venues for social empowerment. **Empowerment** involves helping individuals or groups of individuals to gain power (Staples, 1990). Social workers who have senior citizen clients need to look at the full range of ways to allow seniors to function independently.

A beginning step involves dispelling the myths that contaminate and cloud our perception of older adults in America. Senior citizens are frequently portrayed as inactive, depressed, ill, unattractive, asexual, set in their ways, demented, unable to learn new ways, or withdrawn (Harrigan & Farmer, 1992). These stereotypes are powerful and undermine the image of older adults in America. Social workers should seek to discourage such distorted images.

It is also important for social workers to engage seniors in social policy discourse and the acceptance of responsibilities. Remembering the client-centered nature of social work practice, social workers facilitate policy activity until client leadership emerges. As clients define concerns and policy priorities, social workers become partners with them in social policy analysis and practice (Cox & Parsons, 1994, pp. 64–65).

To assist social workers, Cox and Parsons identify the following five empowerment-oriented tasks:

1. Overcoming workers' and clients' resistance to involvement in the policy process.

2. Obtaining and sharing information regarding existing policies, pending policies, and implementation of policies.
3. Gaining and sharing knowledge about the policy process and policy makers.
4. Developing and testing frameworks for understanding and analyzing policy.
5. Acquiring and sharing practical knowledge about how to change policy. (1994, p. 64)

Although each of the five tasks is difficult to implement, overcoming resistance to involvement is a prerequisite for addressing the remaining four tasks. Seniors often feel in danger of losing control over their lives. Many believe that others are making more and more decisions for them. The elderly, as a population at risk, often feel powerless in solving their own problems. First and foremost, social workers need to reassure seniors that as a group they are a political force and can reclaim control of their lives. Once convinced that social change is possible, older adults are free to explore their shared concerns about issues such as housing, work, health care, income, and transportation.

The Older Americans Act (OAA) of 1965 opened doors, set national objectives, and established mechanisms through **Areawide Agencies on Aging (AAA)** that legitimized the ability of older Americans to pursue their rights. Social workers need to be aware of planning organizations like the AAA in the regions in which they practice. It is vital that they be familiar with the diverse policy and legislative opportunities that will advance concerns of their clients (Hancock, 1990, p. 234).

Looking Ahead

On a positive note, Cox states:

> If the values of the twenty-first century shift along the lines suggested by the social scientists, we should expect an improvement in the status of older persons. Less emphasis on achievement and productivity, in which the young are always viewed as having the greatest potential for development, and greater concern with interpersonal relationships and the meaning and quality of life, in which the old may have the distinct advantage of breadth of experience and wisdom accumulated over a lifetime, should improve the status of older persons. (1993, p. 344)

Older adults are currently confronted with various social risks, including retirement, role loss, age discrimination, negative stereotyping, and dependency. Our commitment is to ensure that future social policies and services are designed to build upon the strengths of seniors and enrich their lives (Cox & Parsons, 1994, p. 28). As with all forms of macro-level assessment, "the social worker's primary responsibility is to clients. . . . The social worker should make every effort to foster maximum self-determination on the part of clients" (National Association of Social Workers, 1990, p. 1).

| # EMPOWERMENT THROUGH THE TIMBERLAND SENIOR CITIZENS CENTER

Mrs. Carla Peters is a social worker at the Timberland Senior Citizens Center. Located in a middle-class section of a city (population 200,000) in the northwestern United States, Timberland offers a wide range of services for older adults. These include health and nutrition programs, an activities program, individual counseling, a peer companion and phone network, and the presentation of various seminars and workshops.

One of Carla's favorite roles is coordinating Timberland's Pulse and Power Program (PPP). Created three years ago in response to concerns over Medicare reductions, the PPP meets weekly to examine and address important local and national issues affecting the elderly. The PPP publishes a monthly newsletter that is sent to all patrons of Timberland. Normally, thirty to thirty-five older adults attend meetings with a leadership council composed of seven members elected annually. The vast majority of members are lifelong residents of the community.

Recently, the PPP has focused on a highly controversial local issue. The county park's wildlife refuge and petting zoo may soon be forced to close or curtail services. This would affect all citizens—the young, school-age children, families as well as seniors. A county budget crunch, coupled with an electorate reluctant to pass new tax millage, has prompted politicians to consider closing the 50-year-old wildlife facility.

At the last PPP meeting, seniors were very vocal. They identified two areas for exploration in connection with saving the wildlife center. First, how could PPP members and others at Timberland effectively lend political support for the county wildlife program? Second, the PPP leadership committee and Carla were asked to assess the possibility of establishing a formal relationship with the wildlife refuge and petting zoo in order to utilize senior volunteers. This association might free personnel and resources at the refuge for other functions. Additionally, a link between the senior citizen center and the wildlife center would have political advantages for the next park levy.

PPP members wanted to become guides and resource people at the wildlife refuge and petting zoo. After formal training by park officials, senior citizens envisioned greeting visitors and being stationed throughout the park to provide educational information concerning various birds, animals, and plant life, and their natural habitats in the region. Several PPP members have expressed an interest in wearing uniforms that represent the timber industry's rich heritage in the area. Others were excited at the prospect of designing and creating authentic Timberland garb.

Carla sensed the great enthusiasm among the elderly. Thinking about ways to support the animal refuge center was meaningful and important for senior citizens. Many older adults viewed participation at the refuge center as an opportunity to share their knowledge of nature and the community and to interact with younger people. Members were encouraged because park administrators and county politicians have also shown interest in exploring this association.

With the park levy due to reappear on the ballot in nine months, Carla saw this as ideal timing for exploring a formalized linkage between the highly motivated senior citizens and the park services. The park system would benefit by acquiring valuable resources and political support. In addition to individual gains, Carla felt that senior citizens would enhance their image as active doers in the community.

TIME TO THINK!

Carla's client in this example is the senior group at the Timberland Senior Citizens Center. While she is interested in their personal growth and development, on a macro level Carla also works to break down common societal beliefs that older Americans are deficient or incompetent.

Along with the PPP leadership committee, Carla has been charged with examining the merits of a formal association with the county park system, with a focus on the animal refuge center and petting zoo. What factors are important for Carla to consider in assessing this situation? How can Carla best orchestrate this process, remembering the social worker's obligation to foster client self-determination? How is social power an important factor in discussions with park system officials?

Macro Systems and Older Adults

Social workers whose practice includes older adults need to evaluate their actions in relationship to both micro and macro systems. Assessing macro systems, like micro systems, is a client-centered process that links client and social worker in partnership. With this perspective, assess and identify important organizational, community, societal, and international factors in creating a program that relates senior citizens to a county animal refuge center. As you do this, maintaining and developing self-rule and integrity for senior citizens should be priorities. You must avoid the tendency to stereotype and place limits on how seniors are expected to act and function.

Organizational Level As PPP members and Carla began to examine the primary organizations involved, two different organizational models became apparent. What initially seemed to be a simple idea for an association between two entities now appears more complex.

Although receiving federal, state, and county funds, Timberland Senior Citizens Center is characterized by professional leadership, a high degree of consumer participation, and flexibility. Timberland's Board of Trustees, most of whom are older adults themselves, maintains and exerts direct control over policy and program development. Timberland's executive director has a positive, professional relationship with the Board of Trustees. The director has informed the Board regarding the prospect of an association with the park system and has received strong support.

The county park system is more bureaucratic and political. The park system is strongly influenced by both national and state policy. Because of the hierarchical authority structure of park personnel, any agreement between Timberland Senior Citizens Center and the park relative to volunteering at the wildlife refuge and petting

continued

zoo must be approved by the chief park officer. In addition, legal counsel representing the park system must evaluate any proposal to ascertain its merits because there are county, state, and federal mandates.

Both organizations favor the concept of older adults volunteering at the refuge center. However, the differences between Timberland's professional model of organization and the park system's public model cause both to approach program implementation very differently. Timberland's Board can make decisions and carry out plans in a timely manner, whereas park officials are bound to rules of procedure. For example, Timberland Senior Citizens Center promptly offered its van for transporting senior citizens to and from the park. Meanwhile park officials struggled with the feasibility of expanding current job descriptions to include training and support of seniors as volunteers in the park.

Members of the PPP leadership committee, however, did not stand by waiting to see if their support for the refuge center died in bureaucratic red tape. Based upon their knowledge and experiences over the years, several seniors have developed important alliances with county commissioners as well as state politicians. Being careful to coordinate their contacts with Timberland and park officials, several seniors made phone calls to assess ways to assist the chief park officer and his staff in bringing this program to fruition. Indeed, over the years, Carla has carefully noted the resourcefulness of senior citizens in identifying influential individuals in key organizations that provide help.

Community Level   Timberland Senior Citizens Center is located in a community experiencing little new economic growth. Although it was once a major timber producing area, employment in the community now relies on four small manufacturing companies. The economic climate in the community has changed little during the past decade. More than 18 percent of the population is over 65 years of age.

Senior citizens in the area are politically active. They vote, they participate in political parties and movements, and a few older adults hold key political offices, including that of mayor. Even though they do not typically vote as a bloc along party lines, older adults can become highly organized on community issues that they regard as in their best interest. Thus senior citizens comprise an important political group for shaping the future of the park system as well as for passing a park levy.

One of the more disturbing aspects of the community involves the segregated nature of housing for older adults. Most seniors live in "Old Pine Town," the name given to the older, center section of the city developed during the timber industry's most prosperous years. Although the senior center has worked to help create a transportation system making the community more accessible to the elderly, many older adults continue to feel isolated. Transportation is an important factor in fulfilling the hopes of those senior citizens who desire to participate at the refuge center. By volunteering at the park, older adults not only interact with different age groups but also potentially enhance their image and stature with children and families.

Interestingly, local newspapers and television have provided positive coverage concerning the possibility of a senior citizen-wildlife refuge affiliation. Seniors are being cast in the community as protectors of animals, heritage, and family activities. While being sensitive not to upstage the efforts of politicians and park officials, senior citizens gain pride from community approval.

At the request of the PPP leadership committee and Timberland's executive director, Carla has also contacted the AAA for their support of the wildlife refuge endeavor. In the past, the AAA has been extremely helpful in providing information, statistics, and resources for community planning and organizing.

Societal Level The OAA of 1965 created a significant national plan outlining goals and objectives for older adults. The objectives included adequate income; the best possible physical and mental health; suitable housing; full restorative services; the opportunity for employment; health in retirement; honor and dignity; civic, cultural, and recreational opportunities; efficient community services; benefits from research; and the ability to exercise individual initiatives in managing one's life (Hancock, 1990, pp. 233–234).

These objectives guide the Administration on Aging as it coordinates programs among government agencies that affect senior citizens. The refuge center program would promote mental health, bringing a sense of value and dignity, as well as recreational and civic opportunities, for older adults. Because the program entails the cooperation of an additional government agency, the park system, Carla will also contact the Administration on Aging to seek their advice and assistance.

Interestingly, both PPP members at Timberland and park officials expressed an interest in exploring the benefits of hiring employees versus those of utilizing volunteers. Low-income elderly would benefit if they were paid for duties performed at the animal refuge center. Carla is aware that the Senior Community Service Employment Program (Title V), authorized under the OAA, was created to encourage part-time employment of low-income seniors to enhance the general welfare of a community (Hancock, 1990, pp. 245–246). She will inquire into the status and appropriateness of any Title V or other grant monies for the proposed program at the animal refuge center.

Finally, Carla is committed to promoting the highest degree of respect for older adults who volunteer. She knows that not all volunteer experiences are positive. Thus, an explicit part of any agreement with the park system for volunteers from Timberland Senior Citizens Center will be AARP's Bill of Rights. A major component in Carla's social work practice with aging people involves empowering older adults and enhancing their societal image as competent citizens.

International Level Timberland Senior Citizens Center is located approximately 120 miles south of western Canada. Therefore, the community is affected both socially and economically by its neighbor to the north. For example, there is direct international competition in both the timber and tourism industries. Nearly 20 percent

continued

CASE EXAMPLE | *continued*

of the visitors to the county park come from Canada. Some of the Canadian visitors speak French, so it is helpful that several senior citizens from Timberland are able to converse both in English and French.

Because seniors at Timberland readily receive Canadian news, many compare their Medicaid and Medicare benefits to those in Canada. This has led to lively discussions contrasting the quality of health care services in the two countries, the meaning of managed health care, and the consequences of increases in Medicare premiums for the elderly in the United States. Clearly, the spiraling cost of medical care for older adults is a major concern for Carla's clients.

Her close proximity to another country motivates Carla to develop a keen interest in international social work. In addition to keeping abreast of changes occurring in Canada that could affect her work directly (e.g., the possible secession of Quebec), Carla has read with interest publications concerned with the role of gerontological social work in other countries. She has found this knowledge valuable in reflecting upon her own practice, especially as it relates to macro practice.

Hang-Sau and Chi (1994, p. 80), working with the elderly in Hong Kong, submit that helping professionals tend to stress the role of teacher while disregarding the role of advocate. They suggest that social workers, overburdened by the daily routine of working with older adults in senior citizen centers, often fail to focus on the significance of advocacy and the need to organize "concern groups."

In her work with the PPE Carla has tended to use the meetings with the seniors as information-sharing sessions and has not adequately stressed the need for advocacy for their issues. In an effort to be neutral, she has felt reluctant to enter political forums and explore controversial issues with senior citizens. Hang-Sau and Chi's (1994) article has persuaded Carla to reevaluate her role at Timberland and to become more vocal in the discussion of political issues as well as to help the senior members exercise more direct political power.

RELECTION ON DIVERSITY: YOUNGER MATURE ADULTS AND OLDER MATURE ADULTS

Like many publications examining human development, this book has conceptualized and analyzed the human life cycle through the use of specific, concrete phases or stages. These have included infancy, preschool, school age, adolescence, young adulthood, middle adulthood, and later adulthood. Developmental categories corresponding to chronological age can be useful in assisting professionals to identify both normative and problematic issues associated with a particular time of life. Yet, it is important to point out that these classification systems are simplified for use in the book's context.

For example, many social scientists prefer to divide adolescence into three parts—early, middle, and late. The argument is that grouping adolescents into a single age category diminishes or deemphasizes the many biological, psychological, and social differences of young people between the ages of 12 and 18. Specificity and insight is gained when researchers distinguish between different phases in adolescence.

Similarly, people often make a distinction between late adulthood and late-late adulthood (Bee & Bjorklund, 2004). Late adulthood is a reference to the relatively "young old," where late-late adulthood refers to the "older old." Although this differentiation might initially seem somewhat superficial, people from age 65 and beyond are not all alike. People in older adulthood are a diverse lot, depending upon health, level of independence, mobility, cognitive functioning, and financial means. Younger mature adults often notice small physical changes (e.g., some symptoms of arthritis and hearing loss), suggesting that a new stage or phase in their life has begun. In contrast, older mature adults often experience a more accelerated form of physical and mental aging characterized by dependency and/or disability that interferes with everyday activities (Bee & Bjorklund, 2004, pp. 372–376).

To illustrate the usefulness of the late adulthood and late-late adulthood distinction for research, findings by Wicks (2004) suggest that younger seniors just entering retirement often seek information differently than their older counterparts. As one might expect, this is particularly true with respect to the use of technology. It appears that younger seniors have a greater tendency to use computers for information gathering, where older seniors may rely more heavily on interpersonal sources to find answers to questions involving medical and financial issues.

As with any form of diversity, including issues related to age, the specificity, accuracy, and helpfulness of any classification system merits scrutiny and careful consideration. Conceptual distinctions are often contextual in nature and should be examined when conducting research or attempting to construct realities. When working with older clients regarding their fair treatment (e.g., challenging assignments and promotion), the 50-plus distinction may be helpful. Similarly, AARP extends membership to those who have reached the age of 50. In contrast, interest in issues of physical and mental frailty by health care organizations is often reserved for people in or beyond their eighties.

Foremost, special care needs to be given so that classification systems do not inadvertently label people in negative, dehumanizing, or undignified ways. As this relates to aging in our society, older adults deserve recognition and acclaim for their knowledge and unique experiential wisdom. It is important to be sensitive to the use of language. When distinguishing between older adults, consider the merits of using the terms "younger mature adult" and "older mature adult" as opposed to "younger old" and "older old."

APPLYING A SOCIAL WORK FRAMEWORK: SOCIAL RECONSTRUCTION THEORY

Chapter 8 started with an overview of social reconstruction theory. Old age as defined by society causes the elderly to feel incompetent and deficient. These feelings occur in part as a result of role loss when seniors are not encouraged to use their talents and skills after retirement. A sense of inadequacy and a decrease in self-esteem are frequently felt by older adults. This results in a loss to society of valuable experience and wisdom. Social reconstruction theory suggests themes of empowerment, self-rule, social power, and maintenance of integrity that social workers with older-age clients will want to integrate into their practice.

In our example, Carla addresses the needs and desires of senior citizens, but she places a special emphasis on seeking ways to advance their power and position in the community and society. Timberland seniors worry about their medical benefits, park system, and isolation from other members of society. They are also concerned about being viewed as second-class citizens whose opinions are seldom considered and whose voices are silenced. Decisions seem to be made about them and for them, seldom by them.

At the request of both clients and agency, Carla entered the political arena to explore ways to advocate for the rights of senior citizens. Her involvement with Timberland's PPP, the AAA, the Administration on Aging, and the AARP enables her to gain valuable information for securing resources and empowering her clientele to reach their goals. Carla's willingness to become involved, to make influential contacts, and to enter political discourse has fostered a spirit of collective participation and action with the PPP and with Timberland.

Using social reconstruction theory allows Carla to look beyond microsystem levels. Older adults at Timberland want to contribute to their communities and society with the enthusiasm of a Jimmy Carter. However, their gifts go beyond helping to establish peace in Haiti or achieving solvency for the animal refuge center and petting zoo. Their accumulated wisdom, available hours, mental energy, and desire to be included in decisions that affect lives are priceless gifts that mutually benefit seniors and the community. Carla has come to appreciate the desire of senior citizens to take their rightful, contributory, and respected place in society.

SUGGESTED ACTIVITIES

1. Ask a grandparent or other senior citizen for an opinion of America's view of aging. Does his or her perception coincide with elements of social reconstruction theory?
2. Does your university or social work program maintain formal linkage with senior citizen groups? What benefits could older adults bring to your college or department? With three other class members, explore your perceptions of the advantages and disadvantages of being old in America. How might a partnership between older adults and a university change or enlighten these perceptions?
3. Invite a representative of a senior citizens organization to speak to your class or school. Become familiar with the various ways that this organization promotes a positive image of older adults. List advocacy programs for the elderly that exist in your community.
4. Identify three or more major advancements in health, social services, and quality of life for older Americans since the Social Security Act of 1935.

REFERENCES

American Association of Retired Persons. (1985). *To serve—not to be served: A guide for older volunteers*. Washington, DC: Author.

Atchley, R. (1989). *Social forces and aging*. Belmont, CA: Wadsworth.

Baker, D. (2005). Bush's numbers racket: Why social security privatization is a phony solution to a phony problem. *The American Prospect*, February, A6–A8.

Bee, H., & Bjorklund, B. (2004). *The journey of adulthood*. Upper Saddle River, NJ: Pearson Prentice Hall.

Blackburn, J., & Chilman, C. (1987). The probable impact of proposed legislative and budgetary changes on the lives of the elderly and their families. *Journal of Gerontological Social Work, 11,* 19–42.

Carter, J. (1995). *Always a reckoning*. New York: Times Books.

Carter, J., & Carter, R. (1987). *Everything to gain: Making the most of the rest of your life*. New York: Random House.

Chambre, S. (1984). Is volunteering a substitute for role loss in old age? An empirical test of activity theory. *Gerontologist, 24,* 292–298.

Christian Century. (2005). What crisis? February 8, 5.

Cohen, G. (2002). Retirement advising older adults who are contemplating this change. *Geriatrics, 57,* 37.

Cox, E., & Parsons, R. (1994). *Empowerment-oriented social work practice with the elderly*. Pacific Grove, CA: Brooks/Cole.

Cox, H. (1993). *Later life: The realities of aging*. Englewood Cliffs, NJ: Prentice-Hall.

Cumming, E., & Henry, W. (1961). *Growing old*. New York: Basic Books.

Dade, L. (1994). *Elderhosteling USA!: An Elderhostel how-to guide*. Ferndale, CA: Eldertime.

Day, C. (1993). The organized elderly: Perilous, powerless, or progressive? *Gerontologist, 33,* 426–427.

Economist. (1989). Paying for granny, *311*(7605), 19–20.

Fischer, L., & Schaffer, K. (1993). *Older volunteers: A guide to research and practice*. Newbury Park, CA: Sage.

Gallagher, S. (1994). Doing their share: Comparing patterns of help given by older and younger adults. *Journal of Marriage and the Family, 56,* 567–578.

Ghilarducci, T. (2002). Forget retirement. Get to work. *The American Prospect*, September, 37–38.

Gist, J. (1992). Did tax reform hurt the elderly? *Gerontologist, 32,* 472–477.

Goldberg, E. (2002). A healthy retirement. *AORN Journal, 76,* 873–874.

Goodman, C. (1984). Helper bank: A reciprocal services program for older adults. *Social Work, 29,* 397–398.

Gough, O. (2001). The impact of the gender pay gap on post-retirement earnings. *Critical Social Policy, 21,* 311–335.

Greenfield, E., & Marks, N. (2004). Formal volunteering as a protective factor for older adults' psychological well-being. *Journal of Gerontology, 59B*(5), S258–S263.

Hancock, B. (1990). *Social work with older people*. Englewood Cliffs, NJ: Prentice-Hall.

Hang-Sau, N., & Chi, I. (1994). Political attitudes and behaviors of the elderly in Hong Kong: Implications for social work practice. *Journal of Gerontological Social Work, 21,* 71–82.

Harrigan, M., & Farmer, R. (1992). The myths and facts of aging. In R. Schneider & N. Kript (Eds.), *Gerontological social work*. Chicago: Nelson-Hall.

Hoffman, S. (1983). Peer counselor training with the elderly. *Gerontologist, 23,* 358–360.

Institute of Management & Administration. (2003). *Human resource department management report,* September 3–9, 12.

Knickman, J., & Snell, E. (2002). The 2030 problem: Caring for aging baby boomers. *Health Services Research, 37,* 849–884.

Kovacs. P., & Black, B. (1999). Volunteerism and older adults: Implications for social work practice. *Journal of Gerontological Social Work, 32,* 25–39.

Kreider, R., & Fields, J. (2002). *Number, timing, and duration of marriages and divorces: 1996.* Washington, DC: U.S. Census Bureau Current Population Reports.

Kuypers, J., & Bengtson, V. (1973). Social breakdown and competence. *Human Development, 16,* 181–201.

Madachy, P. (2003). Serving older people by improving transportation. *Generations, 27,* 23–24.

Marshall, V., & Altpeter, M. (2005). Cultivating social work leadership in health promotion and aging: Strategies for active aging interventions. *Health and Social Work, 30,* 135–144.

McKenzie, R. (1993). Senior status: Has the power of the elderly peaked? *American Enterprise, 4,* 74–80.

Meyer, D., & Bartolomei-Hill, S. (1994). The adequacy of Supplemental Security Income benefits for aged individuals and couples. *Gerontologist, 34,* 161–172.

Modern Maturity. (1995). Halting the decline. November–December, 12–14.

Morris, R., & Bass, S. (1986). The elderly as surplus people: Is there a role for higher education? *Gerontologist, 26,* 12–18.

Morrow-Howell, N., Lott, L., & Ozawa, M. (1990). The impact of race on volunteer helping relationships among the elderly. *Social Work, 35,* 395–402.

National Association of Social Workers. (1990). *Code of ethics.* Washington, DC: Author.

Nunberg, G. (2005). Privatization and the English language. *American Prospect,* February, A16–A17.

Ohio KePro. (2005). The facts about Medicare prescription plans. *For Your Benefit: A Newsletter for Ohio's Medicare Beneficiaries.* Summer, 5–6.

Pena, X. (1996). M.S.U. instructor left out in cold. *Lansing State Journal,* August 14, 1B.

Perkins, K., & Tice, C. (1995). A strengths perspective in practice: Older people and mental health challenges. *Journal of Gerontological Social Work, 23,* 83–97.

Quadagno, J. (1991). Interest-group politics and the future of U.S. social security. In J. Myles & J. Quandagno (Eds.), *States, labor markets, and the future of old-age policy.* Philadelphia: Temple University Press.

Rice, E. (1995). *Human development: A life-span approach.* Upper Saddle River, NJ: Prentice-Hall.

Rittner, B., & Kirk, A. (1995). Health care and public transportation use by poor and frail elderly people. *Social Work, 40,* 365–373.

Rogers, A. (2006). *Human behavior in the social environment.* New York: McGraw Hill.

Schulz, J., & Gorin, S. (2005). Let's not gamble with Social Security. *Health and Social Work, 30,* 75.

Scott, J. (2005). Privatizing Social Security: Can Medicare be far behind? *Healthcare Financial Management, 59,* 30–31.

Shannon, B., Smiciklas-Wright, H., Davis, B., & Lewis, C. (1983). A peer educator approach to nutrition for the elderly. *Gerontologist, 23,* 123–126.

Staples, L. (1990). Powerful ideas about empowerment. *Administration in Social Work,* *14,* 29–42.

Stearns, R., Antenucci, V., Nelson, C., & Glasgow, N. (2003). Public transportation: Options to maintain mobility for life. *Generations, 27,* 14–19.

Storey, J. (1986). Policy changes affecting older Americans during the first Reagan administration. *Gerontologist, 26,* 27–31.

Straight, A. (2003) Public policy and transportation for older people. *Generations, 27,* 44–49.

Stunkel, E. (1997). Rural public transportation and the mobility of older persons: Paradigms for policy. *Journal of Aging and Social Policy, 9*(3), 67–86.

Szinovacz, M., & Davey, A. (2005). Predictors of perceptions of involuntary retirement. *Gerontologist, 45,* 36–47.

Warr, P., Butcher, V., Robertson, I., & Callinan, M. (2004). Older people's well-being as a function of employment, retirement, environmental characteristics and role preference. *British Journal of Psychology, 95,* 297–324.

Wicks, D. (2004). Older adults and their information seeking. *Behavioral and Social Sciences Librarian, 22*(2), 1–26.

Wolf, R. (2005). Poll: Bush losing support for social security reform. *Enquirer* (Cincinnati), June 29, A4.

9 CHAPTER | ACHIEVING SOCIAL JUSTICE AND EMPOWERMENT

Change is the essence of social work practice. Even though the problems confronting many of our clients are influenced by large-scale social ills, social workers often perceive client difficulties only at individual and family levels. This micro orientation to social work practice is frequently reflected in and reinforced by modern media. For example, when analyzing the depiction of social workers in film, Freeman and Valentine (2004) found: "Their interventions were primarily at the micro level of practice with almost no attention to social action or social change" (p. 154).

To assess personal problems without sufficient consideration of social conditions leads to incomplete and inadequate conclusions. An individual or family assessment does not embrace social work's broader vision of human life and the fullness of human interaction. Instead, as Long, Tice, and Morrison (2006) point out: "Social work, uniquely among the helping professions, pursues both macro and micro concerns simultaneously" (p. 76).

To achieve social justice and to empower our clients, we must understand the broad issues and find new and innovative ways to interact with the larger environment while working in therapeutic ways with individuals, families, and smaller groups. A commitment to a **unified approach** requires dedication of social workers to understanding and promoting issues of social justice and social change even when working in a predominantly clinical context (Vodde & Gallant, 2002, p. 439). This is true "whether a social worker feels more comfortable at one level or another" (Long, Tice, & Morrison, 2006, p. 160).

A prerequisite for achieving a more balanced, unified approach in practice is the ability to analyze and develop a thorough understanding of larger systems and their impact in the social environment.

SOCIAL JUSTICE

Social workers have an obligation to promote social justice through the development of a more equitable world. This may seem like an abstract and unobtainable goal. Yet, dedication to the advancement of social justice lies at the very heart of our profession. Concisely, the National Association of Social Workers (NASW) Code of Ethics states that social workers are: "To ensure access to needed information, services, and resources; equality of opportunity; and meaningful participation in decision making for all people" (NASW, 1996, p. 5).

Social work practice is grounded in the ethical principle that every person should have fair access to needed resources, for example, food, housing, jobs, and education. To aid in achieving this goal, social workers need to be skillful in working with clients to evaluate control over resource allocation, the equitable distribution of resources, and whether resources are seen as "rights" or "privileges" (Reid & Billups, 1986).

Standards formulated by the Council on Social Work Education (CSWE), mandate that social workers acquire expertise concerning the dynamics and consequences of social and economic injustice as well as methods and strategies for improving social-economic conditions. CSWE standards challenge social workers and those seeking entry into the profession to examine various forms and mechanisms of oppression and discrimination and identify practical ways to assist clients in finding solutions to social problems. Especially during politically conservative times when resources for social welfare are typically restricted, it is important for social workers to analyze adverse conditions and confront government policies and programs that adversely affect the poor, immigrants, and other disenfranchised groups (Mizrahi, 2004).

In this final chapter, we review how macro practice and content relate to various forms of social injustice. Chapter 1 described the plight of a homeless Appalachian woman with children, focusing on the vulnerability of families in our society. Chapter 2 related economics, unemployment, and politics to the care and nurturing of infants. Clara Sherman's awareness of social change and its impact on the mothers and infants she serves elevates the issues to a macro level. Chapter 3 accentuated the impact of racism upon preschool children. The importance of incorporating parents into seeking solutions to their child-rearing concerns was also highlighted. In Chapter 4, as Melissa Richardson advocated for funds as well as an understanding of the needs of children with ADHD in the community, she accomplished goals on many levels. If her contact had been only an individual, therapeutic relationship with a few children, her work would have had a limited effect. Reviewing aspects of adolescence in Chapter 5, we examined mistreatment that occurs as a result of social labels.

Chapter 6 on young adulthood considered marital status, parenting issues, and sexual orientation, as well as discrimination against people with a homosexual orientation. Gender discrimination in the labor force and role enactment were highlighted in Chapter 7 in the discussion of middle age. Social security, public transportation, and prescription medical cards were examined in relationship to enhancing the position of older Americans in Chapter 8. Combating ageism and the stigma of old age was emphasized as a macro responsibility for the social worker at Timberland Senior Citizens Center. In addition, each chapter contained a section especially designed to challenge the reader to reflect upon human diversity as it impacted each topic.

In the case examples, the assumption was that clients could pay for social work intervention or that service was provided under public or subsidized private auspices. Assessment, therefore, was **client driven**. Primary consideration was given to the needs of clients, not to their ability to secure or pay for intervention and services.

In social work practice, however, clients often are unable to pay for services or are placed on agency waiting lists until resources become available. In such a **resource driven system**, clients often become impoverished while waiting for help. Assessment is frequently limited by what is realistically available through short-term intervention (Netting, Kettner, & McMurtry, 1993).

When analyzing macro-level systems, social workers are advised to be constantly aware of the nature of their own delivery system and the economic realities that surround the availability of services. In recent years, emergency spending bills to fund the War on Terrorism, federal income tax cuts initiated in 2001, and rising costs associated with social security and Medicare expenditures have produced deficit spending and led to an enormous federal debt (Shaviro, 2004). As problems with federal finances have occurred, many individual states have struggled to balance their yearly budgets. Under these conditions, community support via tax levies and private giving has not been able to keep pace with the demand for social services in many locales. A cursory analysis of these conditions illustrates how justice-related issues are enmeshed in the very workplace of social workers. A call for collective social action and public education is needed when clients and agency practitioners sense that resources rather than client needs determine and shape service delivery.

THE TIME CRUNCH

Macro-level assessment and subsequent intervention is an integral function of generalist social work practice. Yet, given the various resource and time constraints placed on social workers, how feasible is it for workers to engage in the kind of macro-level activities described in this book? As waiting lists in social work agencies increase, emergency concerns of clients tend to take precedence over macro-level considerations (Long, 1995).

Recognizing that social workers have excessive demands placed upon them, Brody and Nair (1995, p. 110) advise deliberate and formal planning concerning the use of the professional self to determine priorities for the use of time. Specifically, as related to macro-level social work activities, Brody and Nair suggest the following scheme for priorities:

Priority	Explanation
Highest Priority	An activity that is both important and urgent because it provides the best payoff in accomplishing the organization's mission.
Medium Priority	Important, though not urgent. It is necessary to achieve a significant objective.
Low Priority	An activity that contributes only marginally to the achievement of an important objective.
Posteriority	Neither important nor urgent. It could be delayed, minimized, delegated, or even eliminated. (1995, p. 110)

This model is useful, particularly on an individual basis, for prioritizing macro-level activities. However, it fails to address the broader problem of securing adequate time for social workers to engage in macro-level social work assessment and intervention strategies. The workweek of a social worker can easily be filled with "billable" hours pertaining to individual, family, or group intervention. Care needs to be taken that efforts to change social conditions and promote opportunities for clients are also valued and sufficiently reflected in work schedules.

Long (1995) suggests that beyond individual efforts, collective political pressure from professional groups, including the NASW and various voluntary associations, is crucial to demand that agencies define the role of social worker to include macro-level activities. Cooperation and collaboration of this type among associations and organizations who lobby for macro-level social work activities can been seen in the development and promotion of the National Institutes of Health Plan for Social Work Research (U.S. Department of Health and Human Services, 2003). This report "specifies proposals in the areas of social work research, research infrastructure and training, and the information dissemination and community outreach" and makes recommendations concerning programs and activities to promote social work research as a means of preserving health in the United States (Marsh, 2004, p. 341). Organizations that supported the development of the report and its recommendations included the NASW, the Council on Social Work Education, the Association of Baccalaureate Program Directors, the Society for Social Work Research, the Institute for the Advancement of Social Work Research, the Group for the Advancement of Doctoral Education, and the National Association of Deans and Directors.

Social workers and professional social work bodies need to continue to advocate with funding sources and leadership boards for macro-level activities to be recognized as accountable and valid uses of time. Otherwise, what is to be gained by promoting macro-level assessment and change if social workers have little or no time to dedicate to such activity? Time to participate in program and policy development, collaborate with organizations, conduct research, attend neighborhood gatherings, and defend human rights principles is essential to achieving macro-level change. Social service agencies often encourage social workers to participate in these important activities on their own time rather than incorporating these goals as part of agency policy and mission. Individually and as a profession, social workers and the NASW must continue to assess ways to advance macro practice as a fundamental and integral feature of the social service delivery system.

Unfortunately, the current practice of many agencies to conceptualize productivity and billable units of service in terms of clinical time undermines the unified approach in social work practice. To the frustration of many social workers, progress on this front appears to be slow or nonexistent.

THE DIRECT/INDIRECT DISTINCTION

Traditionally, social work has been conceptualized into direct and indirect practice. **Direct practice** is primarily face-to-face contact with the client and focused on changing the client system, whether an individual, family, or small group. Conversely, **indirect practice** is distinguished as "less contact with a client system on a face-to-face basis . . . managing and developing programs, services, and policies that deal with social structures and resources" (Pierce, 1989, p. 157).

The value of maintaining this differentiation for macro social work endeavors is questionable. Using the direct/indirect distinction, the focus on macro systems in this book would be viewed as indirect practice. In terms of the importance of social work responsibilities, the term "indirect" connotes secondary or ancillary activities. However, we contend that developing and managing programs and policies that match resources and need is a primary function of social work.

The theme of each chapter of this book was directed by a different sociological theory. By using theories of social disorganization, role, normalization, labeling, value-conflict, or social reconstruction orientation, social structure was stressed over the individual and family.

Case examples were focused on macro social work functions. In the first chapter, social workers were encouraged to consider current trends toward managed care and interdisciplinary intervention. In his work with adolescents, Samuel Harris's duties as a social worker at the Santa Louisa Community Center involved more than face-to-face interaction with teenagers. Samuel met regularly with community leaders, employers, and court officials on behalf of his clients. Carla Peters, the social worker at Timberland Senior Citizens Center, challenged herself to become more politically involved and to develop contacts with local, state, and federal officials interested in championing senior causes. Should these be labeled as indirect social work methods? It is clear that macro-oriented activities are what distinguish social workers from other helping professionals.

The direct/indirect dichotomy places the social worker in an awkward position. Does performance of macro-level roles conflict with agency policy? Is the worker encouraged to utilize macro approaches or must she or he take the initiative in developing such intervention? Will Keith Romero, the group social worker in a rural community action agency, continue to feel secure about his job if he participates in a multiagency cluster group? What will be the agency response if he becomes actively involved in evaluating recreational and day care programs that benefit his clients?

At the very least, social workers need to assess macro-level systems and become familiar with community and societal resources so that they may be effective brokers of services. Unfortunately, active involvement in macro practice activities is frequently discouraged by administrators concerned about large caseloads and payment regulations that narrowly define reimbursable services. This falls under the general rubric of what Meyer (1993, pp. 6–7) calls **pressures to think narrowly,** where it is felt that if one cannot resolve these major social problems, nor even grasp the complexity and fluidity of the social scene, the best recourse is to address the least complex, narrowest, most "doable" private or internal aspects of cases so as to demonstrate effectiveness and relieve continuing frustration.

ECOLOGICAL THEORY

Ecological theory emphasizes a complete ecosystems assessment. Different ecology-based paradigms have been presented depicting essential data collection in cases (Meyer, 1993, pp. 114–124). Most versions include culture, physical status, social environment (home, community, school, and work), person (cognitive, emotional, and behavioral aspects), and significant others, as well as historic norms.

Explicit in most social work models for problem solving or planned change is a call for assessment and intervention with macro-level systems. "Practice situations often require practitioners to assess the factors present in a given situation and to relate them to a broad range of behaviors; behaviors potentially associated with more than one model of macro human service work" (Meenaghan, Washington, & Ryan, 1982, pp. 14–15). These authors suggest that social workers should possess technical competencies relevant across models that include "assessing and working with communities, complex organizations, and power configurations." Involvement in political action groups, persuasion of influential individuals to take action on urgent social problems, and promotion of new legislation are macro-level methods for addressing social injustices.

A thorough assessment of the environment also means attention needs to be given to the competition among people over natural resources. In Chapter 8, we explored the merits of public transportation as it relates to older adults. Many professionals would argue that social welfare and human services are inextricably tied to patterns of human consumption, both nationally and internationally. Issues of pollution, environmental degradation, and exploitation of natural resources (e.g., oil, minerals, trees, and water) affect human rights and people of all ages.

As a result of modern information technology, macro-level knowledge and skills now include computer literacy. Hick and McNutt (2002) state: "The Internet has affected all areas of social, economic, and political life. It is having a powerful impact on organizations that are committed to social change and social and economic justice" (p. 1). E-mail, websites, statistical packages, electronic publications, and the ability to share documents as attachments in a quick and manageable fashion constitute powerful tools in advocating for policies and programs that create opportunities or protect rights for disadvantaged populations. Because Internet capabilities are readily accessible around the world, online advocacy can also have a powerful effect in promoting justice on a global level (Queiro-Tajalli, McNutt, & Campbell, 2003).

Students entering field education should carefully examine each agency's tool for assessing clients, traditionally called the social history or its contemporary counterpart—the biopsychosocial assessment. This instrument is an indicator of the field agency's orientation. How comprehensive is the assessment piece in the agency's treatment planning and documentation? Is it rooted in ecological theory or in some other theoretical orientation? Are macro-level elements and components, including an emphasis on social empowerment, specifically included? The student should be prepared to initiate dialogue relative to case issues with supervisors. Such discussion often leads to openness regarding macro approaches. On the other hand, students who are aware of deep investments in entrenched policies and procedures should expect some resistance and should exercise diplomacy in developing social work skills.

THE STRENGTHS PERSPECTIVE

Recent social work publications highlight the **strengths perspective**, a creative and useful alternative to the obsession with problems, pathologies, and deficits. "Practicing from a strengths orientation means this—*everything* you do as a social worker will be predicated, in some way, on helping to discover and embellish, explore and exploit clients' strengths and resources in the service of assisting them to achieve their goals, realize their dreams, and shed the irons off their own inhibitions and misgivings, and society's domination" (Saleebey, 2002, p. 1).

By focusing on client strengths, this perspective shifts assessment away from an individualistic, problem-based approach to "ecological (social, political, and cultural, as well as individual) accounts of human predicaments and possibilities" (Saleebey, 1992, p. 4). Using the strengths perspective, social workers focus on identifying previously unrecognized individual and/or group resources, and are less inclined to define clients only in terms of ego deficiencies, behavioral problems, or family dysfunctions. Social workers are challenged to discover the power and resourcefulness that lie within people (individually and collectively) while avoiding the mind-set of blaming the victim (Ryan, 1976).

Saleebey describes the strengths perspective in relationship to social work assessment in the following statement:

> Recognizing client strengths is fundamental to the value stance of the profession. It provides for a leveling of the power social workers have over clients and in so doing presents increased potential for the facilitation of a partnership in the working relationship. Focusing on strengths in assessment has the potential for liberating clients from stigmatizing diagnostic classifications that reinforce 'sickness' in family and community environments. (1992, pp. 140–141)

Assessment from a strengths perspective places a major emphasis on both environmental and individual strengths. Macro-level assessments of organizations, communities, societies, and countries identify, clarify, and articulate resources and possibilities for planned change. As with other forms of assessment, this dynamic process involves a partnership between client and social worker.

Empowerment is a key concept in the strengths perspective. "Empowerment usually means to return a voice to silenced or disenfranchised people" (Tice & Perkins, 1996, p. 9). Beyond the identification of social ills, empowerment entails discovering and unleashing the power that lies within individuals, families, groups, and neighborhoods. "Empowerment-oriented social workers work collaboratively with their clients. They focus on clients' strengths and adaptive skills as well as clients' competencies and potential" (DuBois & Miley, 2005, p. 27). By focusing on resources and power, the strengths perspective fosters energy and vision for developing social policies and programs that enable clients to gain significant control over their lives.

To illustrate this point, we were tempted to concentrate on current, difficult issues facing many middle-aged women. While serious and distressing problems for women occur during middle age, we made a conscious effort to emphasize the positive aspects and benefits of this life segment for females. For many women, midlife is also a time of liberation, providing distinct advantages. One must move beyond perspectives of midlife women that are based on sexism and gender-role stereotypes (Hunter & Sundel, 1994, p. 113). By focusing on strengths and benefits of middle age, as opposed to deficits, social workers can better empower women to seek positive means to enrich their lives.

As we considered older age, a major emphasis was placed on social empowerment. Individual and collective options to influence program and policy development were principal themes. The Pulse and Power Program at Timberland Senior Citizens Center exemplified how client strengths could be directed into active involvement in important community and national issues. The center program encouraged older adults to exercise their collective influence.

Our goal has been to integrate a strengths perspective. We have been eclectic in approaching theoretical perspectives, and we encourage the reader to consider a variety of approaches in assessing the social environment.

When engaged in social work practice, you will find some helping professionals who rely solely on one theoretical orientation and who assess every client within this framework. Do these professionals have superior clinical skills and insight or do they need to embrace a broader selection of theories? Might such single-focus people have simply chosen to avoid the complexities of macro analyses?

Long, Tice, and Morrison (2006) encourage professionals to expand their outlook beyond traditional problem-solving models and seek ways to approach macro social work practice from a strengths perspective. When a strengths approach is applied to macro-level change, consumers of services (individually and collectively) are more fully embraced as partners in creating change. "Seeking the talents and abilities of consumers, be they smaller systems, organizations, communities, or society, is an appreciable change from helping clients to resolve intrapsychic difficulties, interpersonal relations, life transitions, and structural conflicts—that is, from problem solving" (Long, Tice, & Morrison, 2006, p. 63). Effective macro practice using a strengths perspective relies heavily upon the ability of social workers to engage consumers of services as colleagues or collaborators in assessing the need for social change. Viewing consumers as team members and valued partners encourages their abilities and expertise to move to the forefront.

VALUES AND CONTROLLING BIAS

Social workers, like other practitioners, are subject to biases. Each social worker approaches assessment with a distinct background and set of experiences. One's own cultural, political, ethnic, generational, psychological, educational, and gender orientation will influence how the client's problems are viewed. The challenge for social workers is to be objective when entering into partnerships with clients (Meyer, 1993). Assessment in social work should be client-centered. When social workers gravitate toward micro-level analysis as a result of their education and training, macro assessment is often compromised. To offset this inclination, case examples in this text deemphasize micro-level in favor of macro-level systems.

Beyond the effects of educational and theoretical influences, an **organization's culture** influences how social workers think and behave (Brody & Nair, 1995, p. 17). The culture of one's place of employment not only establishes formal goals, but also communicates an informal sense of the correct way of doing things in that setting. Organizational values, therefore, may constitute a potent source of bias.

Recall that Melissa Richardson, a school social worker, found the Hogan City School System to be receptive and supportive of her activities with a collaborative attention deficit disorder group (ATTEND). The school's organizational culture allowed Melissa to consult with school staff and parents in considering program and policy changes that would benefit children with attention deficit disorders. However, if Melissa had been working in a less progressive school system, the organizational culture could have been far less accepting of her macro-level assessment and intervention endeavors. Faculty and school officials often are territorial and protective with regard to teaching practices. In a more restrictive climate, Melissa's efforts to introduce policy changes could have been interpreted as interference in the work of teachers and school officials and construed by them as negative and unprofessional.

Organizational culture and values affect how social workers view assessment and their work. These factors can encourage or discourage social workers from thinking about the big picture with clients. Social workers seeking less hierarchical and more participatory agency environments that foster decentralized decision making should seek or champion the development of organizations that espouse a **"bottom-up" philosophy.** These types of organizations are characterized by a willingness to take risks and a desire to be responsive to the expectations and strengths of their staff and consumers of services (Poole & Colby, 2002, p. 147).

The graduate considering a social work position should be aware of the organizational climate. Is there a primary concern for the client as an engaged and participant consumer? Is there a sense of trust, emotional bonding, and pride in one's work among workers at the agency? Do social workers at the agency embrace a single theoretical orientation or are they eclectic? Are employees committed to macro social work practice and creating social change?

ENTERTAINING AN INTERNATIONAL PERSPECTIVE

Advances in technology, communication, and transportation serve to connect communities, states, and countries in ways never before imagined. The profound effects associated with advancements in technology and an emerging global economy have compelled social workers to be increasingly international in approaching practice.

For decades, social workers have acknowledged that a broader, more global understanding of the social environment is needed in the social work profession (Friedlander, 1975). Social work has a rich tradition in various international relief and disaster management efforts. This has included significant involvement in the International Red Cross Movement (e.g., the International Committee of the Red Cross, the International Federation of the Red Cross, and various national Red Cross and Red Crescent societies), the Peace Corps, and the United Nations Relief and Rehabilitation Administration. Social workers have also actively worked to improve world health conditions and championed international efforts to alleviate the impoverishment of children and families (for example, the United Nations Children's Fund—UNICEF).

Beyond humanitarian efforts to help victims in other countries, social workers now find that a global view is often necessary for accurate and effective assessment and intervention in the lives of their clients. Whether through cultural sensitivity, economic interdependence, or consideration of foreign policies, the social work profession continues to affirm the importance of an international perspective in problem solving and planned change.

Each chapter of this book contains a section devoted to considering relevant international issues in relationship to case examples. In Chapter 6, David's presenting problem during young adulthood is directly related to his desire to emigrate from Jamaica to the United States. **International social work** "should focus on the profession and practice in different parts of the world, especially the place of the organized profession in different countries, the different roles that social workers perform, the practice methods they use, the problems they deal with, and the many challenges they face" (Hokenstad, Khinduka, & Midgley, 1992, p. 4). In contrast, **international social welfare,** sometimes referred to as comparative social policy, is defined as the analysis of socioeconomic policies and human services in different countries. In this book, we have utilized both concepts.

As a result of her study of social work practice in China, Carla Peters (Chapter 8) was motivated to reevaluate her role as a social worker with older adults at Timberland Senior Citizens Center. She decided to give greater attention to advocacy while continuing to share information regarding issues that affect older adults. She utilizes insights from international social work practice as she assumes an advocacy role.

In Chapter 4, Melissa Richardson used the Internet to surf the web and examine policies, research, and the delivery of services to children with attention deficit disorders in other countries. One of her goals was to compare other programs and policies with those of the United States. Her use of these resources confirms the value of international social welfare.

In 2006, the International Federation of Social Workers (IFSW) celebrated its fiftieth anniversary. This association unites social workers from across the world to seek ways to promote client empowerment and choice, eliminate poverty, and advance client rights. The IFSW works closely with other international social work organizations (e.g., the International Association of Schools of Social Work and the International Council on Social Welfare) to promote global partnerships in assisting social workers and concerned groups to become better informed about and seek ways to address the needs of impoverished people in a variety of countries (Fred, 2005b, p. 6).

Recently, the Council on Social Work Education (CSWE) created the Katherine A. Kendall Institute for International Social Work Education (KAKI). The KAKI is intended to be instrumental in the "development of international content in social work education and to increase cross-organizational collaboration in project development as well as research and data collection and dissemination" (Fred, 2005a, p. 4). Although still in its infancy, the KAKI will provide social work educators and social workers with an infrastructure for sharing information and research examining best practices and successes in international social work practice.

Thanks to organizations and institutes like the IFSW and the KAKI, social workers need not be directly involved in international social work or international social welfare to benefit from knowledge of developments and practices in other countries. Because social work is a profession that is sensitive to contemporary issues, assessment should reflect current conditions in the social environment. The social environment needs to be embraced in a wide-ranging and comprehensive manner. This includes a careful examination of local, national, and international conditions and events. Fortunately, as a result of modern technology, our concept of the world continues to expand. Accessing information concerning social conditions, policy development, program implementation, best practices, social action, and the most recent research is now at our fingertips.

REFLECTION ON DIVERSITY: MULTICULTURAL ORGANIZATIONAL DEVELOPMENT

This chapter is dedicated to an examination of achieving social justice and empowerment. An important step toward this goal begins at home. For social workers, this typically means within the social service agency.

Human service professionals and leaders have an opportunity and a responsibility to model justice- and empowerment-oriented practices in their places of employment. To accomplish such an objective, agencies need to become inclusive and multicultural, reflecting the diverse nature of the surrounding community and society. Social workers and consumers of services as well as administrators and leaders should have high expectations of a workplace that encourages and embraces diversity and seeks to eliminate discriminatory practices and policies.

Multicultural Organizational Development (MCOD) represents one model for producing organizational change. It is a process dedicated to organizational transformation. Beyond accepting and celebrating diversity in the labor force, MCOD seeks "full social and cultural representation on all levels; the elimination of sexism, racism, and other forms of oppression; full inclusion and valuing of differences; and the redistribution of power and influence among all stakeholders" (Hyde, 2004, p. 8). MCOD is an intentional, purposeful approach that "strives to create one culture premised on the strengths of various groups (for example, race, socioeconomic status, gender) and perspectives within the organization" (p. 8).

Progressive organizations dedicate resources and time to intentionally assess and direct their organizational cultures toward multicultural development using approaches like MCOD. In human services, this motivation is less profit oriented and more value driven. Social workers and other helping professionals seek multicultural development in the workplace on the basis of respect for the dignity and worth of human beings, meaningful participation in decision making for all people, and the central importance of human relationships as prescribed in the NASW Code of Ethics (NASW, 1996).

Each social worker needs to indelibly etch a mental reminder that one's place of employment should represent the ideal with respect to multiculturalism and inclusiveness. In each of our chapters, we developed a "Reflection on Diversity" section for this second edition of *Macro Systems in the Social Environment*. Our intention was to create regular opportunities for each of us to think about and reflect upon issues of diversity. In Chapter 4, an appreciable amount of attention was given to promoting inclusion in school systems. The examination of labeling theory in relationship to adolescence in Chapter 5 illustrated the negative and destructive consequences of labeling. You will remember the work environment confronting Jean in Chapter 7 as falling far short of the ideal. Wherever your place of employment, regularly, deliberately, and conscientiously consider how you and others can model and promote inclusive and multicultural practices.

MACRO-LEVEL ASSESSMENT AND THE FUTURE

Given the social, political, and economic climate of the times, social work needs to be understood as a function of prevention rather than remediation. How can social workers promote change in the social environment in order to prevent problems rather than focusing on the rehabilitation of clients and their individual needs (Chetkow-Yanoov, 1992, p. 77)?

The case examples in this book primarily reflect remedial service, but demonstrate how a broader, more inclusive approach will benefit both client and society. Social workers were called into action to deal with some specific difficulty (Garvin & Tropman, 1992, p. 182). At a macro level, the concern was for identifying systemic elements causing the problem(s).

The social work profession is challenged to focus on macro-social conditions and to identify various populations at risk. Known as preventive targeting, this approach can greatly reduce the incidence of a particular problem (Bloom, 1981, p. 15).

You will remember that, in Chapter 2, Clara Sherman headed a service organization called Help Me Grow. Following a community needs assessment, women with severe mental illness and their infants were identified as populations at risk. Clara's efforts were directed at improving social conditions through employment and day care to ensure proper growth and nurturing of infants. Preventive targeting enabled the worker to promote health and well-being among a high-risk population in her community.

In Chapter 4 on normalization and children of school age, major attention was given to identifying schools and students at risk. The intent was to challenge the reader to consider strategies for improving educational programs and services, including curriculum, technology, and economic decisions benefiting schoolchildren at risk of academic failure. Preventive targeting encouraged assessment of educational alternatives.

The importance of preventive targeting in the assessment component of social work practice cannot be overemphasized.

> We will never be able to solve collective problems by treating its victims one by one. We should have some helping professionals look at the sources of these problems in an effort to proact, to reduce environmental stresses and to augment the strengths in populations of persons at risk or with potential, rather than having always to react after the fact to persons made miserable by problems and illness. (Bloom, 1981, p. 213)

Finally, as social work educators, we encourage social work students and practitioners to develop creative imaginations. The issues and problems confronting clients and social workers interested in creating a just world and society are numerous and complex. We live in a troubled and violent world. Professor Jeanne Marsh challenges us to contemplate the following: "In a world awash in violence, is it naïve to suggest that social workers can do anything about it? . . . [Social workers have a] commitment to reducing violence and achieving peace through the development of individual dignity and well-being, economic opportunity, equity, human rights, and democracy" (Marsh, 2003, p. 437). Although these challenges may appear immense, new frontiers continue to expand our opportunities to interact with the diverse skills, data, and practices of social workers from around the world.

Technology makes macro contacts possible as we share new insights and information with those who seek our partnerships in achieving their greatest potential. Social workers committed to social change will thrive on the broad horizons opening to us. As macro social work practice continues to develop, it promises significant and life-giving dividends for clients and society.

REFERENCES

Bloom, M. (1981). *Primary prevention: The possible science.* Englewood Cliffs, NJ: Prentice-Hall.

Brody, R., & Nair, M. (1995). *Macro practice: A generalist approach.* Wheaton, IL: Gregory.

Chetkow-Yanoov, B. (1992). *Social work practice: A systems approach.* New York: Haworth Press.

DuBois, B., & Miley, K. (2005). *Social work: An empowering profession.* Boston: Pearson Allyn & Bacon.

Fred, S. (2005a). Building an international field of practice. *NASW News, 50*(4), 4.

Fred, S. (2005b). Building an international field of practice. *NASW News, 50*(5), 6.

Freeman, M., & Valentine, D. (2004). Through the eyes of Hollywood: Images of social workers in film, *Social Work, 49,* 151–161.

Friedlander, W. (1975). *International social welfare.* Englewood Cliffs, NJ: Prentice-Hall.

Garvin, C., & Tropman, J. (1992). *Social work in contemporary society.* Englewood Cliffs, NJ: Prentice-Hall.

Hick, S., & McNutt, J. (2002). Communities and advocacy on the Internet: A conceptual framework. In S. Hick and J. McNutt (Eds.), *Advocacy, activism, and the Internet: Community organization and social policy.* Chicago: Lyceum.

Hokenstad, M., Khinduka, S., & Midgley, J. (1992). *Profiles in international social work.* Washington, DC: National Association of Social Workers.

Hunter, S., & Sundel, M. (1994). Midlife for women: A new perspective. *Affilia, 9,* 113–128.

Hyde, C. (2004). Multicultural development in human services agencies: Challenges and solutions. *Social Work, 49,* 7–16.

Long, D. (1995). Attention deficit disorder and case management: Infusing macro social work practice. *Journal of Sociology and Social Welfare, 12,* 45–50.

Long, D., Tice, C., & Morrison, J. (2006). *Macro social work practice: A strengths perspective.* Belmont, CA: Thomson Brooks/Cole.

Marsh, J. (2003). The social work response to violence. *Social Work, 48,* 437–438.

Marsh, J. (2004). Social work organizations working together. *Social Work, 49,* 341–342.

Meenaghan, T., Washington, R., & Ryan, R. (1982). *Macro practice in the human services*. New York: Free Press.

Meyer, C. (1993). *Assessment in social work practice*. New York: Columbia University Press.

Mizrahi, T. (2004). Are movements for social and economic justice growing? Reports on protest and social action in the United States and Israel. *Journal of Community Practice, 12*, 155–160.

National Association of Social Workers. (1996). *Code of ethics*. Washington, DC: Author.

Netting, E., Kettner, P., & McMurtry, S. (1993). *Social work macro practice*. White Plains, NY: Longman.

Pierce, D. (1989). *Social work and society: An introduction*. White Plains, NY: Longman.

Poole, D., & Colby, I. (2002). Do public neighborhood centers have the capacity to be instruments of change in human services? *Social Work, 47*, 142–152.

Queiro-Tajalli, I., McNutt, J., & Campbell, C. (2003). International social and economic justice and online advocacy. *International Social Work, 46*, 149–161.

Reid, P., & Billups, J. (1986). Distributional ethics and social work education. *Journal of Social Work Education, 22*, 6–17.

Ryan, W. (1976). *Blaming the victim* (rev.). New York: Vintage.

Saleebey, D. (1992). *The strengths perspective in social work practice*. White Plains, NY: Longman.

Saleebey, D. (2002). *The strengths perspective in social work practice*. Boston: Allyn & Bacon.

Shaviro, D. (2004). The new age of big government. *Regulation*, Spring, 36–42.

Tice, C., & Perkins, K. (1996). *Mental health issues and aging*. Pacific Grove, CA: Brooks/Cole.

U.S. Department of Health and Human Services, National Institutes of Health. (2003). *NIH plan for social work research*. Retrieved May 6, 2004, from http://obssr.od.nih.gov/publications/swr_report.pdf.

Vodde, R., & Gallant, J. (2002). Bridging the gap between micro and macro practice: Large scale change and a unified model of narrative-deconstructive practice. *Journal of Social Work Education, 38*, 439–458.

Name Index

Abels, A., 53
Abrams, L., 96
Adams, M., 94
Ægisdottir, S., 85
Allen, K., 62, 63, 155
Al-Talib, N., 99
Altpeter, M., 170
Amato, P., 48, 145
Amerman, T., 73, 75
Anastas, J., 119
Anderson, D., 149
Antenucci, V., 176
Aronson, E., 95
Atchley, R., 165
Aymer, C., 133

Bacchini, D., 99
Baker, D., 174
Balesent, K., 92
Bank-Mikkelsen, N., 69
Barnett, R., 147
Bartle, E., 29, 38
Bartolomei-Hill, S., 172
Baruch, G., 147
Bass, S., 169, 170

Bean, F., 109
Becker, H., 93, 94, 100–101
Bee, H., 142, 170, 183
Bengtson, V., 162–163
Berk, R., 98
Bernstein, J., 55
Beron, K., 126
Berry, M., 124
Biddle, B., 140
Biener, L., 147
Biklen, D., 77–78
Billups, J., 189
Binder, A., 99
Bishop, D., 97–98
Bjerregaard, B., 102
Bjorklund, B., 142, 170, 183
Black, B., 166
Blackburn, J., 172
Blake, A., 145
Blaker, K., 146
Blankenhorn, D., 47
Blau, M., 149
Blau, P., 10
Bloom, M., 200

SUBJECT INDEX

TO THE OWNER OF THIS BOOK:

I hope that you have found *Macro Systems in the Social Environment*, Second Edition, useful. So that this book can be improved in a future edition, would you take the time to complete this sheet and return it? Thank you.

School and address: _____

_____

Department: _____

Instructor's name:_____

1. What I like most about this book is:_____

_____

_____

2. What I like least about this book is:_____

_____

_____

3. My general reaction to this book is:_____

_____

_____

4. The name of the course in which I used this book is:_____

_____

5. Were all of the chapters of the book assigned for you to read? _____

   If not, which ones weren't? _____

6. In the space below, or on a separate sheet of paper, please write specific suggestions for improving this book and anything else you'd care to share about your experience in using this book.

_____

_____

FOLD HERE

 **BROOKS/COLE**
CENGAGE Learning

BUSINESS REPLY MAIL
FIRST-CLASS MAIL   PERMIT NO. 34   BELMONT CA

POSTAGE WILL BE PAID BY ADDRESSEE

Attn: Dan Alpert, Social Work Editor

Brooks/Cole, Cengage Learning

20 Davis Drive

Belmont, CA 94002-3098

FOLD HERE

OPTIONAL:

Your name: _____ Date: _____

May we quote you, either in promotion for *Macro Systems in the Social Environment,* Second Edition, or in future publishing ventures?

Yes: _____   No: _____

Sincerely yours,

Dennis D. Long and Marla Holle

CPSIA information can be obtained
at www.ICGtesting.com
Printed in the USA
FFOW01n1552190118
44538041-44390FF